Interpreting *Star Wars*

Interpreting *Star Wars*

Reading a Modern Film Franchise

Miles Booy

BLOOMSBURY ACADEMIC
NEW YORK • LONDON • OXFORD • NEW DELHI • SYDNEY

Bloomsbury Academic
Bloomsbury Publishing Inc
1385 Broadway, New York, NY 10018, USA

BLOOMSBURY, BLOOMSBURY ACADEMIC and the Diana logo are trademarks of
Bloomsbury Publishing Plc

First Published in the United States of America 2021

Copyright © Miles Booy, 2021

For legal purposes the Acknowledgements on p. vi constitute an extension
of this copyright page.

Cover design by Namkwan Cho

ISBN: HB: 978-1-5013-6475-4
PB: 978-1-5013-6474-7
ePDF: 978-1-5013-6472-3
eBook: 978-1-5013-6473-0

Typeset by Newgen KnowledgeWorks Pvt. Ltd., Chennai, India

To find out more about our authors and books visit www.bloomsbury.com
and sign up for our newsletters.

Contents

Acknowledgements and Housekeeping   vi

Introduction: Possibilities of interpretation   1

1   *Star Wars* versus secularity   13

2   *Star Wars* and the Reagan revolution   35

3   The first interpreters   55

4   The trilogy and the myth reading   81

5   The progressives strike back: *Star Wars* as liberal text   101

6   New twists on old hopes: Prequels and sequels   125

Conclusion: The many lives of George Lucas   155

Notes   165
Bibliography   183
Index   189

Acknowledgements and Housekeeping

In 1977, *Star Wars* was the title of a single film. It was retrospectively re-titled *Episode IV: A New Hope*, and *Star Wars* became the series title. To avoid confusion, it is increasingly the practice of those writing on the films to refer to each by their episode number. Thus, the film of 1977 would be *Episode IV*. This is a neat route around potential confusion, but it would not be appropriate here. Much of this book is about that period of time when the film of 1977 was not given an episode number, but seemed complete in itself. This had aesthetic and interpretive consequences which are crucial to the arguments here. Consequently, both the original film and the franchise which it spawned are referred to as *Star Wars*, and the text makes it clear what usage is intended.

Katie Gallof commissioned and edited this book for Bloomsbury. Erin Duffy and Shyam saw it safely through production. I am obliged to those who passed comments on my original proposal, and to David Booy and Peter Krämer who both subjected the finished manuscript to a forensic analysis. David and my wife Samantha brainstormed with me about a theme for the cover.

Introduction: Possibilities of interpretation

In 1977, Twentieth Century Fox released a film written and directed by George Lucas. It was, of course, *Star Wars*, and in 1977, that was the only title by which it was known. When success generated sequels, that became the title for a whole series of films, each with episode numbers and subtitles. In 1981, the original film was re-released in this new chapterised format as *Episode IV: A New Hope*. There are those who, prioritising their memories of the film's original release, have never really accepted the new title, and some have said it is unexciting. No one to my knowledge, however, has ever declared it inappropriate. Some, indeed, have seen it as the logical emphasising of a concept already understood to be central to the film. In 2016, Harvard professor Cass Sunstein wrote, 'The first release of *Star Wars* wasn't originally called *A New Hope*, but everyone understood it exactly that way, because that's exactly what it was.'[1]

What 'exactly' *Star Wars* 'was', however, has rarely seemed as clear as Sunstein asserts. Back in 1977, some industry hands found nothing there. Literally *nothing*. Irwin Allen, himself a producer of blockbuster films (*The Towering Inferno* [John Guillermin, 1974], *The Poseidon Adventure* [Ronald Neame, 1972]), watched the ecstatic crowds at early screenings with bemusement, 'There's no stars, there's no love story. What are they clapping at?'[2] Even some of those who praised the film thought there was nothing beneath the surface. 'It has no message,' asserted the positive review published in *Time* magazine in May 1977.[3] David Thomson, an enthusiastic writer on films of many types, has consistently stated his inability to see anything other than the same blankness. 'I have nothing to say about *Star Wars*,' he asserted in 2004, arguing that 'there is nothing to be said about *Star Wars* because there is not enough in it.'[4]

In the mid-1980s, with the entirety of the original trilogy to discuss, academic critic Robin Wood contrasted what he saw as the films' barrenness with the aesthetic delights offered by a prior generation of filmmakers whose complexities of theme and image had allowed him and others to make the case for cinema as a significant art worthy of study.

It is possible to 'read' a film like *Letter From An Unknown Woman* or *Late Spring* twenty times and still discover new meanings, new complexities, ambiguities, possibilities of interpretation. It seems unlikely, however, that this is what takes people back, again and again, to *Star Wars*.[5]

Writing like this suggests that *Star Wars* needs no interpretation, that the meaning of the films is both superficial and self-evident since the films are only entertainment or 'kids films'. Let the interpreters haggle over art cinema where symbolism is found, meaning is oblique and the conflicting impulses of human nature are exposed. Wood argues that blockbuster films themselves seem complicit in this, creating a deliberate barrier to adult discussion because

they are so insistently not serious, so knowing about their own escapist fantasy/ pure entertainment nature, and they consistently invite the audience's complicity in this. To raise serious objections to them is to run the risk of looking a fool (they're 'just entertainment' after all) or, worse, a spoilsport (they're 'such fun'). (p. 164)

Viewed this way, *Star Wars* could never be open to multiple interpretations. The film could only constantly restate, to every audience, the same literal recitation of its plot.

The films themselves, if we were to grant them consciousness and a voice, would disagree. They constantly insist that much is opaque, hidden from view and requiring second thoughts or deeper thinking. Yoda asks Luke Skywalker if he would judge him by his size, and the answer is clearly not to do so. The Millennium Falcon looks like rubbish, but contains all types of modifications which allow it to outrun notionally better ships. The original film of 1977 is the story of Luke Skywalker and what is bequeathed to him by Ben Kenobi: his father's lightsabre but, more importantly, the revelation that the world as he knows it is not how it truly is. This theme of a sub-surface meaning is literalised in the prequel films, for at their centre is a prophecy (that one exists who will bring balance to the Force), and the Jedi's interpretation of this (their belief that it refers to young Anakin Skywalker) has immense consequences.

Outside of academic work, makers of meaning encountered other difficulties. Lucasfilm, George Lucas's wholly owned company for making his films, was not shy of deploying lawyers to enforce its right to declare what constituted an appropriate use of the saga's imagery. The company's infamous zeal with lawsuits made it the example which academic Henry Jenkins used in his influential work on fan culture in the early 1990s to demonstrate how corporate owners sought to control the meaning of their films, angering fans who demanded greater interpretive leeway. Jenkins quotes a communication from Lucasfilm.

> Lucasfilm Ltd. does own all rights to the *Star Wars* characters and we are going to insist upon no pornography. This may mean no fanzines if that measure is what is necessary to stop the few from darkening the reputation our company is so proud of.[6]

Jenkins also quotes a fan response: 'Lucasfilm has said in essence, "This is what we see in the *Star Wars* films and we are telling you that this is what you will see."'

For those who were prepared to look for meaning in the films, their massive success raised the stakes. If *Star Wars* spoke to so many, this reasoning went, it must tell us something about ourselves. Consequently, some very large claims were made about human spirituality or the state of American culture. As the early chapters of this book explore, the first interpretations of *Star Wars* were produced in the context of a Western society seemingly in decline, economically and – some thought – morally as well. At such a moment, hope might be something to be wished for. With the passage of time, new social contexts have generated different interpretations, while the addition of new films has taken the saga in new directions. Sequels and prequels provide new themes, but hope – the concept which Lucas so visibly made central to the saga – has proven incredibly resilient as a concept and flourishes today, as central as it ever was, in our modern discourse where *Star Wars* is more celebrated than ever. Beyond film criticism, quotes are made and banners waved at elections, marches and political rallies.

These are contexts in which *Star Wars* is raised as an offer of hope, and this can be interrogated. When we ask *who found hope in Star Wars?* and *why did they find it to be such an optimistic promise in the face of a terrible situation?*, we are asking about people's interpretations of the film. Cambridge Online Dictionary gives two definitions of *interpretation*. The first is an 'explanation or opinion of what something means'.[7] We recognise such an interpretation most obviously in the form of a written account of the film(s), something outlining themes and structure in a given text and expressing a reason for finding value in this. A number of this book's chapters begin by discussing a lengthy essay or a short book because it is in these extended analyses that the principles underlying the act of interpretation are most clearly visible.

Wherever we find interpretations of this sort, the process which produces them is largely one of matching a meaningful idea from the real world with details of the fictional text. Different interpretations arise not only because ideas about which real- world theories or phenomena might be usefully matched against a film expand, but also because the films are a mass of details, any one of which might be used as the basis for an interpretation, even if it seems unlikely to have been intended that way. An early interpreter, Frank Allnutt, discussed in Chapter 1, believed that *Star Wars* articulated the need of human beings to acknowledge and know the Christian God. Another, contrasting early interpreter, Dan Rubey, discussed in Chapter Two, felt that the film was a prime example of how certain political ideologies are present in the popular culture of capitalist societies, and he sought to understand how they were articulated in a film which was presented as entertainment and notionally apolitical. Clearly, these two interpreters had opposed ambitions, but both proceeded to make their case by working through the film, matching details within the film to their chosen topic. For Allnutt, the Force is God, Kenobi's character connotes Jesus Christ, and his surviving death at Vader's hands replays the resurrection. Rubey, presenting a different interpretation, mapped his account onto other points of the film such as the validation of military action, the role of female characters and the attitudes taken towards non-human protagonists. We call these textual cues, and part of understanding the differing interpretations of Lucas's saga is understanding which cues are recurrently used, which parts of the film are neglected and why this may change over time. An interpretation may announce its own originality or cleverness by being based around previously overlooked parts of the film. Of all the analyses overviewed in this book, only Allnutt tells us the symbolic meaning of the name *Millennium Falcon*. Similarly, Rubey is alone in ascribing significance to the fact that after that ship exits hyperspace but before it is swallowed by the Death Star it encounters, and briefly pursues, a TIE fighter.

More usually, critics return repeatedly to moments, characters or themes which are generally agreed to be important. This book returns frequently to what people have found meaningful about several key icons of the original trilogy: the Ewoks, Princess Leia, the Force, the aliens in the cantina. These have all been repeatedly assigned significance, but the nature of that significance has varied over the years. Sometimes a question may be raised which becomes central to subsequent analysis despite the fact that early interpreters did not think to raise it (how the Empire acquires its weaponry is such a question). Twentieth-century interpretations generally prioritise the progress of Luke Skywalker. Twenty-first-century readings consider a more diverse range of characters (even before the prequels and sequels are taken into account).

The Cambridge Dictionary, however, offers a second definition. Interpretation may also reside in 'a particular way of performing a piece of music, a part in a play etc.' This takes us to a second set of texts which may be regarded as interpretations: when *Star Wars* is retold or added to, it is, in this performative sense, interpreted. This second sense includes the ways in which viewers and fans use the films to feed their creativity or jokes, the ways that spin-off books and comics explore ideas which are marginal in the films themselves, and the ways that later films play out familiar tropes using new vocabularies to incorporate different ideas of what might be hopeful or what might be hoped for. In the Disney era, films such as *The Force Awakens* (J. J. Abrams, 2015) work not only as new *Star Wars* films but as interpretation of the older ones, revising representations in line with shifting cultural norms. This is not to say that these films respond to any specific prior reading, but rather that they position themselves with regard to wider ideas about what the saga is believed to mean to its audience. Investigating these interpretations of the *Star Wars* universe takes us to other media – the novels and comics which are known as the 'expanded universe'. When discussing these, I emphasis the ways in which these materials use familiar characters and settings (Luke, the Tatooine cantina), and I have assumed reader familiarity only with the films.

In following the question, *to whom Star Wars offered hope*, this book considers a range of interpretations of the original film and of the saga which it spawned. As the series approaches its fiftieth anniversary, many of those who enjoy it now may have no memory of the decade in which it was released, the context in which early interpretations emerged and the social situation to which they were quite consciously a response. For this reason, some outline of those aspects of America in the period will be useful in understanding the backdrop against which the film was discussed.

The crises of the 1970s

By the summer of 1977, America had experienced a turbulent decade of social upheaval. The anti-communist Vietnam War had become increasingly unpopular in the late 1960s. Although the war formally ended in 1975, questions of its morality and of the methods used by the US military had split the nation. Further, protesters – often young and associated with the universities – were calling into question the traditional foundations of America's social arrangements. The generation which had been hardened by the Depression and fought the Second World War found its values challenged by its own children – children who accused them of being materialistic, repressed, racist and sexist. Social movements such as feminism and gay rights were barely a decade old when *Star Wars* was released and were loudly opposed by many. Simultaneously, the nation was rocked by a series of scandals. Some famous consumer products were found to be unsafe. The reputation of the CIA has never recovered from revelations – largely about the illegal surveillance of US citizens – made public in 1974. Earlier that same year, President Richard Nixon had resigned from office, rather than face an impeachment vote, following the Watergate scandal. After decades of post-war economic growth, the nation entered a period of high inflation and unemployment as the output of low-paid foreign workers made inroads into markets previously dominated by American firms. Large increases in energy prices escalated the sense of economic crisis and made the nations of the West look weak in the face of self-assertion by other countries, particularly those in the oil-rich Middle East. At the height of this 'energy crisis', President Jimmy Carter appeared on television advising Americans to put on an extra jumper rather than turn up the heat, a moment which became infamous as an image of US impotence. Other Western nations experienced similar conflicts, economic downturn and the radical calling into question of the values and Christian faith which had traditionally underwritten their societies.[8]

George Lucas's early answers to the question of *Star Wars*' origins contained his own take on the changing cultural landscape.

> I researched kids' movies and how they work and how myths work; and I looked very carefully at the elements of films within that fairy tale genre which made them successful. I found that myth always took place over the hill, in some exotic far-off lands. For the Greeks it was Ulysses going off into the unknown. For Victorian England it was India or North Africa and treasure islands. For America it was out West. There had to be strange savages and bizarre things in an exotic land. Now the last of that mythology died out in the mid-1950s, with the last of the men who knew the old West.[9]

Pithier versions would be widely quoted in newspapers and magazines. Lucas would frequently lament the absence of mythology in the modern world, believing that storyforms could be explicitly related to social behaviour.

> Rather than do some angry, socially relevant film, I realised there was another relevance that is even more important – dreams and fantasies, getting children

to believe there is more to life than garbage and killing and all that real stuff like stealing hubcaps – that you could still sit and dream about exotic lands and strange creatures.[10]

The excitement of *Star Wars* aside, things only worsened in the years after the film's release. When the Soviet Union invaded Afghanistan in 1979, the best response the United States could manage was to boycott the Olympic Games, held in Moscow the following year, and it was helpless in the face of a hostage crisis when embassy staff in Iran were taken captive by the supporters of that country's 1979 revolution. In Britain, annual inflation rates were in double-digit figures, the left-wing Labour government required a financial bailout from the International Monetary Fund, and 1978/9 saw the 'Winter of Discontent', a large number of near-simultaneous strikes, an iconic image of which were reports of dead bodies supposedly mouldering in the streets because the gravediggers had literally downed tools.

In 1979 and 1980, the public's lack of belief in the power of its leftist/liberal governments to control events brought the election of right-wing parties. The Conservatives would rule Britain from 1979 to 1997, and Republicans would sit in the White House from 1980 to 1992.

These governments would lay the ideological framework for much of our modern society: the privatisation of public sector responsibilities, militarist intervention in the nation's interest, the slashing of tax rates, the abolition of 'capital controls' (government limits on how much money their citizens could spend abroad) and deregulation of industry and financial services so that private enterprise could innovate and save the apparently sinking economies. The impact of these policies continues to be debated today. Did lower tax rates mean governments had less money to spend on social programmes? Or did the lower rates themselves stimulate economic activity, thus meaning that overall tax revenue rose even as individual contributions fell? Britain's prime minister Margaret Thatcher and America's president Ronald Reagan dominated the Anglosphere's political landscape in the 1980s.

This may seem abstracted from Luke Skywalker and his allies, but this book will demonstrate otherwise. At the time of the original trilogy's release, American news periodicals, reviewing the film, were keen to contrast the film with the state of the nation. *Newsweek*'s Jack Kroll confessed, 'I don't know how Lucas could make so buoyant and exuberant a film, without a smudge of corrupt consciousness, in these smudged times.' Three years later, *Time* magazine welcomed

The Empire Strikes Back: 'All the old friends and some favourite enemies have returned to brighten this unhappy spring.' In that magazine's review of *Star Wars* itself, inflation had been a reference point when praising the special effects as even better than those in *2001: A Space Odyssey* (Stanley Kubrick, 1968), a particular achievement, the reviewer felt, because '*2001* cost $10 million in less inflated 60s dollars; *Star Wars* cost only $9.5 million in the punt currency of the '70s.' Outside of the explicitly political press, *Variety*, the trade paper of the American entertainment industry, wrote, 'Like a breath of fresh air, *Star Wars* sweeps away the cynicism that has in recent years obscured the concepts of valor, dedication and honor.'[11]

The social pressures which had caused so much consternation also made themselves felt in cinema. The late 1960s saw the industry rocked by the box-office failure of several large-budget films. Highly budgeted family blockbusters had been central to Hollywood's financial strategies throughout the 1950s and 1960s. Many were musicals. Others were lengthy epic tales drawn from history, either secular or biblical. The failure of several such films in the late 1960s coincided with the surprising success of several smaller-budget films aimed at the youth market, notably *The Graduate* (Mike Nichols, 1967), *Bonnie and Clyde* (Arthur Penn, 1967) and *Easy Rider* (Dennis Hopper, 1969). Their success inspired a cycle of films aimed at audiences attuned to countercultural values and creatively led by young directors who seemed to understand this market. Often described as a 'renaissance' in American filmmaking, the early 1970s saw many films which questioned the traditional values of American film. Westerns explored the violence and racism of the frontier; conspiracy films depicted Americans at the mercy of shadowy powers; crime movies portrayed the nation's cities as a bleak urban jungle; and emotional dramas explored relationship choices previously banned from the screen. The questioning of values in these films was reflected also in the style of stories told. Narratives went unresolved or ended unhappily, frequently with the death of the central protagonist. The use of devices like slow-motion and freeze-frame called attention to the constructed nature of the narrative. George Lucas's debut feature *THX-1138* (1971) – a bleak dystopia depicting a future society where violent authority suppressed individuality, told in a style which resisted overt emotional engagement with the central characters – was a product of this era. These films were acclaimed by critics and put cinema at the centre of intellectual debate, though actual box-office attendance declined in the period. The era has been celebrated in articles and books both at the time and since.[12]

Early interpretations of *Star Wars* were shaped by how their authors responded to this polarising social moment. Many embraced the questioning of political and aesthetic values. They saw in the politics of the 1970s not a crisis but an emerging better society. Their responses to *Stars Wars* are discussed in Chapter 2. Others, however, felt the 1970s to be a period of stasis, if not decline, and of economic and social chaos. They responded positively to the story that Lucas would rename *A New Hope*.

Hope for whom?

Having studied the history of hope as a philosophical concept, Terry Eagleton draws out its defining features which I shall quickly summarise here in order to sharpen our sense of its meaning and, thus, the ways in which it is dramatised in the films and deployed in interpretations.

For Eagleton, hope is distinct from *optimism*. The latter is simply a psychological disposition. One is an optimist or one isn't, and it consequently lacks moral commitment. As an evaluation of future possibilities, the optimist displays positivity, but this may be without any rational relationship to a given situation. Hope, by contrast, rests on a specific reason for thinking that things will improve. This also defines hope against *belief* because believing that something will happen implies a greater certainty than hoping that it will.

The ancients often denigrated hope as an illusion, and it was in Christian thought that it reached its current definition as a largely positive phenomena. In Christian cultures (or post-Christian ones which inherit its spiritual baggage), hope is a theological virtue along with faith and love/charity, and its spiritual opposite is the sin of despair. Hope, then, constitutes a spiritual commitment which may demand something of us. Maintaining it through dark times may be a significant psychospiritual struggle.[13] With this in mind, a working definition for the purposes of this book might be that hope is *the conviction that something specific which is forgotten or simply latent in current social arrangements will manifest itself with positive results*. A hope based on something forgotten implies a relation with the past. Kenobi's desire to see the Republic restored is such a hope. A hope based on something not lost so much as simply latent is Poe Dameron's belief, in *The Rise of Skywalker*, that if a message can be broadcast across the central systems, then people will rise up to aid the resistance in its hour of need.

With Poe Dameron, however, we are getting ahead of ourselves. In the original film, the new hope is Luke Skywalker. Princess Leia initially appeals to the aged Obi-Wan Kenobi. Her plea, 'Help me, Obi-Wan Kenobi, you're my only hope', is one of the film's iconic lines. Kenobi dies before he can offer hope or aid, but not before he has passed to Luke both the immediate quest and the knowledge of the Force, an energy field with mental (and, later, physical) powers. Speaking from beyond the grave in later films, Kenobi subsequently uses the term twice in direct relation to Luke: 'That boy is our last hope' – *The Empire Strikes Back*; 'You were our only hope' – *Return of the Jedi*. Luke subsequently passes the burden to Leia ('If I don't make it back, you're the only hope for the Alliance' – *Jedi*) though, as events play out, she is not required to take it up.[14]

Many of those who passed comment upon *Star Wars* in the late 1970s felt that its mammoth success was due to the 'hope' it offered at a time of crisis. They believed that the hope which Luke represented to the rebellion could be symbolically attached to our own society's needs. Many who felt this way were American, but I have included throughout this study some British examples to show that these feelings and arguments had international reach. There are clear parallels between political events on either side of the Atlantic in the late 1970s, and they were projected onto *Star Wars* in both nations (and I like to think that a book written in deepest Staffordshire would address my own countryfolk.). Chapter 1 concerns American evangelical enthusiasm for the film which was strong in the late 1970s but became more problematic as the Buddhist-influenced sequels appeared. Similarly, Chapter 4 concerns the interpretation of the films through the work of mythologist Joseph Campbell, a reading which Lucasfilm would embrace enthusiastically and promote through events and publications until the end of the twentieth century.

A critique of these spiritual arguments is made by the left-wing critics of Chapter 2 who, during the period of the original trilogy's release, brought political and psychoanalytic vocabularies to bear on *Star Wars* and were highly critical of both the film(s) and the enthusiasm of people's responses. They equated the new hope of *Star Wars* with the new conservativism represented by Ronald Reagan, a president whose connection to Lucas's film was solidified when his plans for defensive weapons platforms in space, the Strategic Defence Initiative, became known colloquially as the *Star Wars Project*. While spiritual readings were often produced by those who felt society was in decline following cultural upheavals in the post-war period, the authors explored in Chapter 2 were concerned that the social gains they perceived to have been made in the 1960s and 1970s might be reversed, and they felt that the rhetoric of *Star Wars* was symptomatic of – and encouraged – this.

Chapter 3 also concerns responses of the late 1970s, considering novels, documentaries and comics. This is the performative dimension of interpretation. After the enormous success of *Star Wars*, it was clear that the story would continue. The exact way in which it would do so – which aspects of the first film were sufficiently central to the core meaning of the text that they must necessarily be taken up in subsequent narratives – was publicly negotiated by Lucasfilm and its audience through the merchandise which appeared in the years between *Star Wars* and *The Empire Strikes Back*. The political and religious meanings which had been critically debated by those espousing the meaning of the films in essay form are clearly found within these products, demonstrating that the ideas discussed were not limited to academic or evangelical arenas but spoke to other audiences.

Chapters 5 and 6 consider later interpretations of the films, largely twenty-first-century ones, including those prompted by the subsequent prequels and sequels. For all that these films created new stories and themes, later interpretations are built on and enter into dialogue with the earlier readings, if not always consciously. To those on the twenty-first-century left who were as concerned with identity politics as with issues of centralised government, even the original films yielded a wholly different set of meanings than those produced by those who applied Marxist analysis to them in the late 1970s. These readings arose in the 1990s and fed into the prequel trilogy and later the films produced by Disney following its purchase of Lucasfilm. The prequels and sequels to the original trilogy come wholly to the fore in the final chapter, which considers the interpretation of these later texts and the impact of their existence upon the meanings to be found in the original trilogy. A conclusion follows these chapters which overviews the development of readings of *Star Wars* and considers a small but related body of literature – biographies of George Lucas.

No book of this size could discuss every interpretation ever made of *Star Wars*. A key criterion in my own selection of what to discuss has been to return to the late 1970s, to the moment of the film's first amazing success, and recover arguments and interpretations which were made then. I have then followed these themes and debates (hope, social renewal, spirituality, militarism) through the succeeding decades. Similarly, I return to those elements of the film(s) which have been ascribed different meanings over the years, but which have always seemed central to the saga's meaning. Princess Leia, the Force and the creatures in the cantina are just three examples of these. Disney unknowingly gave this book a neater structure than I could have otherwise managed by releasing *Rogue One* (Gareth Edwards, 2016), a direct prequel to the original film which brings the book full-circle. It is, for this reason, allocated the privileged space at the end of the final chapter.

We begin, however, not in the Disney era of *Star Wars* but in a time so different to our own that it may as well be a long time ago in a galaxy far, far away – the 1970s.

1

Star Wars versus secularity

George Lucas's early outlines for what became *Star Wars* foresaw that it and any hypothetical spin-offs would be part of a wider text, *The Journal of the Whills*. This book would possibly be seen on screen at the beginning, opening up to reveal the narrative action just as a book of fairy tales began a number of Disney films.[1] Although this never happened, some have concluded that *Whills* was itself to have been a sacred text. This would not have been inappropriate. What finally emerged after multiple drafts was a film heavily invested in the contrast between a rebellion defined in terms of faith and an Empire which, with the Emperor only present as a passing reference, was run by secular technocrats who sneered at the Force. Later films would change this. The Emperor would be revealed as perhaps the most powerful Force-user of all, and as Jedi skills and combat became both more spectacular and closer to the heart of the story, disbelief in the power of the Force ceased to be a real option. The reading which follows is my own. It traces the opposition of secularity with faith in the film of 1977. I offer it to point up those elements which became important in generating religious interpretations in the 1970s and 1980s as well as outlining some elements which were dispensed with in subsequent films. It will be familiar in outline, but not, I hope, in detail.

Star Wars – A reading

Although the Emperor is only referred to twice in *Star Wars* (1977), the first occurrence is in an important and well-known scene (the second is when Tarkin orders Alderaan destroyed). In a conference room on the Death Star, a number of Imperial officials are arguing over the danger presented by the rebellion:

Admiral Tagge: The rebellion will continue to gain sympathy in the Imperial
             Senate –

Governor Tarkin: (*Entering with Vader*) The Imperial Senate will no longer
             be of any concern to us. I have just received word that the

Emperor has dissolved the council permanently. The last
remnants of the Old Republic have been swept away.

Admiral Tagge: That's impossible! How will the Emperor maintain control
without the bureaucracy?

Governor Tarkin: Regional governors now have direct control over their
territories.

The first reference to the Emperor seems narratively important. Lucas would
later claim that the inspiration was Richard Nixon, but for historically informed
viewers, the abolition of the Republic cues a certain reading: events here are
based on the fall of Republican Rome. Indeed, Rome hangs at the edge of the
film as its foremost real-world example of what it means to be an empire. The
film's novelisation and other early spin-off novels were chapterised with Roman
numerals – as later, of course, were the films themselves. Palpatine's name is not
given onscreen, but it appears in the novelisation and was subsequently used in
the prequel trilogy. Perhaps it recalls Palatine, the central of the seven hills of
Rome, and by *Return of the Jedi*, he has his own equivalent of the Praetorian guard.

For all viewers, historically informed or not, the line establishes that galactic
democracy has reached a new low with the complete abolition of a senatorial
system. As befits a film celebrated for the offering of hope, *Star Wars* is a movie
about a crisis point. Things will get worse before they get better, and later in the
film, Vader is in a position to gloat: 'This will be a day long remembered. It has
seen the end of Kenobi. It will soon see the end of the rebellion.' It is often said
that *The Empire Strikes Back* is a film which sees our heroes harried and constantly on the run (which is true), and the Emperor will boast in *Jedi* that his
plan will destroy the rebellion this time, but the rebels really reach their lowest
ebb five or six minutes before the end of this first film. Kenobi is apparently dead,
the Senate is abolished, the rebel base is within range of the Death Star's planet-
destroying weaponry, and their X-Wing fleet has been decimated. The darkest
hour falls in the minutes before Luke learns to deploy the Force for strategic
ends. Once he does that, however bad things get, there is always (a new) hope.

So, we learn nothing about the Emperor here. He is a narrative function,
mentioned simply to enable the plotpoint of the Senate's abolition. The Grand
Moff Tarkin is the focus of the scene at this point. His entry silences the
squabbling officers. As with Leia's later line about his holding Vader's leash, it
is clear that Tarkin is the centre of authority here. Moreover, there are significant positions of local authority – regional governors. The vision of the Emperor

and Vader forming the heart of a dark empire is later revisionism. A whole language of politics peppers this film. *Senate, bureaucracy, council, regional governors*: these terms imply a whole political system, as does the language used during Vader's interrogation of the rebel he kills and then Princess Leia in the film's opening sequence: *ambassador, consular, diplomatic*. These concerns vanish in the sequels – though they return with a vengeance in the prequels – and we will pay attention to the impact of this elision upon the themes and plot as they come and go.

Vader's lowly status in the Imperial hierarchy as seen here has caused *Star Wars* fans some sleepless nights down the years (google a phrase such as 'Why does Darth Vader defer to Tarkin?' to find the debates), but rather than trying to reconcile the conflicting arrangements of different films, we might productively look again at the characterisation of Vader in the film. His entry into the film in black armour through the white smoke of battle is iconic, but his behaviour is very different from what becomes the norm. In subsequent films, Vader keeps his own council, issuing orders to subordinates only after he has thought actions through in the privacy of his own mind. This contrasts with his behaviour on the rebel ship early in *Star Wars*. In this film, he does his thinking aloud ('She must have hidden the plans in the escape pod') and accepts the views of others as worth listening to ('Holding her is dangerous. If word of this gets out it could generate sympathy for the rebellion in the Senate'). In the course of early sequences, he becomes both visibly frustrated ('There'll be no one to stop us this time!') and angry when impotent ('You are part of the rebel alliance and a traitor – take her away!'). This visibly emotional Vader has a frenetic body language. Later films would depict him as essentially still, unmoving except when necessary. This is sometimes the case here, but in emotional moments he is mobile, as when he looks from side to side, clearly frustrated while he gives orders to 'tear this ship apart, and bring me the passengers. I want them alive,' before angrily exiting screen left.

The abolition of the Senate established, the meeting on the Death Star continues, containing the famous sequence of Vader Force-choking Admiral Motti.

Motti: This station is now the ultimate power in the universe. I suggest we use it.

Vader: Don't be too proud of this technological terror you've created. The ability to destroy a planet is insignificant next to the power of the Force.

> *Motti:*   Don't try to frighten us with your sorcerer's ways, Lord Vader. Your
> sad devotion to that ancient religion has not helped you conjure up the
> stolen data tapes. Or given you clairvoyance enough to help you find
> the rebels' hidden fortr –
> (*With a gesture, Vader begins to Force-strangle Motti.*)
> *Vader:*   I find your lack of faith disturbing.
> *Tarkin:*   Enough of this. Vader, release him.

Return of the Jedi would later lead Robin Wood to argue that the Death Star 'was created by the Force',[2] but in this film the two are constructed as distinct opposites. Vader, taking a stand against the omnipotence of technology, is clearly at odds with the military commanders. His major ally at this point is Tarkin. The governor calls him 'my friend' (something no one other than the Emperor would dare to claim in the sequels) and publically supports him: 'Lord Vader will provide us with the location of the rebel fortress by the time this station is operational.' Even he, however, has his doubts about the Dark Lord's strategy. 'I'm taking an awful risk, Vader,' he says after the *Millennium Falcon* has been allowed to escape the Death Star with a homing beacon planted aboard, 'This had better work.'

The antagonism between Motti and Vader opposes a faith in material causality and military power to one in belief/'religion'. The same positions are taken in later discussions between Ben Kenobi and Han Solo on the Millennium Falcon. Ben is teaching Luke the ways of the Force, and Solo sneers.

> *Solo:*   Hokey religions and ancient weapons are no match for a good blaster at
> your side, kid.
> *Luke:*   You don't believe in the Force, do you?
> *Solo:*   Kid, I've flown from one side of this galaxy to the other. I've seen a lot of
> strange stuff. But I've never seen anything to make me believe there's an
> all-powerful Force controlling everything. There's no mystical energy-
> field controls my destiny.

Both sequences end with an act of the Force (Vader's strangulation of Tagge, Luke successfully hitting the flying orb despite being blindfolded) which effectively ends the debate for viewers and foreshadows the film's conclusion. The sequences use another vocabulary – *religion, hokey, conjure, devotion, ancient, faith, sorcerer's* – which is almost without equivalence in the later films. These words are mostly used to characterise Force-believers as misguided and/or outdated. However, the film settles the debate decisively on their side, so the sequels have no real use for them, and religious terminology is subsequently almost wholly avoided. Han Solo's 'Then I'll see you in Hell' and Vader's 'I am altering the deal. Pray that I do not alter it any further' (both from *Empire*) are rare later uses of that vocabulary. *Pray* particularly stood out in 1980. It would not have done so in 1977.

Though later films take different tacks, the universe of *Star Wars*, the film of 1977, experiences a religious divide not unlike the modern Western world. Older beliefs, once dominant, are giving way to a new secularity. The film is rich with the sense of an old order almost completely passed. Kenobi calls it 'a more civilised age', and the language (of *sabres*, *knights* and *republic*) makes it sound archaic but also more virtuous than the technocratic materialism which has replaced it. Solo calls it 'ancient', an odd word to use in this context if one does some very basic math. Luke is roughly aged twenty, so the Clone Wars, in which his father fought, cannot be much more than two decades earlier. Leaving aside the question of why there wasn't twenty-four-hour news coverage of the combat (and, thus, easily accessed proof of Jedi abilities), this is well within the lifetimes of both Tagge and Solo, but neither appears to have any memory of the Jedi. In the real world, the events of the world's sacred texts happened centuries ago, so it is easy to disregard them as mythology. *Star Wars* constructs the same opposition, but in a timeline so compressed as to make little literal sense. The deployment of the word 'ancient', I would suggest, is an attempt to paper over this.

A Force which could be doubted to even exist could not be represented as it would be later. When Jedi leap acrobatically beyond human abilities, levitate objects at will, and sense each other across major distances in space, scepticism becomes untenable. An intelligent person might, however, reasonably disbelieve in the Force as it is shown in *Star Wars*. The small and subtle acts undertaken in its name mainly concern perception. Luke's ability to 'see' his targets when he is blindfolded or turns off his targeting computer; Kenobi's manipulation of the soldiers manning the roadblock into Mos Eisley; Vader's sensing Kenobi's presence on the Death Star – none of these works on the physical plane, just the psychic/spiritual. General Motti's strangulation, small in comparison to later excesses, is as physical as the Force gets, and even this incident is ambiguous: is Vader manipulating Motti's throat or his mind? Is the man being strangled, or does he simply think that he is? Note that when Vader wants to actually kill someone in this film – the rebel whom he briefly interrogates in the opening sequence – he does so physically, snapping his neck with the strength of his grasp rather than via the Force.

There is nothing here that a sceptic couldn't deride as psychological trickery and misdirection. Indeed, when Ben gets Luke's speeder through the roadblock, he says it is because the Force can have considerable effect upon 'the weaker-minded'. It sounds like a comment upon the psychology of the sorts of people who would submerge their own identities beneath stormtrooper uniforms, and implies that their own mentalities are complicit in the process. Kenobi silently pulls the same trick on other stormtroopers later, when, after deactivating the Death Star's tractor beam, he apparently mentally sends some troopers who might discover him in a different direction. This contrasts with his treatment of Solo, Chewie, Vader, Luke, the Sandpeople and the men who set about Luke in the bar. In all of these cases, though engaged in some sort of confrontation, disagreement or negotiation, Kenobi does not attempt the same mental trickery, possibly because they are strong-willed individuals and, thus, not susceptible. In later instalments, this qualification of weak-mindedness is subtly dropped. For these reasons, the 1977 film *Star Wars* sits uneasily as the 'episode four' which it has been subsequently declared to be. What is thematically at stake in the film is whether the Force exists and whether it is more powerful than a heavily armed battle station/'good blaster', but for an audience which has already viewed *The Phantom Menace*, *Attack of the Clones* and *Revenge of the Sith*, the answer is obviously *yes*.

Concomitant with this more restrained vision of the Force and its capabilities is the more accessible nature of its relation to humanity and, by contrast with the later insistence on 'balance' between its light and dark side, its clear affiliation with the side of good. While the Dark Side is mentioned, it receives little thematic attention. Vader aside, the villains are military men who place their faith in technology. Conversely, when the rebel pilots are briefed about attacking the Death Star, the presentation concludes, 'May the Force Be with You'. There is no suggestion that the other pilots have Luke's special affinity with the Force, but they acknowledge it as a matter of course. While Vader's 'faith' makes him an aberration among the Imperials, the rebellion is a community of believers, faithful to the old ways in the new technocratic universe. They have sought out the last surviving Jedi for aid, made their base in some ancient temples of unspecified origin and, in a scene deleted from the final cut but widely circulated in adaptations such as the novel and comic strip, one of the X-Wing flight leaders tells Luke he met his father, implying Jedi connections. Luke himself is accepted as one among equals, but only as that. This reading of the rebellion – as a community of believers, all humbly equal before the Force – is a significant answer to those who charge that the film fetishises fascist supermen. Later films like *Jedi* and *Clones*, where the Force is powerfully deployed by both sides, could no longer sustain the reading outlined here, nor use the opposition belief:disbelief to define good from evil. In these films, secularity will not be a concern of any of the major characters, and the rhetoric of good side/dark side (barely present in *Star Wars* itself, mentioned only in connection to Vader's 'seduction') will be necessarily escalated to define heroes from villains.

Star Wars' conclusion firmly resolves the issues of faith in the Force versus the technocracy. Luke destroys the station by turning off his battle computer (along with having 'lost Artoo' and suffered numerous other technical faults with his X-Wing) and using the Force, but even before this moment, there has been doubt over whether the computer-targeting device is up-to-the-job. 'That's impossible, even for a computer,' declares one rebel at the briefing where the pilots are given their target. The same point is raised ('Are you sure the computer can hit it?') by ace pilot Wedge Antilles as they hurtle down the Death Star trench. The faithful rebels understand the limitations of technology, even their own. On the Imperial side, by contrast, Tarkin shows his true colours. Having previously defended Vader's methods and integrity against the military technocrats, he is finally revealed as being one of them. When told that the rebels pose a danger to the Death Star and offered an escape craft, he scoffs 'Evacuate? In our moment of triumph? I think you over-estimate their chances.' Vader is the only one of the Death Star's personnel to survive the film precisely because he has taken the opposite view, accepted the possibility of the station's vulnerability, and joined the effort to 'destroy them [the rebels] ship-to-ship'.

This account of certain features of the film *Star Wars* as seen in 1977 intriguingly casts Vader as essentially a misplaced good guy (albeit one who killed Luke's father), thus raising the possibility of his redemption (though, by the time this is achieved, the series has shifted its themes significantly). Though rendered untenable by later developments, this notion of Vader as unique within the film's framework was acknowledged in the late 1970s. Dan Rubey, whose critique of the film is discussed in the next chapter, called him 'Faustian', likening him to Nathaniel Hawthorne's Roger Chillingworth (in *The Scarlet Letter*) or Herman Melville's Ahab (*Moby Dick*) – characters who have made a deal with darkness but paid a heavy price for knowledge and experience, not least in their social isolation.[3]

The sequences which I have pointed up are those which played a significant part in generating certain prominent readings which circulated in the years after the film's release. It is often asserted that the Force can be explicated in terms of every religion imaginable. While this is probably true, not all religious interpretations are equally widely held. Some work for small, niche audiences, while others serve wider groups. Some interpretations receive official recognition and some are more convincing than others because of the larger number of elements of the film which the interpretation seems to fit. Some receive wider coverage than others because of the dominant faith in the society within which the film is screened. Given a framework of faith versus techno-secularity, it comes as little surprise that in 1977 in the English-speaking world the most recurrent reference point in interpretations of the Force was Christianity.

The Christian reading

The Lutheran, an Australian periodical serving the church of the same name, reviewed *Star Wars* thus:

> *Star Wars* has an undergirding religious premise that is theologically simplistic but nonetheless impressively reverent and sincerely introduced. Alec Guinness calls his God 'the Force' and inspires young Luke also to become a disciple of and a believer in 'the Force.' It is a combination of the mysticism of ESP and the New Testament doctrine of the Holy Spirit.[4]

Interpretations in this vein were often built around Kenobi, his quiet faith and his Christ-like death and resurrection. His final disembodied words ('The Force will be with you always') echo the words of Jesus which close Matthew's gospel: 'I am with you always, even unto the end of the world.' Lucas would later reflect that Kenobi 'wasn't meant to be Christ-like,'[5] and subsequent detailed production accounts confirm that it was only late in the film's shooting that the decision was made to 'kill' Kenobi in the lightsabre duel, rather than having him be wounded and hanging at the edge of the action in the final act.[6] Once the film took its final form, however, the Christian reading became a strong and inevitable one. The Force in *Star Wars* was easily allegorised as the Christian God because it is unproblematically A Good Thing. In later films it would be necessary to differentiate between a light side and a dark, a good aspect and a bad which appear to be near-equals in strength, are forever present, and always at war unless, perhaps (and I say perhaps because this subplot from the prequels is abandoned and unexplained), they can be brought into 'balance'. Such balance might reconcile the opposing sides, but they would still exist as structural opposites, the one requiring the other. *Star Wars* itself, the film of 1977, has no truck with such thinking. The Force is assumed to be good, and those who talk of what would later be called its good side need not specify 'good' because that is what the Force is assumed to be (No one says 'May the light side be with you'). It is only when talking of the dark side that one needs to specify a shade because that is an aberration from the normal understanding, just as its single known disciple, Vader, is an aberration among people, mocked by Imperial technocrats and despised as a traitor by the rebels/Kenobi.

The most sustained Christian explication of the film was Frank Allnutt's book *The Force of Star Wars*, published incredibly in 1977.[7] Within months of the film's release (and prior to its European debut), Allnutt's short book, approximately 15,000–20,000 words of it, was out. I am aware that bringing the output of an evangelical Christian press – and one over forty years old – to the attention of academics is the critical equivalent of serving up barrelled fish for shooting, and those who wish to sneer will find easy ammunition in the next few pages. However, Allnutt was moved by the film, sought to understand its success, and his book touched far more lives than any academic publication seems likely to. He was an early *Star Wars* interpreter who considered the film through broadly agreed techniques of explication, and I wish to consider his book in that light.

Allnutt's reading is as we might expect it to be from the evidence already gathered. The heroes are believers (he approvingly speaks of 'that small band of religious zealots aboard the Millennium Falcon', p. 127), but he develops his allegory in a more detailed manner than other Christian analysts, drawing vital distinctions from small details. For Allnutt, Luke and Han represent the two specific audiences to which Christianity is addressed in the New Testament. Luke represents Judaic Christians. Just as the Jewish people inherited from their forefathers knowledge of Yahweh and a tradition of His worship, so Luke stands in the tradition of the Force via his father. Han Solo, by contrast, stands for non-Jewish people, the Gentiles. He knows nothing of the tradition from which the truth emerges and is initially sceptical until he is convinced by demonstrations of power. Like anyone working on a highly detailed interpretation, Allnutt finds meaning in the small details that other explicators do not. While most interpreters have neglected to decode the name of Solo's ship, Allnutt reminds us that 'the word "millennium" is actually a technical Bible term which refers to the thousand-year reign of Christ on Earth . . . [a time of] peace and harmony' (p. 177). In as much as the Falcon's re-appearance in the final battle saves the day (without it, Luke is almost certainly killed and the rebel base destroyed), it is a fair point.

The villains form a similarly detailed tripartite vision of evil: The Emperor is Satan, Tarkin the Antichrist, and Vader is both the False Prophet of the book of *Revelation* and the betrayer Judas Iscariot. With the characters allegorised in this way, Allnutt maps the story of *Star Wars* onto a wealth of biblical narrative besides the frequently cited Jesus parallels. The Old Republic is like Israel ('The people of the Republic were given the universe to develop and rule. In similar fashion, God gave the children of Israel their own land which would be theirs forever', p. 33/4), and, like Israel, its fortunes wax and wane in direct correlation to its continued worship of The Force/God. Tarkin and Vader's roles as Antichrist and False Prophet allow for an exploration of the *Book of Revelation* (pp. 135–40), while Senator Palpatine's descent into evil recalls Lucifer's rebellion in Heaven (pp. 62–9) as retold in the book of *Job*.

Atop these biblical parallels, Allnutt gives historical examples of golden eras which decayed from within. This is what makes the film so compelling for him because he fears that the economically troubled and socially divided America of the 1970s could be lost to darkness just as the Republic was. Just as the Republic ceased to worship the Force, so the West has turned its back on God with moral collapse evident everywhere. Pornography, divorce, abortion, homosexuality: it is a familiar list of sins when viewed (to quote Kenobi in *Jedi*) 'from a certain point of view'. Bad enough in themselves, the resultant outbreak of lawlessness 'could push the nation into forming a national police force!' (p. 150). It is easy to sneer at Allnutt's libertarian fear of centralised law enforcement (particularly from my side of the Atlantic), but who can doubt that *Star Wars* offers him the metaphors to discuss it?

Allnutt's distaste for centralised government and his determination to find in it the source of all the ills in the *Star Wars* galaxy leads him to some unusual conclusions. Most commentators take Tatooine's subsistence agriculture and scavenging to be a response to the hard natural conditions on a planet where two suns create what appears to be total desert. Allnutt, though acknowledging the harsh environment, sees them also as the consequence of economic mismanagement – or possibly deliberate economic warfare – from the centre.[8]

Most people accepted the harsh conditions under the New Order, somewhat begrudgingly, of course, but without much resistance. Many of them were reduced to poverty levels, eking out a meagre existence and little else on barren, forsaken planets such as Tatooine. (p. 119)

There were harsh economic controls and widespread religious persecution. People like Luke's Uncle Owen and Aunt Beru were forced into a near-poverty existence. Bandits roamed the wilderness of planets like Tatooine, while Jawas were reduced to existing off junk and refuse. (p. 143)

Assuming that the scavenging life of the Jawas constitutes a falling off from a better standard of living (that they are not the inherently disgusting creatures which C-3PO takes them to be, but a noble race undergoing bad times) may be the nicest thing anyone said about them until the 1990s. In making these assertions about the galactic economy and its consequences, however, Allnutt is interpreting far beyond any information given in the text. His concern is with the economic and moral collapse of the Republic, of which the Jawas's poor state is nothing more than a symptom. This necessarily leads him to discuss the corruption of the government itself:

The people of the Republic slowly drifted away from following the ways of the Force . . . Affluence gave way to materialism, and the wealth and power that once was used to develop new star systems were being concentrated more and more on personal luxuries and comforts at home. Among businessmen honest gain was scoffed at in favour of get rich schemes . . . As usually happens at this point in the life of any society, there appeared evil people. (p. 37)

None of this has any basis in the film, though the origins of some of it can be gleaned in the novelisation (an important text in the late 1970s and discussed as such in Chapter 3). Allnut projects his own views on contemporary America/ Europe as the film's backstory. If the reader assents at all to Allnutt's inventions, it is because of understandings about human nature and history shared by both writer and reader. Apparently casual language ('As usually happens . . .') invites our collusion in sweeping generalisations. Readers who shared his views on the sinful state of humanity might happily agree. Allnutt's foremost reference point, of course, is the role of the Caesars after the fall of Republican Rome.

Roman Emperors, like Palpatine, had visualised themselves as something greater than human. Some of them went so far as to proclaim themselves gods and demanded that their subjects bow down in homage before them.

There is no proof that Palpatine instituted Emperor worship, but that certainly must have crossed his mind for the future. (p. 67)

Against this vision of corruption at the top and a society adrift, Allnutt struck a populist note, foreseeing that a resolution to the ills of America/the West (he uses the terms interchangeably) may reside in the general populace. What prompted him to write his lengthy interpretation was the same question which other people, for other reasons, were asking: What is, to quote the title of *The Force of Star Wars*' opening chapter, 'the secret of *Star Wars*' popularity'? Allnutt's answer (and his new hope) is that although one generation has wrecked America with its self-absorbed immorality, the next may do better:

> Young people of today want to find reality, and they're looking everywhere to find it. Star Wars is a fantasy with a message about reality. It says to the viewer, 'Listen. There's something better in life than wallowing in the mud of pornography, dope, materialism and vain Philosophies. You have a higher calling – a calling to be somebody.' (p. 25)

Recalling 1977 from the perspective of the twenty-first century, Allnutt suggests that the book – evangelical Christianity's nineteenth best-selling book that year despite not appearing until August – found its market not in an evangelical niche but the cultural mainstream.

> Almost all of my books were sold off book racks in supermarkets and other secular retail stores. Christian book stores, for the most part, passed on carrying the title. And that because it was widely held in those days that Christians simply should not engage in such worldly pastimes [*sic*] as motion pictures.[9]

Can we accept at face value Allnutt's account of where his book sold, or is he too partisan a writer, or just too distant now from events? We will almost certainly never know, though it is certainly a possibility. From a twenty-first-century perspective, *The Force of Star Wars* looks like a cheap, opportunistic tie-in, but that was less obvious in 1977 when the merchandising of films was a much-less-polished operation than today. Unlike a lot of other products from the period, the cover uses Lucasfilm's official promotional artwork (by Greg Hildebrandt) and the proper logo. The blurb on the back is printed to look as if it recedes into the distance, affecting the look of the film's famous opening crawl. Inside are photographs from the film and the acknowledgements read, 'The author and publisher express appreciation to Charles Lippincott and to Twentieth Century Fox for supplying information and photographs for this book.' In 1977, *Force* looked a lot like the official tie-ins.

Lucas himself is not thanked for his help in *The Force of Star Wars*, but he would have recognised the argument which the book contained. He was widely quoted at the time as claiming, 'All I was trying to say in a very simple and straightforward way is that there is a God and there is a good and bad side,' a comment frequently ascribed by biographers to his Methodist upbringing.[10] In a 1979 interview, released in 1980 as part of Lucasfilm's promotion of *The Empire Strikes Back*, he discussed the issue with publicist Alan Arnold.

> *AA:* It's been said that in the United States Star Wars achieved an almost quasi-religious cult. What are your views about that?
>
> *GL:* A number of churches in America have used Star Wars as a way of getting young people interested in religious ideas. I think that's good. It gives young people something entertaining to relate to which at the same time may explain concepts of good and evil.
>
> *AA:* You don't see that as a weakness on the part of the churches themselves?
>
> *GL:* Not really. They're obviously trying to get young people to embrace religion. And that can't be too easy, considering how strong the amoral influence of television is today.[11]

Arnold's initial question is itself capable of various interpretations, and a modern interlocutor might assume that he was talking about fan activities or to the sporadic attempts to get *Jedi Knight* formally recognised as a religious category on census forms. Lucas preferred, in this interview, to view it in terms of organised Christianity and its wide social responsibilities. He endorses the church's use of *Star Wars* to interest 'young people' in religious questions. As the quote makes clear, it wasn't just Frank Allnutt who was worried about moral decline.

Lucas's public utterances over the years have shifted from such direct endorsements of Christianity. Careful readers of the book quoted above – which recounts the making of *Empire* during the late 1970s – can see the vocabularies shifting. Christian language is marginally present in comments about Darth Vader ('The Devil looks after him' – Dave Prowse, p. 114) and, more loosely still, director Irvin Kershner's talk of the films as 'morality plays' (p. 16), but a new term enters the discussion. Though it does not feature in *Empire* itself, the word *meditation* becomes prominent in the surrounding paratexts. In Arnold's book, it is used both in relation to the practices of director Kershner and the isolation chamber in which Vader resides when not on the Star Destroyer's bridge. In the film itself, the concept may not be named, but it is an influence as we begin to see Jedi and Sith turning inwards to contemplate their own psychospiritual state.

We can understand why the sequels would shed the Christian vocabulary of the first film. Ongoing secularisation in the West, and the desire to release the films in non-Christian countries, would make thinly veiled Christianity a risky proposition for high-budget films aimed at mass, youthful audiences. Narratively, the increasingly impressive displays of Jedi powers on show in the later films simply invalidated the faith:scepticism debate which that language had been used to articulate. Instead, a new vocabulary based on Buddhism began to circulate around the films. To self-consciously sophisticated and progressive audience members, Buddhism was acceptably liberal where Christianity was unfashionably naff. Nor was it implicated in the power structures of the Western world. Consequently, fans could embrace the new religious reading as a sign of the saga's philosophical sophistication. In his short book on Lucas, James Clarke later wrote:

> For those whose interest in the possibilities of Zen were sparked by Lucas' *Star Wars* stories then seek out the books *Zen Flesh, Zen Bones* and *Zen in the Art of Archery*. Yoda surely keeps these on his bookshelf.[12]

Lucasfilm itself became happy to endorse this reading in official publications. 'Jedi training shares similarities with Zen Buddhism,' reads *Star Wars: The Power of Myth*, a lavishly illustrated paperback guide to the series for children released in 1999, 'which holds that truth and enlightenment can be found through personal insights and self-mastery . . . as with Jedi training, Buddhist knowledge is handed down as an inspiration to students, who are "awakened" by a teacher who has experienced the truth of the teachings.'[13] These ideas formed part of Lucasfilm's preferred interpretation for over a decade, and this is discussed in Chapter 4. Unsurprisingly, the introduction of Buddhist-inspired material into the saga in *The Empire Strikes Back* put strain on the Christian interpretation.

The Christian reading across the decades

As the vocabulary of faith and scepticism was removed from the films, Christian readings of *Star Wars* would become less central to mainstream interpretations of the film before key elements began to return in the twenty-first century. Thus, though it casts a wide cultural net, the companion volume to the Smithsonian

Institution's 1997 'Star Wars: The Magic of Myth' exhibition doesn't mention Christianity until deep into its reading of Vader's redemption in *Jedi*.[14]

However, if the Christian reading of *Star Wars* was less central to mainstream interpretations of the film, within evangelical culture itself, the film(s) remained a reference point. In the years since 1977, evangelicals' interest in pop culture has changed substantially from the disinterest/disdain which Allnutt describes, and they have become keen to discuss media values and to provide practical lessons for church groups around well-known popular narratives. In *St Paul at the Movies* (1993), Robert Jewett contrasts the salvation offered by the film with that offered by the apostle, using *Romans* 1.16 as the peg upon which to hang his analysis: 'I am not ashamed [of] the gospel; it is the force of God for salvation to all who have faith.' In *Praying the Movies* (2002), Edward McNulty ignores the usual Christian reference points (Kenobi's resurrection, the Force) and considers instead the redemption of Han and Chewbacca. Chewie is, unusually, characterised by McNulty as selfish, a reading based on his need to win at the holographic game board in the Millennium Falcon. These are just two examples among many.[15] Frank Allnutt would periodically update *The Force of Star Wars* as the saga continued and provided him with fresh material to analyse. The cover of the fifth edition (1999, '*5th Edition with "Menace"!*') boasted of 200,000 copies 'in print'. A *Star Wars* fan who shopped regularly in America's religious bookstores could have built up quite a collection of analyses and reflections, even during the late 1980s/early 1990s when the films' popularity among mainstream audiences fell considerably. Evangelicals often emphasised the first film with less attention paid to the sequels, a preference which constituted a form of resistance by a specific cultural group to the trilogy-based interpretation which Lucasfilm insisted on so thoroughly. Those evangelicals who did take Lucas at his word, and discussed later films, were far more likely to be critical and far less inclined to allegory.

Reading popular culture allegorically was perhaps not the favoured practice of many evangelicals. In presenting his analysis, Allnutt had characterised *Star Wars* as 'a prophetic parable' (p. 26). Possibly, this was a calculated move to engage readers suspicious of popular culture: symbolic stories were at the heart of Jesus's own teaching practice, and Allnut's language affiliated *Star Wars* with this tradition. A later book, Phil Phillips's *Turmoil in the Toybox* (originally published in 1986, my 1990 edition boasts of 'over 135,000 in print' – no challenge to Frank Allnutt, but eye-watering enough for those of us used to academic print-runs), is an evangelical denunciation of a perceived creeping occultism in children's culture, and he dislikes the *Star Wars* trilogy appropriately. No fan of slippery symbolism, Phillips calls the film 'occult' because 'Yoda does not talk about following Jesus Christ. Instead, he urges Luke to rely on himself and use the power inherent in his mind to do "good"'.[16] Phillips's brand of Christianity must denounce the film because he has no competence at – nor any intention of practising – allegorical reading.

> There are those, however, who insist the movie has Christian ideals flowing through it. That may be true. Then, the danger here is the 'incompleteness of the gospel.' Some of the ideals presented could lead people to stray from the truth of the gospel. The elements that make Christianity a unique faith is the belief in the redemption of man through the death of Jesus Christ and his resurrection. This belief is not seen in the Jedi religion, not even in an allegorical sense. In *Return of the Jedi*, Darth Vader's salvation does not come through his repentance, but through the vanquishing of the evil Emperor. (p. 154)

Depending on exactly what you mean by *repentance*, there is scope to assume that Vader undertakes it in his final moments, but it is clear that Phillips's demand is for an exact recitation of Christian faith. Indeed, his insistence on literal reading makes him assert that Buddhism does not simply hang around the later films as a privileged allegory but enters the text literally. Yoda is 'known as Zen Master', he asserts on page 139 though this is, of course, untrue. Faced with such inept reading, most academics would write his book off as unworthy of attention. However, we should avoid such temptations. Phillips is not the last interpreter we will discuss whose pursuit of a reading leads him to believe that the subtext he is discussing is rendered literal in the films, and nor is this limited to the political right or to non-academics (see next chapter). To further muddy the waters of easy prejudice, let me add that Phillips's concerns about the female body shape promoted by Barbie dolls are well observed, backed up with evidence and fit perfectly with leftist concerns both then and today.

Conservative or not, Phillips's differences with the Christian interpretations discussed previously do not turn just on a refusal to accept symbolic meaning but also on the characterisation of the Force.

'The Force requires faith (not everyone believes it exists), but it does not have a personality,' he writes. 'It "runs strong" in certain people, but it does not have a will of its own' (p. 149). He adopts a tone of certainty in this matter, but is he right? This is a recurrent question across analyses and spin-off texts: is the Force active in a way which would seem to imply sentience, and which is, thus, readable as God? Do we work it or does it work us? Onboard the Millennium Falcon, the film is its usual oblique self.

> *Kenobi:* Remember a Jedi can feel the Force flowing through him.
> *Luke:* You mean it controls your actions?
> *Kenobi:* Partially, but it also obeys your commands.

The later films perhaps privilege the second half of this arrangement, and Phillips dislikes it accordingly as a New Age power of the self. Frank Allnutt, by contrast, had always favoured the first part, and many subsequent Christian commentators have followed him. Decades later, Caleb Grimes, in his deftly titled *Star Wars Jesus* (not a word wasted in that title!), points to apparent coincidences within the film to assert the will and agency of the Force.[17]

> Without intervention by the Force, R2-D2 and C-3PO probably would never have reached Obi-Wan Kenobi; Luke Skywalker would probably still be stuck on his Uncle Owen's moisture farm indefinitely; and Han Solo most likely would be captured or killed by Jabba the Hutt's henchmen. (p. 25)

He expands this view into the spiritual life of Kenobi, who

> must have wondered about the purpose of his watching over Luke on Tatooine, and asked himself and Yoda (through the Force) whether his skills wouldn't be better served somewhere else? The evil Empire is growing stronger every day, but Obi-Wan does not resort to frantic movements or panicked responses, he listens to the Force and remains still. Only in stillness can one learn to hear its voice. (p. 27)

The question of the Force, who it speaks to and who has access to it is not a small one. It has real-world referents. The guardians of the Force, those who interpret its meaning, act upon what they take to be its will and who represent it to the public at large, are the Jedi. They acquire increased presence as the saga develops, moving from the stuff of legend to the centre of the action. Since 1977, however, church-going has declined in America, and the moral understandings bequeathed by Christianity have been significantly challenged to the degree that some prominent public intellectuals argue that religion should have no place in the public sphere.[18] Believers themselves are frequently perceived as being markedly at odds with the mainstream world of liberal secular consumerism. In such a world, can the Jedi still be the people's heroes? It is a question which has troubled the *Star Wars* franchise in the new millennium.

Marginalising the Jedi

From 1991 onwards, a series of Lucasfilm-generated books were published as the official continuation of the saga. Unlike prior novels, released sporadically and written as standalone volumes, this 'expanded universe' plotted the course of the characters' lives over the forty years since *Return of the Jedi* and reached far back into the *Star Wars* universe's timeline. Han and Leia married and had children, while Luke trained a new generation of Jedi to safeguard the New Republic. I do not wish to discuss at length the complexities of this branch of the *Star Wars* universe, but a number of books have consciously dramatised the distancing of religious belief from the apparent mainstream. In the book *Ambush at Corellia*, Luke is asked by Mon Mothma how his new generation of Jedi will relate to the general populace.

> In the years to come, as the Jedi grow from a handful of students into an order of thousands of Knights, will they set themselves up as an elite priesthood or a band of champions? Are they to be cut off from the people by privilege and mystique, answerable to themselves alone? Or will they act in the service of the people, be intimately bound to the people . . . There must be a Jedi on every planet, a Jedi in every city – not a few planets full of Jedi and nothing else. (p. 48)[19]

In the same book, Luke is reminded that Force-users will always be in the minority and that he should always remember this, not generalising about the world from his own privileged position (p. 198). In other post-millennial *Star Wars* novels, the disconnect between Jedi and populace has grown even greater. A trilogy based around a character called Darth Bane takes place centuries before the films at a time when the Jedi have faced off against powerful Sith Lords, apparently vanquishing them. However, if they think that their victory will be welcomed by the galactic powers, they are to be disappointed. The Supreme Chancellor suggests:

> Over the past four centuries we have seen Jedi declare war on the agents of the dark side time and time again. It is a struggle that never ends. And with each conflict, more civilians are swept up in your web of war. Innocent beings die as armies align with you or your enemies. There are many good people who fear the Jedi and what they are capable of. They see the Jedi as instigators of war. You claim your actions are guided by the Force, but to those who cannot feel its presence it appears as if your order is not accountable to anyone or anything.[20]

These extracts dramatise the gap between a religiously empowered minority and the larger populace. We see the same issue in the prequel trilogy. These films do not venture as deeply into the culture wars as the novels, but while the Jedi retain the confidence of the official powers, they are depicted as alienated from the general populace. They have a 'temple', but there is no evidence that it is open for public worship or charitable community service. The ideas around it – their vows of chastity, etc. – connote not an open space but a monastery closed to the uninitiated. Obi-Wan's visit to diner-owner Dexter Jettster in *Attack of the Clones* is the only instance of a Jedi having friends outside the order (and even here he is after information). As he and Anakin pursue an assassin through a nightclub in the same film, the clientele look at the Knights with suspicion, and Anakin curtly tells them 'Jedi business – go back to your drinks'. Even allowing for the fact that they are in a part of town where law enforcement officials are probably not welcome, the sequence demonstrates the gap between the Jedi and the populace they notionally serve. These arrangements have not helped the knights who find that 'our ability to use the Force is diminished'. Naturally, they keep these concerns to themselves, apparently trusting no one outside the order with the information.

This plotline is never developed. Though the representation of the Jedi's distance from the populace is consistent, no one raises it as a theme. As is frequently the case with the prequels, it is impossible to know from the films as we view them if this was intended or not – though if we wish to argue, Frank Allnutt style, that the Republic fell because the people turned their back on the Force, there is potential evidence here. What is not here, by contrast, is anything of the film of 1977. The notion that those without Force powers might band together with those who do and wish 'May the Force be with you' as an everyday blessing is gone. There is no community between Jedi and non-Jedi, just a distrust aimed by the populace at the lightsabre-wielding zealots whose talk of good and evil threatens the prosperous, secular 'end of ideology' community at large.

The same notion is present – playfully, I assume, not least because the author uses the name Comfortably Smug – in a 2015 online essay entitled 'The Radicalisation of Luke Skywalker' in which the original trilogy is viewed through the lens of contemporary debates across America and Europe about the radicalisation of young Muslim men by Islamist extremists. The author asserts that Luke is typical of those young men who are radicalised: his life is without direction, and he lacks both a father and friends outside his family. He is trained by radical Force-users, firstly Kenobi (who recruits him by lying about his father's death) and later Yoda, 'an extremist cleric who runs a Jedi madrasa on Dagobah'. We have shifted here to using Islam as a reference point (something the original trilogy does not deal with), but like the *Bane* trilogy, it draws on the unease about religious practice, and accompanying negative imagery of it, which is now part of contemporary debate.[21]

I presume that this internet essay is a joke interpretation, and that the author intended us to read it, smile and move on. Even jokes have their structures, however, and the humour in this one lies in both the application of a vocabulary which, though familiar to readers, is not one which they are likely to have considered applying to *Star Wars*, and the ways in which standard critical practices are then followed (the theme is, after all, mapped onto familiar moments in the films in a standard critical manner) to produce a reading which is clearly not the one originally intended.

A world in which this constitutes humour might seem unlikely soil for the Christian reading to flourish in, but it is hardy and does not die. The influence of biblical epic cinema re-erupts spectacularly in later films. *The Phantom Menace* features both a reworking of *Ben Hur*'s chariot race and a virgin birth, while *Attack of the Clones* has an ancient world-style arena sequence. The entire saga retains a strong Messianic streak, and in the Disney era, Christianity visibly returns to mainstream interpretation, and this is discussed in Chapter 6. It flourishes also in less public areas: evangelical publishing continues to interpret the text to its audience, and academic theology has taken up the task in the twenty-first century. The former has had to make peace with an increasingly multicultural society, but it has, for the most part, been up to the task. 'I would like to make myself clear,' asserts the author of *Star Wars Jesus*, 'It is not my goal to convert to Christianity those who love *Star Wars*.'[22]

These books may seem marginal compared to more mainstream, authorised *Star Wars* products, but they certainly share qualities with other, more general trends in *Star Wars* interpretations. Frank Allnutt wrote a short book based on the novelisation, some unknown quantity of film viewings and his enthusiasm for what he felt the film pointed towards. He quoted a few other Christian commentators. Grimes writes three times as much and finds parallels with C. S. Lewis and Joseph Campbell. Academic theologian John C. McDowell relates the films to St Thomas Aquinas, Hannah Arendt, Aristotle, Augustine and Brian Aldiss. And that's just the first letter of the alphabet.[23]

Star Wars interpretations, then, Christian or otherwise, increase in size and complexity as history progresses: twenty-first century analysts are armed with

DVDs/Blu-rays and, often, literally decades of enthusiasm. For those with access to every image and every line of dialogue, and who feel it legitimate to bring to bear on them any amount of exterior reference, the films reveal depths of meanings that their earliest interpreters would struggle to believe. With it come radical shifts in interpretation. For Grimes it is not Kenobi, but 'Luke and Anakin whose characters most evidence the person of Jesus' (p. 241).[24]

Grimes and McDowell both loaded their books with detail, but neither author presents a case for the saga being fully coherent the way Allnutt did in 1977. He felt that all that was interesting about the film boiled down to a central point and that that point had been put there, with whatever degree of consciousness, by its writer-director. For Grimes and McDowell, by contrast, the films are ever fruitful, but the elements within them and the reflections they provoke are not fully compatible. These sorts of publications will continue to appear. The *Star Wars* saga is perhaps the most prominent metaphysical vocabulary in contemporary popular culture, and Christians will continually feel the need to address this. Even outside of theology – popular or academic – Christianity has returned, after a long absence, to a major position within post-millennial *Star Wars* studies. Will Brooker's analysis of the film, published in 2009 as part of the British Film Institute's 'Film Classics' series, is not at all interested in religious interpretations, but 'Christians' is the eighth word of the book.[25] In his overview of the saga's influences and meanings, Cass Sunstein pays dutiful attention to both Christianity and Buddhism, but it is the former which escapes from its delegated subsection to permeate the book before the author concludes, 'Is it feminist (Kind of). Is it about Christianity? (Yes) Does it embrace Buddhism (It tries, at times, but nope, not at all, anything but).'[26] Even Frank Allnutt's book has been rescued from neglect by commentators keen to record much that was previously marginalised in *Star Wars* history. Chris Taylor, in his compendious *How Star Wars Conquered the Universe*, records how one fan found in the book a crucial bridge between the film he loved so much and the Christian family within which he was being raised.[27] After neglecting it for decades, Lucasfilm now acknowledges *The Force of Star Wars* in major histories of the franchise.[28]

In the late 1970s, the Christian reading, or large components of it, was not limited to active Christians. Other people similarly understood the film as a call to rejuvenate a staid secularity through a religious revelation, and the arguments of one group of them are considered in the next chapter. The difference is that they were historical materialists – and they did not approve.

2

Star Wars and the Reagan revolution

Star Wars' opening statement ('A long time ago in a galaxy far far away') rejects relevance to our own lives, and many have been happy to accept this, finding in the films only escapism. Analysts keen to draw connections to our own times, by contrast, have been punning ever since in their titles: *A Galaxy Not So Far Away*, *A Galaxy Here and Now*, *Not So Long Ago, Not So Far Away*.[1] Frank Allnutt had interpreted *Star Wars* according to a principle which passes for common sense across much of the world: he assumed that the meanings he found in the film had been placed there, more or less consciously, by the writer-director, and they acquired significance precisely because he had done so. Left-wing political critics of the late 1970s favoured a very different style of interpretation, seeking to reveal a very different level of meaning. They wished to uncover the values which underlay the story – assumptions and implications of which the authors might not be aware. We shall find people in this chapter who think *Star Wars* is racist, sexist, imperialist and violent, but in making these claims, they are not demonising Lucas as any worse than the rest of us. Rather, the argument is that America was all of these things in 1977, and so its most popular entertainment manifested these features as well.

While *Star Wars* contains much language related to diplomacy and bureaucracy, the explicit drawing of parallels between the events of the film and real-world geopolitics is avoided. The closest the film came to such a parallel was contained in a well-known sequence which, though filmed, was edited out. The scene concerns Luke and his friend Biggs Darklighter on Tatooine. After years of pseudo-existence in the spin-off texts, the sequence was finally made available in the Blu-ray box set of episodes I–VI in 2011. Having separated themselves from their friends, the two young men talk about why Biggs is going to try and join the rebellion and why Luke has, once again, deferred his application to 'The Academy'.

Luke: We've got almost enough vaporators to make the place pay off. I have to
stay one more season. I can't leave them now.

Biggs: What good's all your uncle's work if the Empire just take it over? You
know they've already started to nationalise commerce in the central
systems? It won't be long before your uncle's just a tenant slaving for the
greater glory of the Empire.

Luke: Oh that won't happen here. You said yourself, the Empire wouldn't even
mess with this old rock.

Biggs's description of the Empire's economic ambitions opposes nationalised
commerce, ruled from the centre, with what we see on Tatooine: small holdings
owned and worked by individual farmers. By this reading, the Empire stands for
state centralisation on the model of the Soviet Union – meaning that the rebels,
implicitly or otherwise, represent the capitalist West.[2] Even this is not entirely
clear (the Soviet vocabulary of collective work on farms did not include the role
of 'tenant'), but the film's broad opposition of 'nationalise(d)' and free market
commerce would come as no surprise to the critics considered in this chapter.
They understood the film precisely as a product of capitalism, one which sought
to re-enforce the social norms of that economic system and mollify anxieties felt
across Western societies in the years since the 1960s.

For left-wing cultural theorists, capitalist societies are riven by contradictions,
resulting in an anxious populace. In such a context, popular culture's primary (if
unstated and not completely conscious) aim is to produce fantasy solutions to
those contradictions which will, for a short while, seem to resolve the situations,
thus soothing the anxieties of the populace and allowing the reigning political
ideas to continue to dominate. The balm provided by any individual film cannot
sustain itself in the long term, however; so popular culture is required to endlessly reproduce false resolutions to real problems as constant assurance. The
production of sequels (a development which *Star Wars* and Lucasfilm came to be
seen as instrumental in making a mainstream practice) simply formalised this
job of providing repeated reassurance. The resulting analyses were invariably
critical of popular culture, the bad faith of which it was thought to be the critic's
responsibility to expose.

A number of academic critics responded to *Star Wars* in this way in the
late 1970s, setting a framework for understanding which would be continued
in the 1980s by other academics who, with more films to view, could produce
a broader analysis. In Britain, the magazines *Framework* and *Sight and Sound*
printed pieces in this vein, while the longest, most sustained work was done by

Dan Rubey in the US academic journal *Jump Cut*.[3] *Framework*'s reading was the pithiest: '*Star Wars* has sold because it has helped to alleviate anxieties caused by the 1960s. Its success is part of a huge, instinctive endeavour by the media to put away forever that troublesome decade' (p. 43). Dan Rubey's, however, was more thorough, and it is his I shall discuss here.

Rubey wrote his lengthy analysis while completing a dissertation on the ideological underpinnings of medieval romances. *Star Wars*' vocabulary of knights and princesses constituted a clear link to that form of storytelling, and he was drawn to the film as a way of understanding how those ideologies (which he regarded as archaic) continued to work in modern popular culture. Rubey argues that the United States is committed to the celebration of individual action, but that the emergence of a high-tech mass society has rendered it impossible for the individual to make a difference. Moreover, the moral norms and social arrangements of American society were the products of religious beliefs which have been discarded by post-war secularity. Those Christian norms, however, notionally remained in place as laws, cultural norms and social expectations, even though their metaphysical foundation had been abandoned. These are the cultural contradictions, he argues, of modern America. For him, the interest of *Star Wars*' imagery and narrative workings is precisely that they are symptoms of a wider cultural condition – symptoms from which that wider condition can be diagnosed.

Given this as a starting point, it is not difficult to guess what Rubey makes of *Star Wars*. The film does present a hi-tech environment run by faceless Imperial technocrats with a 'bureaucracy' and enforced by masked stormtroopers. On Tatooine, Luke does indeed feel unable to make a difference. Though his alienation may be escalated by his being stuck on a desert planet, his feelings of social impotence differ from the rest of us only by degree. His world is redeemed, however, by the Force which, re-igniting the metaphysical justification for action, allows him to play a pivotal role, as an individual, in galactic politics, without much in the way of training, specialised knowledge or practice. The film must be a war movie, Rubey argues, because combat is an arena within which outdated notions of heroism and individual action can still be displayed. He also points to the convenience of the Death Star's thermal exhaust port. The rebel alliance could not really overthrow an Empire so dispersed that it was administered by a network of regional governors and bureaucracy, so its power must be incarnated in something they can destroy (p. 7). Subsequent films have made full use of the same narrative strategy: both Death Stars can be taken out by snub fighters; the battledroid army on Naboo is controlled from a single source; the Jedi can be wiped out near instantly by issuing the clone army with Order 66; Starkiller base can be destroyed by overloading the thermal oscillator; the communications tower in *Rogue One* has a 'masterswitch' conveniently located at its base; the First Order tracks the resistance fleet through hyperspace in *The Last Jedi* via a system located on only one ship; and the new Imperial fleet in *The Rise of Skywalker* is controlled from a single point. In *Return of the Jedi*, the Emperor himself becomes such a nodal point, a being ascribed such power that the whole Empire will apparently collapse following his death. In his book on *Star Wars* fans, Will Brooker records that some suggest that the Emperor 'was controlling the Imperial Forces with his mind', an interpretation which was treated with 'friendly contempt' by others.[4] However, if one were to attempt a full narrative explanation of how the massive forces incarnated in these nodal points actually worked, or why the death of a single individual can bring the trilogy to a happy close, one would be dragged into this sort of answer (which is surely why the films avoid explanations).

In destroying the Death Star, Rubey suggests, Luke validates the social order by showing that it is still possible to take decisive action within it, and to acquire the proper rewards (a medal, the chance to court a princess). The film must be an adventure film because that is the only genre where individual actions can be played out as meaningful. 'The film's dogfights and one-man fighters are an attempt to recapture the glamour of WWII films and disassociate ourselves from the destructive role that our bombers and rockets actually played in Vietnam' (p. 4). For Rubey, as for others, the Vietnam War was the one which could not be openly acknowledged in *Star Wars* (hence no ground-level combat), but the scar which it left upon America could be revealed by a symptomatic reading.[5]

This generic affiliation with the war film means that the contradiction which *Star Wars* must spend most of its time negotiating is that of violence. American moral discourse disapproves of violence, Rubey argues, but the nation is itself an aggressive society, and the state operates its own systems of violence through armed law enforcement, the death penalty and military adventurism. Rubey demonstrates how the film negotiates the problem of violence by suggesting that rebels and the Empire carry out equivalent actions, as follows:

Vader chokes the general: Kenobi mind-manipulates stormtroopers

The Empire destroys Alderaan: rebels destroy the Death Star

Stormtroopers enter Leia's spaceship: heroes enter the Death Star

Vader breaks a rebel's neck: Kenobi slices a man's arm off

Star Destroyer pursues Leia's ship: Falcon pursues TIE fighter

Are these really equivalent actions, as Rubey asks us to believe? The film insists that they are not, and uses a moral language to contextualise events so that the rebels always have a justification for their action: Kenobi is defending Luke in the cantina; the Death Star was built for destruction unlike 'peaceful' Alderaan; while Vader actively pursues Leia's ship, the Falcon's 'pursuit' of the TIE fighter is a quick marginal moment in the film (this is the only critical piece I know of which uses this brief event as part of its reading; nobody else attaches interpretive significance to this minor action), etc.

Rubey understands these arguments, but he refuses to take the film's moral vocabulary at face value, just as he critiques US intervention in foreign countries which he sees as based on similarly misapplied ethical claims, and he argues that the two are related: that popular culture contextualises certain violent actions as justified, heroic, undertaken for the liberation of others and/or self-defensive, and this salves audience anxieties over their own lives while providing a vocabulary through which American governments can justify their own actions in combat.

With the two sides morally equivalent, Rubey argues that *Star Wars* can offer nothing to its audiences. A reversal of fortune – whereby the Empire was overthrown – would simply perpetuate more of the same. 'There is no revolutionary change, no reordering of priorities, no new knowledge which fundamentally transforms reality,' Rubey writes (p. 10). This is, of course, a direct assault upon the film's obvious meaning, which is precisely to show how a world can be transformed by the revelation of the Force. Frank Allnutt embraced that message, but Rubey insists that no real change is offered as the religious terms upon which it is based are fraudulent.

Allnutt and Rubey could not be further apart on the issue of whether *Star Wars* offers hope of social transformation, but this should not blind us to all the common ground they share. Both view the 1970s as a period of crisis and see the huge success of the film as resulting from its offering a response to that. For Allnutt, the Force is a legitimate clue to a very real spirituality which viewers need to embrace, but for Rubey, it is a desperate attempt to alleviate unresolvable anxieties by reinstating bankrupt 'metaphysical justifications'. It is hard to imagine Rubey sitting down to read *The Force of Star Wars*, but he would not be surprised by its content and would regard Allnutt as a competent, if extreme, reader of the film's fraudulent rhetoric.

This argument reaches its heart in the film's final sequence where Han and Luke are honoured with medals. This scene has been a magnet for political critics because it seems to implicate the rebels in exactly the sort of military imagery used throughout the film to characterise the Empire.

> Martial tones dominate the scene and the accompanying music. The military position of 'attention' and the practice of lining troops up in precise rows is an attempt to deny the human' body's weakness and vulnerability, to make human beings hard-edged and precise like their weapons. Up to this conclusion, the bad guys have been associated with their rigid body-armour, impenetrable mask-like helmets, and heavily-armoured Death Star. (p. 6)

This militaristic interpretation of the rebels is encouraged by Lucas's decision to model it on a sequence from a prior film, Leni Riefenstahl's *Triumph of the Will* (1935). Riefenstahl was a German filmmaker who shot films which she later asserted to be neutral documentary-making, but which most viewers have found to glorify the Nazi public spectacles which they record so artistically.[6] In her footage of a rally, Hitler and other senior Nazis make their way down a central aisle towards a raised dais, flanked on either side by the faithful called to attention (in this case, raising the Nazi salute). Upon reaching the dais, they ascend it and turn to face the crowd. This is the framework upon which Lucas models his conclusion, and his decision to do so has granted hostile analysts a textual cue upon which to hang arguments about the evil at the heart of *Star Wars*.[7]

That the medal-awarding ceremony rewards Luke and Han, but not apparently Chewie, has worried some commentators from 1977 onwards. It suggests that the film is rife with what a later generation would call *white male privilege*, and this spills over into the representation of other races. From the Jawas and Tusken Raiders in 1977 through Jar Jar Binks and Watto in 1999, the *Star Wars* films have been accused of including elements of negative racial stereotyping in the characterisation of certain aliens. In the twenty-first century, the common practice is to take demeaning stereotypes of specific groups and map them onto *Star Wars* aliens, thus apparently exposing the limits of white America's imagination. 'Sandpeople, or Tusken Raiders, are Tatooine-based vicious brutes who live out in the desert. They wear long pale robes and keep their faces covered,' writes one twenty-first-century website, before continuing, 'That's right, the Arabs are next on the long list of groups that *Star Wars* apparently has a problem with.'[8]

Arguments of this type are conspicuously absent in writings of the late 1970s/ early 1980s. Even when individual racial slurs are perceived, they are not made the centre of the analysis. This is not to say that they are completely absent. Jonathan Rosenbaum wrote of the Jawas:

> While the original 1936 FLASH GORDON serial could allude to the to the 'Yellow Peril' directly through Ming the Merciless without any sort of embarrassment, the styling of the Jawas as stingy Jewish merchants – 'Munchkin Shylocks' in Richard Corliss's apt phrase – is much more oblique and subtle: one might even have to see the relationship of 'Jawa' to the Hebrew 'Yaweh' in order to catch the clue. (p. 106)

This sort of analysis, however, was the exception not the rule. Rather than making much critical effort to match caricatures to real-world referents, and believing that that was enough, critics of the period are much more concerned to make a wider, more structural point. *Star Wars*, Rubey argues, privileges white males – Luke and Han – as the agents of change, and everyone else has subordinate roles. The demeaning nature of any individual characterisation can easily slot into this argument, but it was rarely the point, and the wider issue was always emphasised. Even if the alien beings exhibited no racist traits, they would still function as a subordinate 'other' to the white males at the narrative's centre.

A primary concern here is the subordination of women to men. Depending on how you gauge the gender of the aliens in the cantina (a question which nobody was asking in 1977), the film famously only has two women in it: Aunt Beru and Princess Leia. The first is easily dismissed by Rubey as acting only in the domestic sphere: 'When Luke's aunt isn't stuffing artichokes into the Cuisinart, she serves first as a mediator between Luke and his uncle and then as a motive for revenge' (p. 8). Leia is a more complex case, a major role which necessarily brings with it a range of actions. As ever in interpretation, the question is which aspects of the text's many features to prioritise. Rubey acknowledges the conflicting messages sent by the character before making his judgement:

> Princess Leia, despite her attractive spunkiness and toughness, basically fulfils the same male-oriented roles. She is the traditional damsel in distress . . . Although she does grab a laser gun at one point and fires a few shots, she remains dependent on male rescuers, and the only action she initiates during the

rescue almost gets them killed in a garbage crusher. Her most memorable line, repeated over and over by her holographic image, is 'Help me, Obi-Wan Kenobi, you're my only hope'. (p. 8)

Rubey does note Leia's empowering moments, though he undervalues them relative to later interpreters, such as when he views the garbage-masher incident as an example of her leading the team into danger rather than being a brilliant improvisation. In his writing, Leia's positive qualities are always placed in the first halves of sentences, and the crucial second halves undercut their value. The film's flaunting of its traditional basis in fairy tales and myths allows Rubey to project traditional notions of female servitude onto the character. 'Damsel in distress' is a phrase we shall follow across the decades through various understandings of Leia's character. Rubey returns several times to her retreating into the background of the plot as the film reaches its final act: 'During the attack on the Death Star, she merely stands as a spectator' (p. 8).

Similarly, Rubey sees the droids and Chewbacca as happy to serve in subsidiary roles. Luke may gain audience sympathy by his compassionate dealings with the droids, but they remain his property (as Threepio's frequent references to 'Master Luke' attest), while Chewbacca is seemingly content to get no medal, and none of them enters into the competition for Leia's affections, which is the terrain only of Han and Luke. We should note that though his relationship with Chewie is later idealised as a life-bond and a partnership of equals, in *Star Wars* itself, Han always talks of 'I' not 'we'. It is Han – not the pair of them – who owes Jabba money. In the recurrence of such relationships, Rubey argues 'not that the treatment of robots in STAR WARS is racist, but that the film makes use of and supports racist habits of thought when it divides its characters up into hierarchical levels based on their physical attributes'. Reading the medal-awarding ceremony as the ultimate re-imposition of traditional values leads Rubey to make a notable error. He regards Leia's subordinate position to be a consequence of a patriarchal structure, and, consequently, his analysis assumes that the rebel commander standing at the top of the raised steps at the final ceremony is Leia's father and that her position within the ceremony is to mediate between this parental authority and the younger generation represented by Luke and Han. Like the evangelical Phil Philips, who thought Yoda was literally referred to onscreen as 'Zen master', Rubey projects the deep metaphors he uncovers into a literal presence within the text's narrative.

Rubey's was the most sustained political analysis of this period, but the issues he was discussing were far from unique. 1978 saw the same concerns sketched out in a shorter piece in the British journal *Framework*.[9] The magazine analysed the film in a section labelled 'Hollywood corner', effectively marginalising mainstream American filmmaking as effectively as *Star Wars* allegedly marginalises its non-humans. Using a Freudian model, the journal assumes that the sexuality which the film's child-friendly nature minimises manifests itself elsewhere in the text, both as the Force ('obviously unconscious and libidinal') and the final action, which it summarises thus: 'In the climax of the film Luke must prove his manhood by guiding his spacecraft through a long narrow corridor to plant his bomb into a two-metre hole, so exploding the Death Star' (both quotes p. 42).

The articles discussed here found a general political conservatism within *Star Wars*. They had only a single film and a general, though acute, sense of national crisis to work with. Analysts who followed them subsequently refined the interpretation in the light of subsequent films and political events. When Ronald Reagan was elected president in 1980, conservatism had a new centre – and political critiques of *Star Wars* had a new focal point.

Ronald Reagan and *Star Wars*

The Democratic administration of Jimmy Carter (in office 1977–81) had seemed weak in the face of foreign aggression. It was unable to deal with the problems which beset the American economy, notably an energy crisis which led him to request that Americans turn to energy-saving measures such as car-pooling, 'live(ing) thriftily' and lowering the thermostat and wearing a sweater instead. From the multiple economic dramas of the 1970s and the crisis of American confidence following the Vietnam War and the Watergate scandal emerged a 'New Right' which sought economic deregulation, increased defence budgets, traditional social norms and harsher dealings with lawbreakers.[10]

The Reagan administration (1981–9) became the talismanic symbol of this movement – its biggest electoral success – and the narrative and values of *Star Wars* were easily mapped onto this political re-alignment by left-wing analysts. Luke had, after all, begun the film in a malaise. He was trapped inside Tatooine's subsistence economy where work is hard, luxuries few and energy units are powered down overnight. He is pulled from this environment (easily interpreted as an allegory for the energy crisis-ridden West) to a brighter world where heroism is possible and the existence of the energy required to power giant starships is so taken for granted that no one bothers to talk about it.

That last detail is mine, but it would mesh perfectly with the views of those who saw the film as embodying the New Right and anticipating Reagan's victory (indeed, in his essay, Rubey mourned the destruction of the Lars moisture farm which he viewed as the only ecologically sensitive institution in the film and, as such, something to be emulated, not fled). The addition of the film's chapter heading made it easy to affiliate the film with the rise of the New Right. Critics Michael Ryan and Douglas Kellner made the connection: 'films like *Star Wars* offered what many white middle class Americans were seeking in the late seventies – "A New Hope".[11] Although the trilogy was two-thirds complete before Reagan was elected, enthusiasm for the mood of *Star Wars* was seen as an indicator of people's desire for dramatic action, a desire which subsequently manifested itself in votes for the Republican party. For these critics, the action-adventure format is distinctive, for it makes conservatism – as Reagan made it – into something other than a passive acceptance of the status quo, recasting it instead as something dynamic which has been lost and must be heroically striven and fought for.

Like Ryan and Kellner, Robin Wood writes from a later point than Rubey and can extend his arguments to encompass the matter of sequels and other products of 1980s cinema.[12] The move towards sequels by Hollywood and its audiences alike allows Wood to expand Rubey's theme of the reassurance provided by the film in the face of an anxious and complex social reality. Like his predecessors, he uses psychoanalytic language to construct his argument, likening audience behaviour towards these films to that of a child playing. Young children, he asserts, find reassurance in repetition and, for this reason, will play the same game again and again until it grows bored and requires something new – a new game very like the old favourite but with some element of novelty. Wood projects this psychic process onto the viewing of *Star Wars* and other 1980s blockbusters. Those who viewed the film many times were like the youngest child, endlessly playing the same game, and when they required something new (something a bit different but not very), there were *Empire* and *Jedi*. Also, by extension, there were similar films such as the Lucas-produced *Raiders of the Lost Ark* (Steven Spielberg, 1981) which replayed the same heroics. The mindset of those who would use cinema in this way – to revert itself to the state where a young child's pleasures are an acceptable comparison – is one which is turning away from the problems of the complex world and is, Wood argues, ripe for manipulation by the New Right whose simple answers and reassertions of old values parallel the actions of the film.

Central to Wood's perception of the 1980s Hollywood blockbuster was his understanding of genre. Dan Rubey was a medievalist, and he had viewed *Star Wars* in terms of its reuse of the narrative forms of the Middle Ages. Wood's background was in the study of cinema itself, and he looked at the trilogy in terms of its reuse of the genre forms of the 1930s and 1940s. In both cases, the argument was the same: Lucas presented his sources as eternal stories, something primal and always present. Rubey and Wood assert that they are not: they are the political ideology of a certain age crystallised into an exciting narrative format, and those ideologies were repressive and had been shown to be so by the liberationist political movements of the post-war period. Wood's essay appeared in a book where he applauded the films of Robert Altman and Michael Cimino, directors whose films not only questioned the traditional structures and meanings of American society but did so by destabilising the conventions of Hollywood genres, the narrative format within which the national ideology was played out. The politics which they were attacking was precisely what Lucas was reinstating under cover of . . . well, the Ewoks.

> Consider also the exotic adventure movie: our white heroes, plus comic relief, encounter a potentially hostile tribe, but the natives turn out to be harmless, childlike, innocent – they have never seen a white man before, and they promptly worship our heroes as gods. You can't do that any more: such movies (mostly despised 'B' movies anyway) don't get shown now, and if we saw one on late-night television we would have to laugh at it. But dress the natives as koala bears, displace the god identity onto a robot so that the natives appear even stupider, and you can still get away with it: the natives can still be childlike, lovable and ready to help the heroes out of a fix; the nature of the laughter changes from repudiation to complicity. (p. 167/8)

Wood's argument is informed by developments which earlier commentators knew nothing about. His contextualisation of the meeting of rebels and Ewoks, for instance, is quite possibly influenced by Lucas's involvement with the *Indiana Jones* films – films set in the 1930s where American adventurers travel the developing world for ancient artifacts which are subsequently, at best, publicly displayed in American museums (though they also fight Nazis). In all important respects, however, Wood's argument reiterates Rubey's. The earlier critic's concern with the first film's construction of 'hierarchical levels' which prioritise young white males is repeated in Wood's critique of the trilogy's revitalisation of generic conventions which privilege white adventurers who, in a strange environment, encounter simplistic 'natives'.

What remains largely absent is the direct matching of specific characters against the supposedly racist caricatures which they allegedly repeat. The Ewoks are not said to represent any specific race, just a type of 'native' other. Should we be surprised? I think not. While the cultural analysis of the mid-1980s had inherited from feminism a vocabulary sufficient to make lengthy arguments about Princess Leia's perceived passivity (and the consciousness about the Jawas quoted earlier brings to bear the vocabulary of decades-long debates about anti-Semitism), the wider vocabulary for discussing racial representations that we know today had not yet been fully developed (as evidenced, I think, by the fact that Wood himself was happy to write of 'natives', rather than, for example, 'indigenous people', and he did not feel obliged to put quotation marks around the terms, unlike me). The emphasis is on how the films impose large structures of privilege rather than policing individual infractions in the name of specific groups. The days of loud public denunciations of a single character (such as those which greeted the release of *The Phantom Menace*), internet lists which explain exactly which ethnic groups are being caricatured, and twenty-five-page essays on the relationship between Tusken Raiders and the Bedouin people[13] are decades in the future at this point, though the same concerns are clearly being aired. Wood was concerned with larger structures – structures which had been called into question by post-war politics and which the New Right was seeking to reinstate rather as Lucas affirmed traditional narrative storytelling rather than questioning it. Borrowing a phrase from another critic, Andrew Britton, Wood labelled *Star Wars* and similar films 'Reaganite entertainment'.

It is not difficult to make stylistic connections between *Star Wars* and Reagan. A prominent television ad of his 1984 campaign became known as *Morning in America*, a phrase subsequently associated with the president (although the ad actually ran 'It's morning again in America'), and the same symbol of a new day is at work in *Star Wars*. The first day's actions conclude in frustration with a family supper sequence from which Luke exits declaring, 'Looks like I'm not going anywhere' and the evening ritual of powering down. Up at sunrise the next day to search for the missing R2-D2, Luke is catapulted into a new life wherein there is no time for mere sleep. However productive we might find such comparisons, we do not ultimately need to work hard to forge such connections. Reagan himself, not wholly intentionally, would end up indelibly associated with the film through his administration's plans to develop a space-based defence project, officially named the Strategic Defence Initiative but popularly known as the 'Star Wars Project' or, more simply, 'Star Wars'. Although aerial defence systems had been mooted by American defence theorists as early as the mid-1940s (when the concern was German V2 rockets), its development had been shelved when super power strategy had turned towards a 'balance of power' theory that America and the USSR would not dare attack each other for fear of each other's nuclear reprisals. In the 1980s, Reagan's game-changing proposal was to establish platforms in space which would use laser technology to destroy missiles in the upper atmosphere. Peter Krämer has researched how the language used to describe the project aped that of Lucas's film.[14] That a 1978 issue of *Aviation Week* described the project as a 'battlestation' (as the Death Star is described) might be just coincidence, but later usage was clearly deliberate.

In 1983, Reagan sought to finance the development of the Strategic Defence Initiative. *Star Wars* had become available for home-viewing the previous year on video, laserdisc and pay cable television, and in March, when the connection with SDI was made, the release of *Jedi* was two months away, so *Star Wars* awareness was high. Reagan himself, Peter Krämer argues, effectively set the scene on 8 March when he addressed the Annual Convention of the Association of Evangelicals and stressed that the real crisis gripping the world was 'a spiritual one'.

I have argued that the diminishment of a Christian vocabulary in the films made after 1977 reflects the growing secularity of American culture and political discourse. The evangelicals whom Reagan addressed that day were concerned precisely about this process, and he addressed their concerns about abortion and a perceived growing disregard for traditional values before turning to international affairs. In a speech loaded with moral terminology, he called Russia 'an evil Empire', a phrase often taken as a direct quote from Lucas's film (actually 'evil galactic empire', contained in the opening crawl, is the closest usage) and, using another image which had also become central to the trilogy by this point, characterised the Soviet Union as totalitarian 'darkness'. It is, indeed, a potent speech, a cornerstone of the Reagan era and perceptions of it, which appalled the president's domestic opponents but enthused dissidents behind the Iron Curtain. The speech fused themes of moral responsibility, temptation, religious salvation and military technology. Reagan attacked proposals for a freeze on the deployment of nuclear weapons as posing a false moral equivalence between the

United States and Russia and asked his audience and the wider nation, using the language of both combat and metaphysics, to commit itself to 'the struggle between right and wrong, good and evil'.[15]

When Reagan submitted his budget to Congress two weeks later, a plan which included funding for SDI development, he went on television on 23 March to appeal to Americans for support, again constructing the case in moral terms. The SDI programme would, he said, be defensive. The current strategy of threatening aggressors with nuclear retaliation could only avenge lives, he argued, and he offered instead 'a new hope' for the twenty-first century: a defence system which would stop missiles before they reached their targets. On the floor of the Senate the next day, Democratic senator Edward Kennedy brought all these submerged references to the surface when he accused the president of pedalling 'Red Scare tactics and reckless *Star Wars* schemes'. The link with the film was intended to make the plans appear ridiculous, and this succeeded to the extent that newspaper cartoonists would, in SDI-based jokes, depict Reagan in the Oval Office surrounded by film characters, the president seemingly unable to differentiate fact from fiction. However, Reagan himself, though keen to emphasise that peace – not war – was his intention, embraced the phrase to the extent that, discussing SDI in March 1985, he said, 'If you will pardon my stealing a film line – the Force is with us.' Reagan's conservative supporters also embraced the connection. Phyllis Schlafly, famous for her anti-feminist campaigns, regarded both the film and Reagan's vision as concerning the 'drama of the battle between good and evil, and of the triumphs of the good over evil through adventure, courage and confrontation'.

Reagan's appropriation of the film would play back into subsequent leftist criticism. When Jonathan Rosenbaum included his 1978 piece on *Star Wars* in a 1995 selection of his work, he, perhaps aware that the films were finding an enthusiastic second life after a period of public disinterest, sought to deflect criticism of his negative opinion of their values by pointing out:

> Those who question my description of *Star Wars* as 'a guiltless celebration of unlimited warfare' may want to consider that my piece was written well before that movie title was used to identify a U.S. military weapons program. (p. 3)

In this case, Reagan's usage of the term allows Rosenbaum both to make his point clear – that there is a connection between what is offered as entertainment and wider military objectives – as well as deploying a political name despised on the left as validation for his critique of *Star Wars*. In the years since, Reagan's usages have become a part of the saga to be analysed or evoked. In 2007, theo-logian John McDowell contrasts the way that the Jedi always wish the Force as a blessing upon others ('May the Force be with *you*') with Reagan's appropriation of it for himself and his allies ('The Force was with *us*').[16] The implication is that the president was guilty of heresy. A decade later, Reagan's variation on the film's opening fed back into film criticism when Britain's *Daily Telegraph* was widely quoted (not least on the film's DVD/Blu-ray packaging) as having declared, in its coverage of *Rogue One*, 'The Evil Empire is back with a vengeance.' Note that one of the quotations I used in the previous chapter, one by Caleb Grimes, also uses the phrase 'Evil Empire'.

This left-wing reading of *Star Wars* discussed in this chapter sustained itself throughout the 1980s. It would be called into question because more films were released and because, in the twenty-first century, many on the left proclaimed a politics not primarily couched in economic terms (and not situated in academia) while near-simultaneously changing their model of how audiences responded to, and interacted with, film.

These shifts meant that while the issues which the 1970s Marxist critics had explored did not go away, the question of their articulation within the film(s) required rethinking. While Rubey, Wood and others assumed that the Vietnam War had to be treated as an unseen pressure which the film sought to forget by turning back to more obviously heroic eras of warfare, later interpreters saw that conflict as a conscious theme of the saga. It is pos-sible to see the *Star Wars* films as replaying the humiliation of the United States in Vietnam through showing how a hi-tech top-down military oper-ation (America/the Empire) is beaten by a smaller group which is nimble on its feet, and which blends easily into the surrounding universe, making it difficult to find. By the mid-1980s, Lucas was happy to encourage these parallels with the Vietnam War, and they came to the fore in *Return of the Jedi* where the battle switched to the type of forest terrain which Dan Rubey felt was being studiously avoided and the indigenous Ewoks proved capable of overrunning an Imperial facility.[17]

This reading of the films as being consciously about the Vietnam War was slow to find articulation by viewers despite the fact that it had hidden in plain sight, along with an implicit ecological theme, in the official novelisation of *Jedi*. Written by James Kahn (a science fiction writer and medic originally brought into Hollywood's orbit by the producers of *ET: The Extra-Terrestrial* [Steven Spielberg, 1982] who solicited his advice on how aliens might be resuscitated), the novelisation was reportedly the best-selling book in the United States in 1983.[18]

The book emphasises the degree to which the Imperial base is despoiling the forests of Endor's moon:

> Harsh, metallic, octagonal, it seemed to cut like an insult into the verdant beauty of the place. The bushes at its perimeter were singed black from repeated shuttle landings; the flora beyond that was wilting – dying from refuse disposal, trampling feet, chemical exhaust fumes. (p. 122)

When the Ewoks attack this outpost, the novel evokes the anti-American Vietnamese forces by describing them forming 'cadres' (p. 152) and emphasising their ability to hide in natural terrain, invisible to Imperial forces. As the battle commences, the Ewoks use the smallness of themselves and natural artefacts to gum up the strategic points of Imperial technology ('The little bears were hanging on the legs of the Imperial walkers, hobbling the appendages with lengths of vine, or injuring the joint mechanisms by forcing pebbles and twigs into the hinges', p. 152) before the book engages in a full-on description of how nature may take on technology.

> They [the Ewoks] felled trees on their foes. They dug pits which they covered with branches, and then lured the walkers to chase them until the clumsy armoured vehicles toppled into the dug-outs. They started rockslides. They dammed a small, nearby stream, and then opened the floodgates, deluging a host of troops and two more walkers. They ganged up, then ran away. They jumped on top of walkers from high branches, and poured pouches of burning lizard-oil in the gun-slits. (p. 160)

This reading of *Jedi* (film and book, for he explicitly cites the latter) became the starting point of Peter Biskind's reading of the work of Lucas and Steven Spielberg, published in 1990 in a collection of essays on American cinema in the 1980s. Although he had spent the preceding years working in mainstream publications, Biskind's background was in left-wing academic analysis. He had, for instance, published in *Jump Cut*, the journal in which Dan Rubey had given *Star Wars* such a thorough analysis in 1978. As such, his writing is rich in familiar themes: the trilogy, Biskind argued, shows how young people (Luke, Leia) must fight through the chaos of their parents' generation (the 1960s radicals, represented here by the father figure Darth Vader) to reclaim the lost wisdom of the older, pre-1960s generation (Obi-Wan, Yoda). The maths is a bit fuzzy (in 1977, Luke and Leia would likely have been perceived as the tail end of

the baby boom rather than their children), and this is a rare instance of a generational reading of the films in the 1980s, but there is much that is familiar here.
Frank Allnutt had seen the films as evidence that young people were rejecting
the self-indulgence of 1960s politics, and applauded accordingly. Dan Rubey
and Robin Wood had characterised the political movements to emerge then in
wholly different terms, and disliked *Star Wars'* perceived attempt to turn the
clock back.[19]

However, in large rhetorical flourishes, Biskind simply cuts some of the links
which had informed previous analyses. 'The *Indiana Jones* films were always to
the right of the *Star Wars* trilogy,' he asserts (p. 121), thus absolving the science
fiction films of the sins of the colonialist-adventure series. This allowed him to
argue that, whatever *Star Wars's* stylistic conservatism, it was not simply a rejection of the values of the 1960s – rather, it was drenched in them. The films'
ideas about ecology and their spiritual opposition to Western materialism were
derived from the counterculture. Emphasising the moment when the rebels on
Endor first met the Ewoks had allowed Robin Wood to construct a 'first contact'
scenario, aligning the films with decades of Imperialist discourse. Biskind turns
the argument on its head, emphasising instead the Ewoks' importance in the
subsequent battle to paint them as full partners in the rebellion.

Citing Lucas's background as a student in the 1960s and his public
pronouncements about parallels between the Emperor and Richard Nixon
allowed Biskind to mine the films for liberal-left meaning. He contextualises this
within the cinema of Spielberg and Lucas's youth (though the latter was hardly
a film buff in his early years) – the pictures of the 1950s which he characterises
as centrist. That political centre had been fragmented by the social upheaval of
the 1960s, but, Biskind argues, by utilising elements of both left and right in
mass entertainment, the Lucas/Spielberg movies attempt to reconstruct the lost
centre.

This would not necessarily impress a prior generation of leftist critics. Without
wishing to put words in anyone's mouth – or their conference papers – Ryan and
Kellner saw in the films 'a model of a corporatist social structure that includes all
groups – women, blacks, small businessmen, leader executives, the military, even
"third world" people (the Ewoks) in a fantasy of renewed consensus' (p. 234),
and Robin Wood explicitly compared *Star Wars* to 'melting pot' Second-World-
War movies, where a group of American soldiers would provide a strangely neat
demographic cross-section of American society all united behind the stars and
stripes. However, because they regarded the consensus politics of the 1950s, and

their cinematic avatars, as essentially bankrupt, these critics grant the *Star Wars* trilogy no credit for attempting to revive it.

Biskind can look upon *Star Wars'* ideological project in a similar vein, but find a more positive meaning because he sees its reconstructed centre. The films offer not a simple return to a pre-1960s consensus, but a new remaking of the centre ground with the values of the 1960s enshrined in its philosophy. Biskind's reading, therefore, is a crucial step between the old condemnations of *Star Wars* by the academic left and the hope that later activists found there. His highlighting of the ways in which the small Ewoks fight back against a colonising technological invader would be escalated in later decades.

More than any interpretive work, however, the link between the films and President Reagan would be severed simply by the passage of time. In the twenty-first century, it became possible to recall the troubles of the 1970s, and *Star Wars'* hope of release from them, without needing to map these feelings onto actual historical political programmes. I began this book with a short quote from a book by Cass Sunstein. Here is a fuller version from page 41 of his book.

> The first release of *Star Wars* wasn't originally called *A New Hope*, but everyone understood it exactly that way, because that's exactly what it was. Lucas intended it for young people – for fourteen year-olds or under – and the movie connected with the kid in each of us, who needed the attention, and some optimism and exhilaration, at just that time. After the terrible tumult of the 1960s – the assassinations of two Kennedys, of Martin Luther King, of Malcolm X – a new hope was exactly what people wanted.[20]

Or, later, from page 103:

> *A New Hope* was made in the United States, in the aftermath of the 1960s and in the shadow of the civil rights movement, the Soviet Union, and the Watergate era.

The author had served in the White House of the Democrat Barack Obama and had every reason to be attentive to the film's political history, but Reaganism is clearly of no interest to him. The hope that *Star Wars* offers is still seen as a political one – because the country has been traumatised by the events listed and the film is a cure for that – but that hope is divorced from any connection with the Reaganite political response. Nor, as psychoanalytic vocabulary retreated into Film Studies' past, is Sunstein worried about films which play to 'the kid in all of us'.

There do remain individuals who still regard *Star Wars* in the manner of 1980s critics: as a dangerous idealisation of a right-wing renaissance and a per-nicious infantilisation of its audience. Broadly speaking, however, the political left has shifted away from the readings presented here. Chapter 5 considers why the political left of later decades view the films in a positive light. Part of this was generational (some of those who had thrilled to *Star Wars* when young ended up writing about it decades later), partly it was because later films made different readings easier. Remaining, for now, in the late 1970s, we are required to consider other readings of *Star Wars* which circulated at the time in the form of merchandise. In the three-year gap between *Star Wars* and *The Empire Strikes Back* books, comics and toys became the media through which Lucasfilm and its audience defined and refined the meaning of the original film. Was all new *Star Wars* narrative to concern the rediscovery of faith amidst a secular world? Did the merchandise confirm or refute the notion that the saga inherently marginalised non-white non-male agents? How was this broad audience understanding the issues which Allnutt and Rubey had raised? And what other questions arise from a consideration of the late 1970s merchandise?

3

The first interpreters

The interpretations considered in the previous chapters were the work of people who sat down and wrote lengthy essays, consciously analysing *Star Wars* for an inherent meaning, possibly one which would explain its huge success. However, quick off the mark though those essayists were, they were not the very first interpreters of the film. That honour fell to those professionals who were charged with promoting the film, either as the providers of studio-used publicity or as the producers of the novelisation and the comic strip adaptation which preceded the film's release.

Do such materials constitute interpretation? Yes, in the performative sense of the term. Working from the film, or from Lucasfilm-provided working documents, these products emphasised those elements deemed important, neglected others and put into circulation images of what the film was or might legitimately be expanded to include. They thus constituted a prominent part of the film's public image in the late 1970s. The priorities of the merchandise and new stories released in the period did not necessarily tally with those on screen. Governor Tarkin may have had authority over Vader on the Death Star, but, oddly, nobody thought he was worth incarnating as an action figure until 1997. The question we can ask of all these materials is the one we ask of interpreters: *what did they think that Star Wars meant?*

Pre-release promotion

The posters for films, displayed outside cinemas, often in advance of a film's release, put into public circulation images of and ideas about the films which they promote by emphasising some elements to the exclusion of others. After some early promotional concepts were done by Ralph McQuarrie and comics artist Howard Chaykin, Lucasfilm commissioned artist Tommy Jung to paint what would become the iconic poster of the film's North American release. Jung had a substantial history of film poster work across a variety of genres, and discussing his career may be the only opportunity ever to put *Plan 9 From Outer Space, Dr. Zhivago, La Strada* and *Star Wars* in the same sentence.

Given the theme of good versus evil to work with, Jung's art, easily found online,[1] depicts Luke and Leia in the bottom right corner, while Vader's helmet hangs ominously above them. In the top left-hand corner is the Death Star and below that a flight of fighters in formation. The image juxtaposes darkness and light with Vader/outer space/shadows on the dunes, giving a generally dark three-quarters against which Luke and Leia stand out. The characters are sexualised in ways in which they are famously not on screen. Leia's arms and legs are bare and her chest emphasised by the low cut of her dress and the stretch lines of the material around her breasts. Luke's torso is bared, and he holds his lightsabre above his head – the position in which a sword is so often held in fantasy art. The sabre extends a shining blade in three directions – up, left and right – forming a cross. Many internet sources quote – without proper attribution – Jung's view that the contrast of a bright cross with the darkness of Vader would capture the theme of good versus evil which Lucas had asked him to emphasise,[2] implying that the Christian theme was active in the film's promotion at this point. Perhaps the most Messianic feature is the sheen of yellow light which surrounds the heroes. This image (and the variations on it which Lucasfilm commissioned from other artists) refined the film's imagery into something less metallic and more romantic than the finished movie actually is, emphasising its affiliation with myth and fairy tale. The muscular, torso-baring Luke and glamorised Leia emphasise romantic elements which are muted in the film itself.

All of the above can be contrasted with the actual film, but what is most striking about the image is its static nature. Luke, holding a lightsabre above his head, seems posed rather than in movement. Space itself is silent and still. The fighters fly gracefully in formation, not in combat, and while the film emphasises the barrenness of Tatooine, Jung depicts it as sandy rather than rocky, recalling more romantic desert fantasies such as the *Arabian Nights*.

Jung's poster accompanied the US release of the film. By the time *Star Wars* was released abroad, months later, it had been supplanted in many countries by a new painting by British artist Tom Chantrell. Chantrell had the advan-tage of having seen the film by the time he did his work and of knowing some-thing of its success. Consequently, his imagery cleaves far closer to the film. The characters are now in their proper costumes, and while the earlier posters had shown Leia holding a blaster much like Han's, here she wields the stormtrooper rifle which she uses in the film. Facial likenesses are excellent, a significant improvement over Jung, and Chantrell's grasp of the characters' body language is skilfully displayed. This is necessary because, while Jung's image had been static, Chantrell inserts all of the film's dynamism and movement which early posters had repressed. With the film a proven success by the time this poster was painted, it had nothing to gain by hiding either its action elements or its hardware, and Chantrell paints a far greater number of elements. It emphasised the environment of space rather than the planetary ones (Tatooine still features but only in a small image at the edge of the main picture) and movement. Han is running, Leia fires a rifle, and Luke faces the viewer with a laser pistol. The X-Wings have been joined by TIE fighters and engage in combat. To the right is an explosion in space. The stillness and spirituality implied by the earlier posters are replaced by an emphasis on the film's kinetic pace and action. The clash of good and evil is represented not in a clear Christian symbol but in the vaguer contrast of Vader's black armour with the white costumes of Luke and Leia. Those critics who felt that *Star Wars* sought to re-energise traditional ideas of masculinity would presumably be drawn to discussing the size and position of Luke's lightsabre. The weapon which had been, in Jung's work, the axis around which the religious imagery worked now hangs phallically between his legs. The thematic shift from the first poster to the new one is near total. The religious imagery has been replaced with laser beams and space battles. The public image of what people should expect from *Star Wars* was evolving.

Beyond the posters, Lucasfilm could promote the film, and cue certain readings, by feeding fans an account of the film's origins. Initially this took the form of a behind-the-scenes book published by Del Ray and, in Britain, in magazine form by Marvel Comics. This was followed, after the film's success, by an hour-long television documentary, *The Making of Star Wars*. Broadcast on the ABC network on 16 September 1977, the project was overseen by *Star Wars'* own producer, Gary Kurtz, and presented by Artoo and Threepio, played by Anthony Daniels and Kenny Baker. These products, along with hundreds of magazine articles and merchandise of all kinds, fed the demand for the film's imagery – lavish colour photos in the book, clips from the film itself in the television programme.

Despite the different media for which they were made, book and television show share many features. Both retell the story, assuming that reliving the narrative is part of the appeal of their products, and both locate the origins of the film in pulp fiction and Hollywood's own history, particularly B-movies.

A voice-over by narrator William Conrad informed TV viewers that 'Lucas wanted to recapture the spirit of romance and adventure he found in the movies of the past . . . westerns and old *Flash Gordon* serials,' while the book/magazine reproduced the front covers of old pulp magazines (*Thrilling Wonder Stories, Amazing Stories*) and Alex Raymond's *Flash Gordon* comic strips. The book similarly locates predecessors for the film's content. Governor Tarkin is likened to Flash Gordon's adversary Ming the Merciless; Han Solo to Western characters played by John Wayne and Gary Cooper, the lightsabre clash to old swordfight sequences and the droids to all manner of prior cinematic robots. In both book and television special, B-movies and decades-old comic strips were celebrated for their spirit of adventure rather than criticised for their dated social attitudes or formulaic narratives. Indeed, the book took pleasure in familiar phrases. The opening spread of the book's retelling of the story, dealing with Princess Leia's capture, is headed *Damsel in Distress*. This phrase is used, without irony or criticism, as a legitimate and enticing narrative trope, a promise of danger and excitement with heroism to come.

Early adaptations

Production accounts of *Star Wars*, Lucas's biographies and histories of the American comic industry all agree on the basic facts about the ways in which *Star Wars* was promoted prior to its release. In the summer of 1976, publicist Charles Lippincott, along with Roy Thomas and Howard Chaykin, the writer and artist of the Marvel adaptation, attended the San Diego Comic Convention, giving a presentation to fans about the upcoming film and the comic – the first people to do what is now a major part of that event. Other conventions were targeted with props and promotional artwork. A science fiction fan wrote to Mark Hamill in January 1977 comparing the recently released trailer for the film with what had been on display at a Kansas City convention: 'Darth Vader's costume seemed more menacing at K.C. than it did on screen.'[3]

While such responses are rarely recorded (sadly), they do exist, and examples such as this show how ideas about the film circulated prior to release (and also, in his case, how Vader was already becoming central to the saga's meaning). They did so because science fiction fans were targeted as a key audience not only through convention appearances but through Lucasfilm's careful selection of merchandise partners. The company entered into early arrangements with publishers whose strong reputations within that market would enhance the film's prestige by association. Del Ray was America's foremost science fiction paperback imprint and Marvel, the market leader of comics, was a company whose superhero characters directly targeted the boys and young men who would be one of *Star Wars*' primary audiences.[4] Each company would adapt the story into a different medium (a paperback novelisation and a series of comics, respectively[5]), and these were put together while the film was in post-production. Lucas and the film's publicist Charles Lippincott met with Marvel writer Roy Thomas and artist Howard Chaykin to discuss the comic adaptation on 27 July 1976, only eleven days after principal photography had concluded. Working from a copy of the *Star Wars* script, Chaykin would draw the story in pencil, dividing it into six issues of seventeen pages each and ending each instalment at an appropriate juncture, usually a cliff-hanger, before handing the completed pages to Thomas to write narrative captions and dialogue. At the meeting, Chaykin laid out a schedule which would see the comic's production running hand-in-hand with the film's editing. He would conclude the artwork by December 1976 and spend January working on the colouring.[6] Foster's deadline was shorter, and the novelisation was published on 12 November 1976, significantly in advance of the film's eventual release (though a Christmas '76 debut had been initially planned). In non-US markets, the novel was often released only after the film was a success and, the courting of science fiction specialists no longer necessary, it was often issued by larger, mainstream publishers. All reports suggest that Marvel aimed to produce three issues of the comic before the film was actually released, but apparently authoritative sources vary over whether this was achieved. Lucasfilm's history of the franchise suggest it was, but writer-editor Roy Thomas asserts that only two were released prior to the film's release. If Lucasfilm are correct, American comic fans knew the story up to and including the rescue of Princess Leia from her detention cell. If Thomas is correct, they had only read as far as the Millennium Falcon's jump into hyperspace (here envisaged as a series of different-coloured vertical bands) after leaving Tatooine.[7]

As early entrants to the suddenly emerging market for *Star Wars* materials, the novelisation and comic met huge sales. Despite being largely disregarded as shoddy work by comics fandom,[8] each issue of Marvel's adaptation was reprinted several times and the content was subsequently repackaged in different formats to enable it to circulate further still – a sales bonanza now claimed by leading industry figures to have saved the then-failing company. In his history of Hollywood in the 1970s, *Easy Riders, Raging Bulls*, Peter Biskind records that the *Star Wars* novelisation had sold two million copies by 25 August 1977, while Lucasfilm publications report that a later novelisation, that of *Return of the Jedi*, was the best-selling book in America in 1983.[9]

Based on the film's screenplay, the adaptations of *Star Wars* included information which was never on-screen – information which, in these and in press coverage, soon reached a wide audience. Anyone who cared knew, in 1977/8, what Luke's home planet was called – Tatooine – and it comes as a shock to realise that this information is given nowhere on-screen.[10] Absent from the film, the name is all over the adaptations, appearing on the first page of the comic and the third of the novelisation. Ditto *cantina* – uniformly understood by fans as the site of Luke and Ben's first meeting with Solo and Chewbacca, though again no one uses the term on-screen; that TIE fighter stands for Twin Ion Engine is revealed only in *The Star Wars Sketchbook*, a collection of production sketches released for the Christmas 1977 market.[11] By the turn of the millennium, so many fans had convinced themselves that they'd actually seen filmed sequences of Luke's childhood friend Biggs Darklighter returning to Tatooine to confide that he was going to jump ship and join the rebellion (rather than just read about it in the adaptations) that the 'Frequently Asked Questions' section on Lucasfilm's official *Star Wars* website had to specifically deny that the footage was ever shown on TV or 'early' screenings. Frank Allnutt, as we have seen, spent a lot of his pages interpreting the novel. When the film was only available to see in cinemas, that is understandable. More surprising is that as late as 1990, when the films had been available on home video for years (and thus easily viewed), Peter Biskind was still backing up his arguments about *Jedi* with reference to the language used in the novelisation.[12] These books had influence.[13]

These initial adaptations have been scrutinised down the years by fans looking for evidence of whether Lucas really had a narrative plan from the start, particularly the novelisation to which his name was appended. For our purposes, however, it is more historically useful to search for differences. The logo on the front of Marvel's first issue – released on 8 March – is mostly that of the film as we know it. The font is correct, the *Star* sits above the *Wars* – but the S and the T of *Star* and the R and S which conclude *Wars* are not joined up. That didn't happen until issue 3. Unthinkably from our current perspective, neither of the adaptations of 1977 begins 'A Long Time Ago in a Galaxy Far Far Away'; Foster begins with 'Another galaxy, another time',[14] which manages to be even vaguer but less engaging; and Marvel's opening captions record Lucas's original opening crawl rather than the now-familiar version, rewritten during the film's post-production phase by Brian de Palma and Jay Cocks.[15]

Although the idea of *The Book of the Whills* was dropped early in the scripting process, it appears in the novelisation, where the prologue, recounting the fall of the Republic, is supposedly extracted from it. To read these texts is to watch the now-familiar film being finalised before our eyes.[16]

A number of features are common across the two adaptations. Both retell Luke's discussion with Biggs about his joining the rebellion, but the political vocabulary of the scene was effaced. Dean Foster's novelisation turned 'nationalise commerce' to 'imperialise commerce' (p. 30), while the comic missed the line out altogether. Both include the material of Luke and other young people on Tatooine (which is named) that was cut from the film, and in both, Luke watches the sky through his macrobinoculars, seeing two ships exchange gunfire. In the comic version, he appears as early as the second page. This provides a very different narrative experience as we have a flesh-and-blood character to follow through the early part of the story rather than, as in the film, only following Artoo and Threepio. This necessarily impacts subsequent narrational devices. In the film, Luke's first scene is immediately prior to the droid sale, and non-diegetic elements – a lengthy take, swelling music – emphasise his entry. Neither the comic nor the book places similar emphasis at this point because he has already been introduced.

However different these moments are from the film as we know it, they resulted from writers/artists attempting to remain faithful to the script as they were given it. Beyond this, both adaptations added a layer of meaning, referring self-reflexively at several points to the film's origins. Both (but Marvel most conspicuously) use the term 'hidden fortress' several times, acknowledging the film by Akira Kurosawa (*The Hidden Fortress*, 1958) which inspired some aspects of the plot. The comic evokes Lucas's previous science fiction film *THX-1138* by using TX-138 to denote an area of the detention block (issue 3, a subtle escalation of the film's 'cell block 1138'), while Foster nods to the origins of his own book as a publicity project by having Han reminisce briefly about someone called Tocneppil (publicity director Charles Lippincot's name spelt backwards). Other elaborations are also apparent. Frank Allnutt, as we have seen, expanded upon the role of Palpatine, likening him to the Roman Emperors who were worshipped as gods. In his prologue, Dean Foster fancies a different sort of corruption, writing of Palpatine that 'soon he was controlled by the very assistants and boot-lickers he had appointed to high office, and the cries of the people for justice did not reach his ears' (p. 1). Despite his small role in the film – three mentions, no appearances – the Emperor almost instantly acquired significant importance in any narrative expansion of the story, presumably because he sits at the apex of the Empire's power structure and its qualities derive from him.

Working from a script, neither Foster nor Marvel knew what the model work or special effects looked like, or how scenes would be presented on-screen. Elements of that script which were lost in execution (such as the fact that the rebel ship is disabled by a blast to its 'solar fin') are dutifully recorded in both novel and comic, but much which became subsequently iconic is missing. The novel opens with a description of Tatooine rather than the now-famous scene in which a rebel ship swiftly enters the screen pursued by a massive Imperial cruiser (not labelled a 'star destroyer' until 1980) which takes over ten seconds to come fully into view. Later comic adaptations all make something of the contrast between its massive size relative to the rebel ship which it pursues, and the juxtaposition of sizes across the trilogy became crucial for later generations of analysts. The adaptations of 1977 knew nothing of this. Chaykin drew the two ships of similar size. Foster described the rebel ship as a 'cruiser' (p. 3) as if it were similarly bulky. Neither adaptation records that the Imperial craft swallows the rebel ship. Foster declares that the stormtroopers enter by cutting through a bulkhead in the ship's roof. Chaykin's troopers have entered in the second panel; text reads: 'Grappling rays have joined the two vessels, and suddenly the Imperial troops come pouring through a wide-gaping hole,' so the iconic term *tractor beam* had not established itself by this point. Neither adaptation depicts a tense stand-off as rebel troops line up at 180 degrees to the bulkhead to try and fight off the attackers.

It is only with the entry of Darth Vader that we see the adaptations reflecting their source text's understanding of what will be a seminal moment. Vader, as we have seen, gets very little screen time in the film and is subordinate to other authority figures. Despite this, the film gives him a striking entrance, walking through the smoke of battle onto the rebel ship. Foster similarly makes his entrance impressive. After some lightly humorous business with the droids on the ship, there is a scene break (a blank line or an asterisk, depending on edition) and the story resumes.

> Two metres tall. Bipedal. Flowing black robes trailing from the figure and a face forever masked by a functional if bizarre metal breath screen – a Dark Lord of the Sith was an awesome, threatening shape as it strode through the corridors of the rebel ship.

Fear followed the footsteps of all the Dark Lords. The cloud of evil which clung tight about this particular one was intense enough to cause hardened Imperial troops to back away, menacing enough to set them muttering nervously among themselves. Once-resolute rebel crew members ceased resisting, broke and ran in panic at the sight of the black armour – armour which, though black as it was, was not nearly as dark as the thoughts drifting through the mind within.

One purpose, one thought, one obsession dominated that mind now. It burned in the brain of Darth Vader as he turned down another passageway in the broken fighter. (p. 9)

The very short sentences – fragments, really, for they are not whole sentences – which open the scene are a stylistic break with the writing style so far and thus denote something impressive, a moment of sufficient significance to shift the style of storytelling. Vader's distance from other characters is conveyed through the use of the word *it* to describe him in the first paragraph and the complete avoidance across the first two paragraphs of personal pronouns. Only in the third paragraph is he referred to as *he*, and normal storytelling procedures begin to settle in around him.

How did these adaptations deal with those issues which religious and polit-ical criticism has raised? Would a reading of the adaptations provide more evi-dence for the complaint that the story marginalised non-humans? Both Foster and Marvel were sufficiently self-conscious about Chewbacca's exclusion from the awarding of medals to see that he too was rewarded. Foster wrote that Leia 'placed something heavy and golden around Solo's neck, then Chewbacca's – having to strain to do so – and finally around Luke's' (p. 219). Marvel added a caption reading 'Chewbacca the Wookie, too, will have his medal . . . but he will have to put it on himself. Few space princesses are that tall.'

The comic offers us few opinions about the non-human characters. The cantina's patrons are displayed in the pictures, but there is no written com-mentary. The novel necessarily requires more description and enters into the thoughts of the human characters who interact with them. Those who sought to condemn the film for its depiction of peoples other than non-white humanoids would find ammunition with this description of the Jawas.

Three travesties of men scurried out from behind concealing boulders. Their motions were more indicative of rodent than humankind, and they stood little taller than the Artoo unit. When they saw that the single burst of enervating energy had immobilised the robot, they holstered their peculiar weapons.

Nevertheless, they approached the listless machine cautiously, with the trepida-
tion of hereditary cowards.

Their cloaks were thickly coated with dust and sand. Unhealthy red-yellow pupils
glowed catlike from the depths of their hoods as they studied their captive. The
jawas conversed in low guttural croaks and scrambled analogs of human speech.
If, as anthropologists hypothesised, they had ever been human, they had long
since degenerated past anything resembling the human race. (p. 32)

Foster clearly had no more time for the creatures than does Threepio. We will see
later that even Jawas were capable of rehabilitation as the long history of the saga
played out, but fans have always looked elsewhere for evidence that the film is
not intolerant. From the beginning, they have found it in the way that the heroes
relate in a friendly manner to their droids by contrast with other characters who
show no such respect. The seminal scene is the Mos Eisley cantina where the
owner angrily declares, 'We don't serve their kind here,' and indicates that Artoo
and Threepio must leave, a sequence rife with connotations of segregation.

Chapter 5 will discuss how this sequence is regarded in the twenty-first century as an important moment in the film, one which is trumpeted by fans and
recurrently emphasised in critical analysis. That these elements would acquire
such importance was not apparent to those creating the comic, which elides it
completely. Luke and Ben are in the cantina and the droids left outside with no
explanation. Indeed, the whole sequence is downplayed. Chaykin makes little of
what we know now to be a famous scene. There is no wide-angle picture of the
bar's many drinkers, no close-ups on alien physiognomy. The film briefly paused
its narrative development to display the drinkers. The comic doesn't. Dean
Foster's novelisation is more alert to the dramatic possibilities of the sequence
and gives extensive description: 'There were one-eyed creatures and thousand-
eyed, creatures with scales, creatures with fur and some with skin that seemed to
ripple and change consistency according to their feelings of the moment' (p. 94).
Luke is the viewpoint character here, and the narrative continues from his perspective through the barman's declaration, and young Skywalker concludes that
'this wasn't the time or place to force the issue of 'droid rights' (p. 95). Note the
apostrophe in *'droid*, acknowledging the origins of the term as a shortened form
of *android*. In later years, this would be dropped as *droid* became an acceptable
word on its own terms.

Luke is the viewpoint character used again when the Millennium Falcon
arrives with the data-carrying Artoo at the rebel base.

Luke was then treated to a sight unique in his experience, unique in most men's. Several rebel technicians walked up to Artoo Detoo, positioned themselves around him, and gently hoisted him in their arms. This was the first, and probably the last time he would ever see a robot being carried respectfully by men. (p. 178)

Whatever it made of the Jawas, Dean Foster's novelisation, then, was alert to the significance of the relationship between the human protagonists and their droid companions. Marvel was less so, but its adaptation has its own aesthetic and history. Though not highly regarded by fans at the time, it has nonetheless constituted a significant shift in the relationship between films and their comic strip adaptations, although some of the larger claims require qualification. A number of histories claim that this six-issue length was a significant break with a tradition that comic adaptations of a film would only run to two or three issues. This is not quite true. Between October 1976 and February 1977, Marvel had published a five-issue adaptation of another recent science fiction film, *Logan's Run*, a comic which was not ultimately a success, though no one would have known that when arrangements to adapt *Star Wars* were made. The *Logan's Run* comic, however, had debuted four months after the film was released, so Marvel was selling a familiar story. Between December 1976 and September 1977, the company also ran a comic based on *2001: A Space Odyssey* (though the film was originally released in 1968, re-issues in 1974 and 1977 gave it more recent currency). Those comics had been short-lived, but greater success had been had with a black-and-white magazine based on the *Planet of the Apes* films. Negotiations on a *Star Wars* comic which was to be issued prior to the film's debut were initially held up because Marvel was happier releasing comics based on known science fiction properties than trying to gauge a hit pre-release. This release of comic issues in advance of a film was a new development.

The six-issue adaptation diverges from the film in significant ways, some of which we might expect. Leia kisses Luke twice in the film – once before they swing over the plunging vertical shaft on the Death Star and again as he prepares to man his X-Wing fighter. In the film itself, neither of these moments are emphasised. The Death Star kiss is shot from waist up and is clearly less important than the chase-and-escape action which it so briefly interrupts. The second is a quick peck on the cheek, an attempt to cheer Luke up as he gets maudlin going into battle ('I just wish . . . Ben was here'). The comic gives these kisses more emphasis. The first takes place in a wide panel – it stretches across the whole page, unusual for Chaykin – while the second is rendered as a shared action, a kiss on the lips, and accompanied by another panel which shows their hands passionately clenched together. Later, as Luke touches down after destroying the Death Star, scripter Roy Thomas writes, 'A lithe figure, robes flowing, rushes up to embrace Luke in a very unsenatorial fashion.' Marvel clearly felt they understood which way the romantic wind blew in the story and emphasised these moments accordingly.

The novelisation had shown no interest in the film's religious themes and had not engaged with it through, for instance, liturgical or biblical language. By contrast, the religious vocabulary which we traced in the film is actually amplified in Marvel's comic adaptation. This is not wholly surprising. Roy Thomas had arrived at Marvel in 1965 when writer Stan Lee sought to pass on some of his large workload. Thomas soon became writer on several headline series such as *The Avengers*. Although the language of the King James Bible was clearly an influence, Lee's writing had been largely secular in its content. Thomas was happier to use religiously resonant words, and vague, metaphorical references to *prayer* or *faith* were common in his dialogue and captions across a range of comics. He applied this vocabulary liberally to his *Star Wars* adaptation. Thus, the Imperial conference room is called 'soulless'; the fireball of an exploded X-Wing is described as 'the terrors of the damned . . . the hot winds of hell'; and Han Solo, ensconced in the Millennium Falcon's gun turret, 'finds out that space-mercenaries too can pray'. In both the comic and the novelisation, Vader, when he is about to strike the killer blow against Kenobi, is given the extra line 'Prepare to meet the Force', a play on the traditional phrase about meeting one's maker (i.e. God). Since Foster's novelisation makes little attempt to incorporate the Christian elements of the film, the line sits more comfortably in the comic.

Continuing the story

While *Star Wars* was in production, the idea that its story was part of a larger narrative was never far from the surface. *The Book of the Whills* was abandoned as a framing device, but the contextualisation of the narrative continued. The novelisation carried the subtitle *The Adventures of Luke Skywalker*, and the same line was subsequently appended to the earliest spin-off novels: *Splinter of the Mind's Eye* and, somewhat more oddly, a trilogy of Luke-free books about Han Solo.[17] In 1977, this subtitle might have seemed appropriate. Whatever else they might have disagreed about, the Christians and historical materialists of the previous chapters both took it as read that the film's primary focus was Luke's ability to make one redemptive journey for the rest of us. This also made sense at a production level, where Harrison Ford was the only lead not to have signed a three-film contract and might, consequently, never reprise his role. Even when that issue was resolved, the subtitle hung around. It can be found on the title pages of the novelisation of *The Empire Strikes Back* before vanishing from Lucasfilm's vocabulary. It does not appear in *Return of the Jedi* products from 1983, though Harrison Ford used it in interviews. 'The story that Han Solo was part of,' he told *Starburst* magazine in 1983, 'which is *The Adventures of Luke Skywalker*, in my guise as best friend is over.'[18] This was a rare usage of an umbrella title which had been discarded several years earlier. For Ford, eager to put the films behind him and move on, its value might have lain precisely in the way that it glossed over his own character's role. What had led to the abandoning of this Skywalker-centred understanding of the narrative was the way in which the saga had expanded, both on- and off-screen, and Luke was not always central to them. When *The Empire Strikes Back* splits him off from the other main characters, for instance, it is clear that both plotlines have equal weight in the story. By that point (1980), the merchandise which sought to continue the story of the rebellion after the destruction of the Death Star had already shown that he need not be the main focus of storylines.

Narrative continuations were quick to appear. Dean Foster's contract for the novelisation had stipulated that he would write a second novel, one which might form the basis for a cheaply filmed sequel.[19] It saw print in February 1978 as *Splinter of the Mind's Eye*. Marvel's monthly publication schedule demanded that they be even quicker off the mark. After the six-issue adaptation, new adventures following the events of the film would have to be on the magazine rack in October 1977. Both the new novel and the comics would take their initial bearings from ideas which had featured in *Star Wars*' earliest drafts but been abandoned. *Splinter of the Mind's Eye* would feature the Kaiburr crystal, a gem which amplifies the powers of the Force, an idea which Lucas had abandoned at an early stage but which Dean Foster resurrected. In the comic, writer Roy Thomas would take 'Starkiller' (an early surname for the character who became Luke Skywalker) and, in his first new story (issues 7–10), build a new character, the self-proclaimed 'Starkiller Kid', around it. Both continuations would assert their legitimacy through constant reference back to the film. *Splinter* has Luke musing on Ben's lightsabre duel with Darth Vader on its opening page.

The comic would make numerous references to the plot of the film and present lengthy flashbacks in issues 8 and 16 (with the character otherwise deemed off-limits, these flashbacks were Vader's only appearance in the comic in the years immediately after the film). Although set on new planets in different parts of the universe, familiar images and technology are deployed. From issues 7 to 10, the comic featured an Imperial cruiser, banthas, a spacers' cantina, new droids with grating personalities and a young man from a farm who is itching to get off-world. Landspeeders and X-Wings feature in *Splinter*. Such links to the original film notwithstanding, these initial expansions of the *Star Wars* universe feature some unlikely choices from a twenty-first-century perspective. Where are the TIE fighters? Where are the stormtroopers?

In *Splinter of the Mind's Eye*, Luke and Leia, piloting an X and Y wing, respectively, crash, with the droids, onto the swamp world of Mimban. Foster had written an opening space battle, but this was removed by Lucasfilm.[20] That judgement was based on the expenses of a potential film, but it is still a shock to see how completely planet-bound it was assumed that new *Star Wars* fiction could be. Once crashed on Mimban, Luke and Leia meet an elderly woman, Halla, who boasts of her Force sensitivity and produces a shard of crystal – the titular splinter – which hugely magnifies the power of Force-users. When they are captured by local Imperials, a 'regional governor' (the novel continues to use the political arrangements which were laid out in the first film) confiscates the crystal, alerting Darth Vader, who travels to the planet, and a climactic battle occurs in an abandoned temple where the main body of the crystal resides. Characterisation turns on Luke's feelings for the princess, his emerging control of the Force and the mental scars left on Leia by her harrowing Imperial interrogation. Use of the Force to levitate objects makes its first appearance, and Vader is still sufficiently emotive to wave 'a threatening fist in Luke's direction'.

For stories of Han and Chewie, readers would have to turn to Marvel's *Star Wars* comic. The front cover of issue 7 (on sale in October 1977) depicted them cornered, shooting at unseen assailants, while their names and pictures are listed on a Wanted poster in the background.

'Han Solo and Chewbacca,' the cover copy read, 'on a world the law forgot!' This was a promise of Western tropes – a logical direction given Lucas's public reflections on his inspiration – but readers passed through other genres to reach it, notably the encounter with space pirates, 'cosmic buccaneers' dressed in a motley arrangement of clothes: 'ray guns glitter next to archaic cutlasses'. When the pirates take the reward that Han and Chewie had been given by the rebels, it is referred to as 'treasure'. There has been little like this since. Though Solo and his ilk continue to be sporadically referred to as 'space pirates' in later merchandise, few have sought to identify with the genre so completely. In 1977, however, such an approach was entirely compatible with Lucasfilm's public discussion of *Star Wars*' distillation of genre fiction.

This engagement with pirate narrative over, the Western begins once Han and Chewie head for a planet so remote that even Jabba won't find them – Aduba-3, a classic Western ghost town blown up to the size of a planet. There was once a 'chromium rush', but that has subsided. Almost immediately, they witness an alien priest street-fighting with local pilots. 'Can't identify the exact religion,' Solo says, adding, in a sentence which surely wouldn't have been written in later years but fits well with much else from 1977, 'I guess I shouldn't have skipped so much Sunday School as a kid.'

After receiving Solo's aid, the priest explains the cause of the fight:

> He is a borg who died last night. You know the term I'm sure . . . half human . . . half mechanical droid. Yet the man half of him had a soul or so my faith believes. The spacers, as you know, have an age-old prejudice against any kind of robot and refuse to let him be buried on Spacers' Hill, as is his right as a one-time pilot.

The sequence will sound familiar to anyone who knows John Sturges's *The Magnificent Seven* (1960). Desperate for work of any kind, Han and Chewie see that the borg is laid to rest, just as two of the seven saw that an Indian was properly buried in Sturges's film. Although Marvel had failed to understand the importance of the cantina sequence and its theme of prejudice first time around, they are clearly the basis of this new narrative. Once the borg is buried, Han and Chewie retire to the local cantina (which is called that), entering through the classic waist-high double-swing doors of the Western bar and engaging in a free-wheeling brawl which leaves furniture smashed. Amidst the chaos, they are approached by a group of farmers from outside the town. They need 'a champion' who will protect their village and farmland from an outlaw gang who come yearly to seize their crops and young women. Solo agrees to the job, even though it will pay a pittance.

A sheen of technological sophistication is overlaid the story's Western tropes. When the outlaws appear, they swoop in on anti-gravity bikes, though they speak pure bad cowboy: 'If you persist you will soon be nothing,' their leader tells Solo, 'Just one more lifeless corpse, twisting in the desert wind!' This continues as Solo assembles his team, including Amaiza, a cynical gun-slinger fresh from the now-defunct 'Black Hole Gang'; and a clear Luke-substitute in Jimm, the self-proclaimed Starkiller Kid, a droid-accompanied farmboy who wants off the planet and is disappointed to find that the job Solo advertises entails protecting his own village. Other characters are less familiar types: a porcupine-like alien who can fire his spines as an offensive weapon; a doddery old man who wields a lightsabre and insists he is a Jedi; and a six-foot-tall carnivorous rabbit with green fur. They all operate under Solo's command, and their banding together is accompanied by no politicised vocabulary of marginality, but those who disliked the formal and militaristic ceremony which concludes *Star Wars* might feel that this loose alliance is more to their political tastes. The woman and the rabbit even banter flirtatiously.

Their obvious differences aside (one is defined purely as desert, the other as swamp), both Aduba-3 and Mimban from *Splinter* are extrapolations of Tatooine. Mimban is an extreme environment defined by a single landscape just as Tatooine was – and just as Hoth, Dagobah and the moon of Endor will be. It has few human settlements, and they are mostly based around Imperial mining sites. In the comic, Thomas and Chaykin re-created Tatooine's subsistence agriculture, raiders, spaceport cantina, banthas, its distance from galactic civilisation and the adolescent frustrations of farmboys. Similarly, the film's broadly Christian plotline about the affirmation of faith continues into these early spin-offs through the introduction of older (Kenobi-aged) characters who speak of spiritual or religious meanings about which younger characters are sceptical. In *Splinter*, it is a local woman called Halla. In the comic, it is two old men who, in different ways, cling to ancient religions which are ignored or actively derided by the younger characters but who turn out to be correct in their views and genuinely in touch with higher powers. In the comic, Solo's team includes Don-Wan Kihotay, an old man who wields a lightsabre and claims to be a surviving Jedi. Upon reaching that agricultural outpost, they meet an aged man who claims that there is no need for hired mercenaries as he can summon the people's ancient protector from inside the surrounding mountains. Around these characters is played out the same vocabulary of religion and its dismissal that we traced in *Star Wars* itself. The comic uses *holy mission, worshipped, blasphemy, righteousness, Hell-spawned, shaman, crazy, mad man, legendary, fairy tales, old codger* and *senile fool. Splinter* gives us *wizard, magicians, prayed, miracles/miraculous, demons, meditation, superstition, myth, crazy, legendary* and *delusions* along with Christian-charged words such as *atone* and Vader's comment after dispatching an underling 'Whoever is your Lord now, it is not me,' implying a divinity in the world of the dead. In the conclusion of *Splinter*, Luke is apparently killed but is resurrected by the powers of the Kaiburr Crystal. The word *witch* is never used of Halla, but that is the image which hangs around her, as when Leia talks of her turning an Imperial officer 'into a frog' (p. 138).

As we might expect, Halla really can use the Force, and the village shaman really can call forth a mighty reptilian behemoth to protect his people. The beast does its job of destroying the raiders until the shaman himself is accidently squashed underfoot, causing the monster to lose focus and rampage wildly. Whether Don-Wan Kihotay is a real Jedi or, as Han thinks and as the Cervantes allusion clearly implies,[21] a deluded man who has stumbled across a lightsabre is left unresolved, but he proves the key to the monster's defeat. He calls it 'a dragon' and, having thus brought it into his mythic/romantic worldview, attacks it with his lightsabre, causing clear pain. He is not nimble enough to strike the killer blow, but Solo is, disintegrating the beast by pushing the sabre deep into its belly. As with *Star Wars* itself, the affirmation of faith comes to operate around an initially sceptical Solo, in whose spiritual odyssey this is another forward step. 'Right now I sure wish we had some of that Force I keep hearing about,' he had thought to himself in the early stages of the battle. Later, having saved the day using a lightsabre, he reflects in the concluding panel that 'If only for a minute, I got a little feel of what it's like . . . to be a Jedi Knight.'

Splinter is less interesting than the Marvel comic, I think. It has a sceptic plotline, but because none of the characters at the heart of the story (Luke, Leia, Vader) are disbelievers, the stakes are never high. Similarly, if the comic story is the richer text, it is also perhaps because it continues the scattergun deployment of genre references as the film to cue readings – knights, pirates, farmhands and cowboys, all collide across its narrative, while Mimban is sparse in such accoutrements. Those who read these stories at the time remain nostalgic for them (fans of the Marvel Comic are particularly easily found online, and they have been reprinted several times over the years), but they are undoubtedly odd *Star Wars* stories to modern eyes. Though lengthy in duration, they remain planet-bound. Sequences in space are limited to the characters' arrival at whatever low-tech farming/mining world the story is set on. The comic is most explicit in this agenda in the character of Jimm. One among the oddball team which Solo assembles to protect the village, Jimm is likened to Luke Skywalker. He is a farmer's son who yearns to get off his agrarian world and fancies himself an adventurer despite the fact that he's never shot anything bigger than a dune cactus (wamp rat was Luke's equivalent). Jimm is initially more proactive than

Luke. He comes to the spaceport town specifically looking for work which will take him off-world. Disappointed to find that the job Solo is advertising is actually protecting his own village, he nevertheless plays his part; and when Merri, the local teenage beauty, shows some romantic interest in him, he decides to stay. He re-appears some issues later, a married farmer with a child on the way. If *Star Wars* the film was about the energy of getting off-world, these issues play out a trajectory whereby maturing through combat leads one to settle down to adult life within the community.

The comic would not stay this way for long. With issue 11, a new writer, Archie Goodwin, replaced Thomas. His first story was another four-issue planet-bound story, this time on a world covered in water. 'A reverse of *Dune*' was how he described it in Marvel's self-published fan magazine *FOOM*, so Herbert's novel still haunted the discourse around the film at this point.[22] After this and some one-issue stories to tie up loose ends, Goodwin – along with a dynamic new art team in penciller Carmine Infantino and inkers Gene Day and Tom Palmer – redefined the comic. In issue 18 (cover dated December 1978, but available on newsstands three months earlier), with all the major characters reunited, the Millennium Falcon stumbles across the wreckage of an Imperial transport ship with the bodies of dead rebel soldiers floating amidst the debris. Attacked by TIE fighters operating out of an Imperial star destroyer, Han seeks sanctuary on The Wheel, a massive circular space station given over entirely to gambling palaces and the industries which serve them. In its hi-tech corridors, Artoo must access the master computers, Luke suffers from mental contact with Darth Vader, and Han and Chewie rough-house their way through zero-g gladiatorial games. Like the Aduba-3 story, this narrative has taken its cues from the original film, but it has chosen a wholly different set of reference points. Out goes farmland, in comes space stations, computers and Imperial shenanigans with a full complement of TIEs, star destroyers, stormtroopers, scheming Imperial governors and the Dark Lord of the Sith himself. Space was no longer just something which the characters passed through in the opening pages, en route to the next planet-bound narrative, but a dynamic environment for exploration and combat. Words like *soul* and *metaphysics* appear only sporadically from now on, and then only in relation to Vader, and Solo's spiritual development is cut off as a theme. So long as what people had taken from *Star Wars* was its frontier agrarianism, the affirmation of faith was always viable, and perhaps even likely, as a narrative component. A line such as Han's about Sunday School seemed resonant in such a context. That context was significantly altered, however, once spin-off texts took their cues from entirely different aspects of the film. Roy Thomas would later reflect that Goodwin 'proved much more attuned to the whole milieu than I had been'.[23]

Thomas's self-deprecation may miss the wider point. The difference is not simply that between two comic writers. Rather, the question is how the choice of those moments in *Star Wars* which were thought to be worth developing/ repeating changed. We have seen how promotional posters for the film shifted from a static and messianic Luke forming a cross with his sabre to an emphasis on kinetic action, often set in space. Similarly, the comic moved away from planet-bound tales of faith vindicated towards hi-tech space adventure. The comic even discovered what would later be a recurrent motif in the films: the implication of organised gambling in the power structure.[24] With whatever degree of consciousness, the comic had moved towards those same elements of *Star Wars* which would become dominant in Lucasfilm's subsequent sequels. Although there is no evidence of direct collusion (beyond the fact that the nature of licensed products was vetted by Lucasfilm), the franchise may be said to have found its own reading of itself. In a bizarre coincidence, the issue of the comic where this all comes together, and where the Wheel story begins, is entitled *The Empire Strikes*.

The Wheel is an environment of a wholly different type to those previously offered by the *Star Wars* comic. It is not an agrarian backwater but a holiday destination for those doing well in a diversified industrial economy. It exists in a delicate political balance, being located inside Imperial space but notionally independent of the Empire's interference. As such, it is a plausible extrapolation of the film's vocabulary concerning levels of regional government and bureaucracy.

With the authorities, however, prepared to overlook Imperial stormtroopers discreetly searching for Luke and Han in the maintenance levels away from public view, how can the story be resolved? The rebels can hardly launch a fleet of X-Wings against a station inhabited by innocent pleasure-seekers. Instead, a different sort of action is taken – and from an unexpected quarter. Alarmed by the presence of stormtroopers in a space from which they were notionally barred, the diverse patrons of the Wheel rise up against them: 'On their homeworlds, they wouldn't dare this, but The Wheel has always been a sanctuary . . . a safety valve for an oppressed galaxy to let off steam. To find it violated and tampered with sends its thousands of frustrated pleasure and thrill seekers wildly rampaging!' That was from issue 23, cover dated May 1979.

This ending set the precedent for much which was to follow. Stories would frequently turn on this new rebel tactic: seeking to inspire oppressed local populations to rise up against the Empire. Issue 30 finds Leia on a solo mission to Metalorn, an Imperial 'factory planet', to make contact with an old acquaintance, an historian from Alderaan, who she hopes can be convinced to spread sedition on the planet which is given over completely to armament production. Ecological themes had played a small but noticeable part in the comic to this date: the effects of technology on the natural environments of the *Star Wars* universe had been sporadically noted. Here, however, it becomes a major part of the imagery as the story is set on a planet where the natural landscape has been completely replaced.

> The surface of Metalorn is chaos. Shifting grey ash, barren rock, great fiery pits of molten slag. But below that surface is order. Clean, gleaming metal, filtered air, unending artificial light. And the disciplined hand of the Empire.

Occasional patches of uncovered earth can be found, and there an apparently single mother finds her daughter, Tammi, planting a seed which she has saved from her fruit at breakfast. 'Nothing can grow on Metalorn,' she tells her daughter. 'All its resources are drained for industry. When it's all used up . . . the Empire will move us to another world.' Tammi protests, but a stormtrooper declares her seeds 'garbage' and kicks them away.

Leia infiltrates the factory like an action heroine which the comics always portray her as being. She outshoots stormtroopers and cleverly fools the planetwide tracking system. To those late 1970s critics who argued that Leia was passive and *Star Wars* inherently chauvinistic, the comic was a monthly riposte. She makes only brief contact with her old tutor, but the fleeting appearance is enough to burst the Imperial lie that all the royal house of Alderaan were killed in the planet's destruction. Forced to escape quickly, Leia shields herself behind Tammi and, mistaking her for the child's mother, the stormtroopers pass her by. Tammi instantly bonds with Leia, someone else who gets into trouble with the authorities, and asks if she isn't scared only to be told that fear is real but 'when you believe in something enough – you do it anyway'. Making her escape off-world, Leia insists, when her pilot objects that the mission failed, that she has achieved something on the planet, that the people there can be a subtle force for sabotage within the Imperial system, but first they 'needed to be shown there was a rebellion . . . to see that its leaders survive and continue to fight . . . To give Metalorn what it's been lacking before – hope.' The story concludes with four panels in which Tammi, inspired by Leia, returns to the patch of earth and plants her seeds again. 'Task accomplished, she sits down and waits. Waits for her seeds to grow ... Patiently. Hopefully.'

This commitment to cross-cultural alliance extended to those races seen, and allegedly disrespected, in the original film. While Leia is on Metalorn, issues 31 and 32 (January and February 1980) find Luke, Han and Chewie on Tatooine, seeking to recruit smugglers to aid the rebellion. They discover that the Imperials are testing refrigeration weapons. The Omega Frost will literally freeze starships to destruction, and where better to test its capability of generating sub-zero temperatures than beneath the planet's unforgiving twin suns?

The first thing to note is that both these stories take place in environments where the Empire is developing weaponry. This is a process which is glossed over by the original films, but one which will be surprisingly recurrent in surrounding discourse. Where the Empire gets it weapons from will become an important question in the twenty-first century – not because the fantasy names given to the Death Star's components or its designers mean anything, but because the construction process will become one of the major ways in which the franchise discusses the material conditions under which the Empire sustains its rule. In the late 1970s, the comic's answer to the question of weapons procure-ment was a classic military–industrial complex: The Omega Frost is developed by The House of Tagge, a technology corporation working hand-in-hand with the Empire to develop the terror-tech that it requires. After a run-in with Imperial stormtroopers, Luke, Han and Chewie become stranded in the desert. With no other way to avoid baking in the hot suns, they negotiate a lift from passing Jawas. What begins as a simple negotiated and paid-for ride becomes a more genuine partnership when the threat to the planet is made clear. This is the first story ever written about an alliance between two of Tatooine's species, though its limitations are clear. Luke can, in the final panel, talk of 'our friends the Jawas', but there is no attempt to understand or subvert the planet's wider social arrangements, no reference to ongoing change and the Jawas' dialogue remains untranslated (it is written in vaguely Arabic symbols).

For all the chase scenes and blaster fire which punctuate Marvel's stories, what we see here is a rebellion which employs strategies far removed from military action. It reaches out to citizens (children, Jawas, aged historians) and bonds with them quickly through shared concerns. The rebellion inspires 'hope' and expects that an apparently passive populace can be encouraged to act from its position within the Imperial system. The rebellion is associated with nature – against an Empire shown to be rapacious for raw materials to construct technology – and, in the Leia story, seems to define the rebellion in primarily female terms. While the imagery of *Star Wars* is frequently ambiguous, this story features clear symbols (a child, seeds) which readers are meant to understand as metaphors for the possibilities of growth. In the late 1970s, no other form of *Star Wars* was portraying the rebellion as working through cross-cultural alliances. While the dismissive critique put forward by Robin Wood and others was influential in academic institutions, at the popular level – in texts which vastly outsold academic journals – a wholly different view of the saga was circulating.

Han Solo

What is elided in a saga which is proclaimed as *The Adventures of Luke Skywalker* is, of course, Han Solo. (As we have seen, Harrison Ford used it that way to put the films behind him.) However, it is through Han that many of the qualities which people enjoyed in the film were manifested. Flippancy, camaraderie, improvisation, impatience, laser guns, piloting skills, self-interest, sex appeal, speed, sarcasm, flirtatiousness: all the things which contrast with the piety of Luke and Kenobi are Solo's specialities. Roy Thomas's decision to initially follow Solo's story rather than that of the rebel alliance was implicit acknowledgement of the narrative richness to be found in the character. 1979 made it official with the publication of two books by Maryland-based author Brian Daley concerning Han and Chewie. Although set before the film and with its characters working outside Imperial space, *Han Solo at Star's End* and *Han Solo's Revenge* still manage to give us *Star Wars* as we would come to know it in the following years.

The plot of *Star's End* is as follows. Working in the non-Imperial Corporate Sector, circumstances and personal relationships require that Han and Chewie uncover the truth behind the disappearance of dissidents who opposed the ruthlessly capitalistic authority which runs the sector. When they are betrayed from within the dissidents' own ranks, Chewie is captured by security forces, requiring Han to organise the infiltration of the authority's hidden prison facility, the Star's End of the title. There they find the missing dissidents and, in the escape, the facility is destroyed and many staff killed.

Star's End contains no long-talking scenes (as did *Splinter of the Mind's Eye*) and no homaging classic Westerns in land-locked stories (*a la* the comic). It begins with the Millennium Falcon under attack in space. The action flows fast in sentences like 'He began relaying fire-control data to the ship's weapon system' (p. 7) which assume reader familiarity with a dogfight in space. The conflict soon takes the Falcon down into a planetary atmosphere where the narrative attempts to replicate the frenzied kinetics of the film. Only five pages in, we get for the first time what will later be a common image: the Falcon tipped 90 degrees onto one side to get through a narrow gulley. If that was a hint of the future, much of the book's pleasure lay in its speedy re-creation of what the audience had declared to be the film's most spectacular moments. 'Han engaged the hyperdrive,' we read on page 23. 'Stars seemed to fall away in all directions as the ship outraced sluggard light.' In 1977, the adaptations of the film itself had no reference to the visual look of the special effects sequences. Now a major feature of spin-off books would be their ability to re-create them as Han and Chewie move from one danger to another, brilliantly improvising escapes, such as when they confuse a tractor beam in which their ship is caught by losing their cargo of grain, disorientating the mechanism's operations with the multiple minuscule granules. Chewie's bowcaster and the Falcon's gameboard are also present. This is the first novel by someone who, writing after the film's success, knew what big moments to replicate and served them up to an audience who understood these actions with minimal description. The front cover of *Star's End* was not a few characters, static, on a planet's surface, but Han and Chewie, weapons firing, against a backdrop of stars and planets.

While *Star's End* offers up as much action as any reader might want, that material co-exists with some familiar religious themes. When asked by rebels if he will help them against the controlling Corporate Authority, Han laughs, 'Consult your clergyman' (p. 19), and later goes into combat with the declaration that 'Church is out' (p. 122). When they run into Jessa, an old flame of Solo's, she sarcastically asks where he has been keeping himself: 'No doubt you've been busy with religious retreats?' These religious references circulate around Solo because this is yet another version of his redemption, and all the parts of *Star Wars* relevant to that plotline are re-run. The story begins with Han and Chewie down on their luck, running supplies for a local rebel group not out of commitment but because they need a job. It ends with Jessa asking Solo if he'll stay and help them against the Authority. Because Solo's full metamorphosis to hero can't be played out here – this is, after all, only a prequel – the book ends ambiguously. He makes no show of commitment to this cause, but the promise of an overhaul for the damaged Falcon and Jessa's romantic company will keep him around for a while. Like all the prequels of this era, all that the stories can show us is hints of what we know comes in the film. A Solo prequel invariably hints at his suppressed idealism, as in this hint about his past in *Star's End*.

> I already know all about morality, Jess. A friend of mine made a decision once, thought he was doing the moral thing. Hell, he *was*. But he'd been conned. He lost his career, his girl, everything. This friend of mine, he ended up standing there while they ripped the rank and insignia off his tunic . . . his commanding officer committed perjury against him. There was only one witness in his defence, and who's going to believe a Wookie? (p. 71/2)

I think we all know who is being discussed here.

In this chapter, I have traced the evolution of the interpretation of *Star Wars* by those professionals charged with creating materials which either promoted the original film or spun-off new material from it. From posters to books, via comic strips and accounts of the film's production, an initial concern with reusing genre tropes gave way to an engagement with the film's own arrestingly stylised imagery, and a focus on planet-bound frontier environments was replaced by an emphasis on technological interiors and the kinetic travel through space itself. All of this would be enough to consign the subtitle *The Adventures of Luke Skywalker* to history.

Ironically the text which offered least to this process was the one actually seen by the most people and which included both actual footage from the original film and new material featuring the original cast. This was the notorious *Star Wars Holiday Special*, broadcast in the United States and Canada on Friday, 17 November 1978. The two-hour programme mixed *Star Wars* material with light-entertainment veterans. While other narrative forms were successfully refining elements of the film into profitable products, this attempt to fuse the *Star Wars* universe with television entertainment genres failed. Lucas had his name removed from the credits and subsequently claimed to have had next to no involvement. For decades afterwards, Lucasfilm publications did not acknowledge its existence.

Lucas's claim to have had little involvement in the holiday special has been contested, but none can doubt that he was busy preparing a very different version of what *Star Wars* was about from that screened on television. With the creation of the trilogy structure, *The Empire Strikes Back* came packaged as *Episode V*, and *Star Wars* was re-released the following year as *Episode IV: A New Hope*. While promoting *The Empire Strikes Back*, Lucas outlined a history of the saga's creation and shape which would more or less be accepted for the rest of the century even though it veered widely from his 1977 contextualisations of the film within pulp fiction and science fiction serials. Lucas's engagement with the thought of Joseph Campbell would up the cultural ante, shift the spiritual meanings of the text away from Christianity and give *Star Wars* what it had never had before – an authorised interpretation for the meaning of the hope which it offered.

4

The trilogy and the myth reading

When viewed in 1977, *Star Wars* was experienced as a complete story (albeit one where the villain escapes and, particularly strangely, the romantic triangle remains unresolved). To this day, it retains that status in many 'how to write a screenplay' manuals where it is frequently used as a prime example of a successfully executed three-act drama.[1] Its subsequent reclassification as *Episode IV* radically recast the value of parts of the film. As originally released, certain information is purely functional. Leia appeals to Kenobi as a retired military hero; therefore, she must refer to his prior battles. In 1977, the Clone Wars were of no interest save that their having happened in the past validated the character in the present. Once *Star Wars* became *Episode IV*, those same details were revealed to be an essential part of the saga itself, content of equal weight to the film we were watching (even if the first three episodes remained entirely hypothetical for nearly twenty years). The narrative of *The Empire Strikes Back* similarly, and spectacularly, opened up the immediate past as a site of struggle and ambiguity when Vader reveals (and I trust I'm not spoiling this for anyone) that he is Luke's father.

While Lucasfilm's promotional materials for the first film had concentrated on the inspiration which Lucas had found in pulp fiction and movie serials, *Empire* and these new arrangements, found a confident Lucas expounding on a masterplan. This 1980 interview with Alan Arnold, publicist and official chronicler of *Empire*'s production, is representative.

AA: Tell me more about the overall concept of the *Star Wars* saga.

GL: There are essentially nine films in a series of three trilogies. The first trilogy is about the young Ben Kenobi and the early life of Luke's father when Luke was a little boy. The trilogy takes place some twenty years before the second trilogy which includes *Star Wars* and *Empire*. About a year or two passes between each story of the trilogy and about twenty years pass between the trilogies. The entire saga spans about fifty-five years.

AA: How much have you written?

GL: I have story treatments on all nine. I also have voluminous notes, histories, and other material I've developed for various purposes. Some of it will be used, some not. Originally, when I wrote *Star Wars*, it developed into an epic on the scale of *War and Peace*, so big I couldn't possibly make it into a movie. So, I cut it in half but it was still too big, so I cut each half into three parts. I then had the material for six movies. After the success of *Star Wars* I added another trilogy but stopped there, primarily because reality took over.[2]

Few directors ever speak like this. Fewer still, of course, are ever asked. Regardless of arguments about genre or formula, *Star Wars* had been perceived as an authored text, the work of George Lucas, something which gave it a status above many other mainstream films produced by Hollywood which were viewed in ignorance of the creative efforts of individual workers. Even accounts of the film which placed its origins in myth or comic strips stressed Lucas's own creative agency as he reworked these old stories for a modern audience. Interviews like this escalated his claim to be imbuing the films with a personal vision, something which would allow him to remain the author of the text even as he ceased to actually direct the films.

The truth of Lucas's claims to have the saga all worked out has been debated over the years, but, in answer to a question about Darth Vader put by *Rolling Stone* magazine in 1977, Lucas had been perfectly capable of outlining a backstory which (with allowances for his hiding the familial relationship) is recognisably the climax of *Revenge of the Sith*, released twenty-eight years later.

> He kills Luke's father, then Ben and Vader have a confrontation, just like they have in Star Wars, and Ben almost kills Vader. As a matter of fact, he falls into a volcanic pit and gets fried and is one destroyed being. That's why he has to wear the suit with a mask.[3]

Some parts of the saga were clearly written in stone, if only in Lucas's mind, but did the nine treatments ever really exist? Later researchers have not found them, though one post-millennial writer, Chris Taylor, notes that Lucas's first biographer, Dale Pollock, claimed to have read the plots for episodes VII–IX.[4]

Regardless of whether they actually existed, the notion of a pre-planned saga implied the saga was something special, something apart from everyday cinema. The film student in *Scream 2* (Wes Craven, 1997) who is told that *Empire* is the exception to the rule that sequels are always inferior to their originators is shot down by the film's authoritative voice on these matters: 'Not a sequel, part of a trilogy, completely planned.' The trilogy structure, and its attendant pre-planning, in this view, sets *Empire* and *Jedi* above other mere sequels. For other fans the pre-planned nature of the series became a way of understanding production decisions, as in this rather defensive account of why a black actor was rejected for the role of Han Solo.

> Knowing – if he ever got to make his planned sequels – that a romance for Han and Leia was planned, Lucas didn't want the controversial, and probably non-commercial, element of an interracial relationship, a love that in the mid '70s still barely dared to speak its name.[5]

Whether we agree with this or not, such explication was fully in line with the reading which Lucasfilm was keen to promote: the three films should be viewed as a pre-planned and coherent whole. Doing so involved remaking the films (literally so in the case of the CGI-enhanced *Special Editions* released in 1997) into an altogether more substantial piece, capable of sustaining more ambitious readings and of streamlining and standardising the meanings generated by the first film.

Towards that end, *Empire* and *Jedi* significantly shifted their vocabularies, generic affiliations and narrative arrangements. It is here that a lot of the saga's familiar language is set in place (e.g. star destroyers). Planet names are no longer effaced (Hoth is named several times, even in the opening crawl), though we should note that the Ewoks are never named as such on screen. The repetition of crucial elements of the opening ('*A long time ago. . .*', the opening crawl, the consistent use of star destroyers in the opening shot) implied a coherence across the different films and rendered the images iconic by repetition.[6] Han and Chewie became a partnership of equals, and both dispensed with the antisocial characteristics demonstrated in the first film. Chewbacca is no longer quick to anger over minor things such as the chess-like holographic game, and is rendered aggressive only by threats to his friends. Han no longer shoots innocents, not even the Tauntaun which he requires to save Luke's life on Hoth (the creature conveniently keels over and dies from exposure). The most contentious element in this process was the 1997 amending of his shoot-out with Greedo in *Star Wars*, turning his killing of Jabba's messenger into an act of self-defence. Heroes don't kill, so Greedo had to have shot first. The casting of Billy Dee Williams as Lando and of a woman as rebel leader Mon Mothma, who spoke with greater authority than Leia was ever given, addressed some of the political issues around the first film, though Lucasfilm would not acknowledge these arguments.

No one, however, moves more completely to the centre of the saga than Vader. Now firmly defined as a major villain, his body count and powers increase massively. He is clearly in command of those around him and, standing statically without a body language of frustration, he no longer discusses tactics with Imperial officers as equals but simply gives orders and Force-chokes those who fail him. His new centrality is marked by the appearance of his own theme, 'The Imperial March', which will be musically prominent from now on. When not required on the bridge, he shuns company and retreats to a black isolation module. No one questions his powers, no one talks dismissively of 'sorcerer's ways', and he has a direct line to the Emperor. They are the centre of the Empire, and their plan is to convert Luke to their cause.

These changes necessarily impact some of the readings we have considered so far. With the Empire no longer defined by its technocratic secularity, the belief:non-belief opposition – central to the Christian reading – is abandoned. The rebels are no longer a community of believers. When Han parts from Luke on Hoth, he wishes him 'Good luck', and Leia uses the same words having briefed a group of rebel pilots who will receive covering fire as they seek to slip through the Imperial blockade. The equivalent scenes in *Star Wars* would be Han's taking leave of Luke on Yavin and the rebel briefing mission, both of which concluded with 'May the Force Be with You'. Han's redemption in the first film was explicitly tied to his finding belief in the Force, and being able to utter that phrase, but in *Empire*, Lando's similar trajectory contains no such element. The rebels seem to no longer believe that the Force is an active entity which might offer protection. That is now the sole preserve of individual Jedi. Vader declares, 'The Force is with you, young Skywalker', but the iconic 'May the Force Be with You' is spoken only once in the film – the very last line, bar a growl from Chewbacca – by Luke to the departing Millennium Falcon. As we saw in Chapter 1, some later stories would define the Force-users by their distance from common humanity. That process begins here.

The reward for distancing themselves from the common herd is a massive upscaling of Jedi/Sith powers. Kenobi's tricks in *Star Wars* were largely mental, but the levitation of objects now becomes recurrent and, when the plot requires it, Force-users monitor each other across wide distances. The Force itself, however, is no longer spoken of as an active instigator of events – rather, for all the talk of letting the Force 'flow through' you, the Jedi are now the seat of their own abilities: 'You have only begun to discover *your* powers' (my emphasis), Vader tells Luke. Perhaps no other line in the film so completely signifies the change which has occurred from being films about submission to a higher good, to being stories of self-actualisation.[7] The similar shift from a galactic Empire defined by its secularity to one incarnating a 'dark side' would be a crucial marker of the films' new interest in psychoanalytic interpretations, but, as with the loss of the language of Imperial governance (the whole language of administration vanishes), it also diverts from cultural concerns. The first film raised theological questions (*Is there a God?*) or social ones (*Is society best organised around a religious principle?*), but the new arrangements are more easily relegated to the framework of an individual psychology.

These developments severely curtail the Christian reading, a reading which was under pressure from other directions too. It had been sustainable through comics and evangelical publications so long as the story was nostalgic for an American past defined by farmland settings and the imagery of the Western. These are dispensed with as part of the wholesale rearrangement of genre tropes within the films. No location introduced in *Empire* – ice-world, swamp planet, asteroid field, flying gas mine – connotes a specific genre in the same way that the desert connotes the Western, and none of them resonate with America's past like a farmland homestead. Solo's 'gee up' motions as he mounts a Tauntaun hardly makes up for the fact that he no longer wears his waistcoat (nor Luke his poncho). Lando Calrissian has the dapper cloak of a riverboat gambler and the exaggerated manners of a southern aristocrat. Anyone drawing on their familiarity with Westerns to deduce that such a man cannot be trusted would find their generic competence well rewarded, but it is not a reading which audiences are encouraged to prioritise. Attention is given instead to his in-world references: the important thing about Lando is not his adherence to a character type but that he used to own the Millennium Falcon. Similarly, the notion of the bounty hunter may draw on real-world or generic references, but the visual look of those hunters assembled on Vader's star destroyer draws not on Western imagery but on *Star Wars'* own reputation for strange aliens, humanised robots and armour-clad villains. This may be the point where *Star Wars* becomes a genre unto itself.

As generic imagery is shed, other themes come into focus. Dagobah, world of swamp, snakes, caverns, darkness and overgrown nature is as richly constructed a semiotic environment as Tatooine, but it does not point towards prior films but to widely circulated discourses concerning human consciousness. 'Like something out of a dream,' is how Luke describes it. Alan Arnold was not usually a man to turn to interpretation in his account of *Empire's* production, but in describing the jungle/swamp set of Dagobah, he takes a similar tack, calling it both 'the forest of our subconscious' (p. 203) and the 'jungle of the mind' (p. 242). The camerawork of the *Star Wars* films rarely calls attention to itself. Perhaps the most striking moment when it does so occurs on Dagobah: the blurry slow-motion effects used when Luke enters a subterranean grove and confronts a vision of Darth Vader which, once decapitated, appears to have his own face. When sent inside by Yoda, he had asked what was inside and obliquely told, 'Only what you take with you.' We might say that if the dark swamp infested by reptiles is our unconscious, Yoda's power is that of the analyst: he raises to the surface what the subconscious/swamp has swallowed up (Luke's X-Wing).

This imagery has subsequently supported decades worth of analysis, from Arnold's casual descriptions, through Dale Pollock's assertion in 1983 that Vader's slicing off of Luke's hand constitutes 'a clear expression of boys' castration fears', to the lengthy analyses contained in 2015's essay collection *Star Wars Psychology*.[8] The common observation that *Empire* is the most sophisticated film of the original trilogy reaches an apex here, for the Dagobah sequences provide the framework for all later readings of the saga's psychospiritual content. No other environment attempts such imagery as Dagobah is constructed of. While forests may be mysterious places (sudden sounds, mists, dark shadows), there is no attempt to represent the moon of Endor in these terms. Dagobah would also come to be the basis for an entirely different account of the hope offered by *Star Wars* – the notion that the film constitutes a form of mythology.

Star Wars as myth

The term *mythology* has various uses in literary/cultural criticisms. Analysts generally use the word to refer to stories or meanings which circulate widely within a society, reflecting back to that culture a picture of the values which it upholds. A number of responses to that circulation of meaning are possible. Some use the term to refer to pre-scientific understandings of the universe, and this often contains an implication that however engaging the stories of mythology are, they are not in any major sense true but are related to religious or cultural rituals. Such usages of the term – common enough in conversation or journalism – assume that *myth* relates only to the stories of the ancient world. Many accounts of myth cover only these stories, and Odysseus, Anubis and Odin are all recognisable characters within this framework.

Other usages of the term myth connote more recent stories. By this definition, all accounts of the world which circulate are myths. Appeals to human
nature, the way things are, grim realities or the facts of life are all mythologies, so this argument goes, attempting to take something which was culturally
determined and make it appear to be an inescapable fact of nature. Such actions,
the critic usually asserts, serve the interests of those in power who make their
own worldview and interests appear to be indisputable givens, the natural way of
the world. Roland Barthes, who gave the term currency in this manner, wrote, in
his book *Mythologies*, of how an exhibition of photographic images of the world's
diverse peoples presented in Paris in the 1950s showed that common ideas were
clearly present across diverse cultures, and concluded that by 'scratching the history of men . . . one very quickly reaches the solid rock of a universal human
nature'.[9]

George Lucas, in an interview which I used in the introduction, was happy to
scratch surfaces in exactly this way.

> I researched kids' movies and how they work and how myths work; and I looked
> very carefully at the elements of films within that fairy tale genre which made
> them successful. I found that myth always took place over the hill, in some
> exotic far-off lands. For the Greeks it was Ulysses going off into the unknown.
> For Victorian England it was India or North Africa and treasure islands. For
> America it was out West. There had to be strange savages and bizarre things in
> an exotic land. Now the last of that mythology died out in the mid-1950s, with
> the last of the men who knew the old West.[10]

Greece, Victorian England, the American West: beneath the differences, Lucas
claims, lies a common experience. His borrowings subsequently became the
object of study. Academics explicated references to historic literature: Homer's
Odyssey, Virgil's *Aeneid*, *Beowulf*, Dante's *The Divine Comedy*, and Milton's
Paradise Lost are just five of the texts that Todd H. Sammons finds the 'epic lit-
erate' Lucas using in the trilogy.[11] This activity coalesced into a fully explicated
theory of the meaning of *Star Wars* because Lucas would find solid academic
backup for his belief in the compatibility of the world's mythologies in the schol-
arship of Joseph Campbell.[12]

Campbell was an American scholar, born in 1904. He initially studied art
and literature, particularly that of the Medieval period, before turning to the
analysis of legends. He largely invented what is now termed *comparative mythology*, making famous (and intellectually respectable) this view that beneath the

differing surface details of diverse mythologies lay a common core of meaning, shared features which could not be explained by the historical processes through which societies influence each other. From this, he postulated that all humans undergo the same psychic progress: the need to locate a source of energy which exists outside everyday phenomena. This energy pre-exists language itself, Campbell argues, so cannot be directly talked about but is discussed instead through the allegories of myth. Seeing this as a common need across humanity, Campbell distilled the content of diverse mythologies into one story, the Monomyth (taking the term from James Joyce's *Finnegan's Wake*), which he outlined in various books, most famously *The Hero with a Thousand Faces*. That book sets out seventeen recurrent plot points which recur across the world's mythologies. As such, various pathways can be found through it, depending upon which points one chooses to map an individual story onto. The most recurrent theme, however, is that which has become known as *The Hero's Journey*. In this, a hero undergoes an adventure which is as much psychic as physical, travelling outside of his – and it was invariably *his* – everyday society, to find a magical talisman or power which will rejuvenate a jaded society when he brings it home.

Can we really believe that the same psychic process manifested itself across numerous cultures? Doing so requires a theory which postulates massive continuities across human psychic experience. Campbell found it in the psychology of Carl Jung, who argued for the existence of archetypes in humanity's collective unconscious. These were a series of primal images/patterns which, like Campbell's Monomyth, manifested across humanity, adapted for local circumstance but still identifiably the same. 'Perhaps it will be objected,' he wrote,

> that in bringing out the correspondences I have overlooked the differences between the various Oriental and Occidental, modern, ancient and primitive traditions . . . but this is a book about the similarities; and once those are understood the differences will be found to be much less than is popularly (or politically) supposed.[13]

Transcultural understandings of this type and the positing of continuities between ancient semi-forgotten rites and present-day narrative patterns no longer commends itself to our finest minds, but it was once central to the cultural debate, and Campbell's work is situated within a once-vibrant field. Books such as *The Golden Bough* (James George Frazer, 1890, a major influence on Campbell's thinking), *From Ritual to Romance* (Jessie L. Weston, 1920), *The White Goddess* (Robert Graves, 1948) and *Anatomy of Criticism* (Northrop Frye,

1957), along with the anthropology of Claude Levi-Strauss, are all examples of similar thought, and were all once famous.

Whatever we make of the ways in which *Star Wars* is thought to map neatly onto Campbell's schema, his work is easily situated within the debates we are following because, like others before him, Campbell perceived Western culture to be undergoing a crisis. His argument was that the symbols he had uncovered have resonated in all ages because they are the working through of the maturing process. However, he finds that very process blocked by contemporary society. The rituals which led prior generations successfully through life have been forgotten or diluted. Once the full-immersion baptism of adolescents has been diluted into infant christening, or the moment of the first hunt has given way to the socially insignificant hi-jinks of adolescent hazing, can these moments retain any of their power to mark meaningful transitions in a person's life? Campbell did not think so. Rather, he argued that modern Western society retarded our self-actualisation. He diagnosed the modern world thus:

> It may well be that the very high incidence of neuroticism among ourselves follows from the decline among us of such effective spiritual aid. We remain fixated to the unexorcised images of our infancy, and hence disinclined to the necessary passages of our adulthood. In the United States there is even a pathos of inverted emphasis: the goal is not to grow old, but to remain young; not to mature away from Mother, but to cleave to her. (p. 11)

The writing quoted above is from 1949, but his observations in later decades suggest that he did not think that the situation had improved. Such comments perhaps make him sound like Frank Allnutt, despairing of our current malaise and pining for a better age when a particular set of principles held cultural centrality. This is not true, for the energy source which the hero accesses in Campbell's schema is not a specific set of spiritual teachings but a power which the hero uses, upon his return, not to re-create a past golden age, but to generate some new arrangements which meet the new needs. The modern world needs healing, Campbell argues, because people have forgotten that the truths of the mythic journey are allegorical. It is instead split between those who take mythic stories literally (by arguing, for example, that the resurrection of Christ was an historical event rather than a myth of renewal) or who reject them completely because they are not empirically true.

The first person to find in Campbell a route into *Star Wars* was the critic Andrew Gordon in his essay '*Star Wars*: A Myth for Our Time', first published in late 1978.[14] He maps the original film against Campbell's nineteen narrative points. Luke is the orphaned son of royalty, or at least a knight, who lives a dull life far from the centre of things, but a 'herald' (R2-D2) arrives with a 'call to adventure' (Leia's hologram). Consequently, Luke meets a wise mentor (Kenobi) who introduces him to a wider world and hands him a magic weapon (though, oddly given the implied significance of its first appearance, Luke never uses his lightsabre in combat in *Star Wars*). In the early stages of the film, they meet a number of 'threshold guardians' who bar their way but are dispatched (the Sandpeople, the stormtroopers at Mos Eisley, and the criminal in the cantina who accosts Luke). When the Millennium Falcon is absorbed into the Death Star, Luke enters 'The Belly of the Whale'. There, his adventures constitute a symbolic death and rebirth before he and his associates escape with new redemptive knowledge (the Force and/or the station's schematics). Having both been inside the beast and lived outside it, Luke is now 'master of two worlds', the one who is not part of the Death Star but still knows it well enough to be able to return and destroy it.

Beneath this mythic quest lies a more personal psychic struggle: the Oedipal need of a young man to form an identity by establishing himself as an adult. At the start, Luke's adventurous identity is stymied by parental authority, but Vader acts out the patricidal instinct (he has previously killed Luke's biological father, then kills the surrogate Kenobi, and his stormtroopers have killed Owen and Beru), thus enabling Luke to come into his own. Central to the notion of Luke being reborn is the sequence in the trash compactor. Gordon quotes Campbell's story point where 'the dreamer is absolutely abandoned . . . in a deep hole of a cellar. The walls of his room keep getting narrower and narrower, so that he cannot stir. In this image are combined the ideas of mother womb, imprisonment, cell and grave' and find the obvious parallel. 'Luke encounters these two perils after his plunge into the inferno of the garbage room' (Gordon p. 80/ Campbell p. 104).

The heightened language ('plunged', 'inferno') underlines the importance which Gordon ascribes to the moment. It is perhaps surprising that he describes the sequence in a single line, but he was writing before home video made the film available for constant scrutiny, so perhaps we can expand the idea. In a film largely made up of dry spaces (desert planet, space station interior), the only place we find fluid mess is in the compactor. Although Luke shares most of his adventures on the Death Star with at least one companion, he alone is pulled under the water by a single tentacle, an umbilical cord in a reverse birth, before being let free to return to the surface.

Campbell's schema found a champion in George Lucas. The anthropology which he studied at college immediately after high school would likely have given him some grounding in myth and ritual, but biographies cannot agree when Lucas read Campbell's work. From the mid-1980s onwards (notably at the National Arts Club in February 1985, when Campbell was presented with the club's Medal of Literature), Lucas would talk of reading the book during the long writing process of the first film and finding it key to crystallising his thoughts. References to Campbell, however, had been notably absent from his accounts of the film's production given in the 1970s. Biographer Brian Jay Jones is not alone in suggesting that it was not until the drafting of *The Empire Strikes Back* that *The Hero with a Thousand Faces* became influential upon Lucas.[15] This seems a compelling argument, not least because of the transformations worked on the narrative between the first and second films. Part of Campbell's schema involved the hero retreating from society to a world of more primal symbols where he must conquer his own darkness and return to the social world with a new redemptive knowledge. Luke's time on Dagobah fits this well.

Campbell himself expressed enthusiasm for *Star Wars*, despite showing no other interest in popular culture. He apparently did not own a television set, and had not watched mainstream cinema in years. He had, however, spent time working with avant-garde filmmaker Maya Deren, an experience which would surely commend him to Lucas (whose work at film school was highly experimental and rarely narrative-based). After making Lucas's acquaintance, he accepted an invitation to Skywalker Ranch. In the version which has emerged for public consumption, Campbell, when invited to watch a film, insisted on viewing the whole trilogy in one day. Seeing in the films the playing out of the symbols which he thought are crucial to our psychic development, he declared afterwards, 'You know, I thought real art stopped with Picasso, Joyce and Mann. Now I know it hasn't.'[16] Robin Wood had accused *Star Wars* of aiding the process of infantilisation. Campbell saw the exact opposite: its value lay precisely in the way that it offered a psychic route to maturity in a world otherwise all too keen on infancy.

Campbell's ideas, and his enthusiasm for *Star Wars*, were something which Lucasfilm became keen to promote. In 1988, PBS aired *The Power of Myth*, six-hour-long interviews between Campbell and political journalist Bill Moyers. Shot at Lucas's Skywalker Ranch, the discussions covered both Campbell's theories in general and *Star Wars* in particular. Campbell still took a pessimistic view of contemporary society. We had lost contact with the truth of myth, he argued, resulting in a chaotic society where young men were not properly socialised because the rituals which had allowed prior generations to properly enter adulthood had been abandoned or watered down. His own take on the *Star Wars* trilogy was that it resolved the modern dilemma of life in a world where our tools – technology – and administrative systems have come to own us.

> I think that the *Star Wars* is a valid mythological perspective and the problem is of the machine (and the state is a machine). Is the machine going to crush humanity or serve humanity? And humanity comes not from the machine but from the heart. In *The* [sic] *Return of the Jedi* Skywalker unmasks his father. The father has been playing these machine roles, a state role, and the removal of the mask [revealed] an underdeveloped man there. By being an executive of a system, one is not developing one's humanity. I think that George Lucas really did a beautiful thing there.

What Dan Rubey had diagnosed as a technophobic fear of new innovations becomes, in Campbell's reading, a healthy and humane balance.

Beyond this broadcast were a slew of publications. In the 1990s, Princeton University Press released an edition of *The Hero with a Thousand Faces* featuring Luke Skywalker among the mythic icons on the front cover, while Lucasfilm itself would use its power to issue authorised books as a way of promoting the reading. Various volumes were released, all with near-identical titles: *Star Wars: The Power of Myth*; *Star Wars: The Magic of Myth*; *The Power of Myth*.[17] The last of these tied in with Moyers's television interviews. The others were companion volumes to exhibitions of *Star Wars* costumes, models and design artwork.

In 1997, *Star Wars: The Magic of Myth* was an exhibition at the prestigious Smithsonian Institution's Air and Space Museum. The presentation contextualised those exhibits within the myth reading, taking images from traditional tales from across the globe and making connections to the *Star Wars* narrative. Mary Henderson's companion volume reproduced the argument and imagery. In the book, pages preceding the text proper depict a series of starscapes, implying not only a galaxy far, far away but the primal nature of the materials discussed and the wide cultural context upon which it draws. Myths arose, we are told, because

> ancient people struggled to answer the most fundamental questions about their humanity, such as why are we here? How can we live up to our highest potential? Is there a Force that exists within and beyond us that we may call God

. . . In attempting to address these larger issues, certain archetypal stories, in which some elements of plot, character types, and locale all remain basically the same, have described the human experience with such universality that they have become lasting myths. (p. 4)

While the exhibition draws extensively from Campbell, it does not endorse his wide view of the crisis of Western civilisation. Instead, it contextualises its interpretation within a more familiar narrative about the specific traumas of the 1970s.

In 1977, the ancient myths no longer seemed relevant for many people in this culture; pressing present-day problems absorbed our attention, and hope itself seemed in short supply. The economy was on the downswing, the recently ended Vietnam war had left no clear victor and many troubling issues in its wake, the Cold War continued, and Watergate had instilled a profound disillusion with government in the minds of many Americans. (p. 6)

As the foremost explication of the myth reading, the exhibition perhaps makes the largest aesthetic and psychological claims that have ever been formally made for the trilogy. What might otherwise be seen as the repetitions of routine narrative mechanics become imbued with meaning:

The motif of the hunt is repeated in different guises throughout the second film of the trilogy. Predators stalk, snare and even consume their prey, while the victims manage to wriggle away only to be captured again. (p. 60)

Unknowingly he [Han] has set the ship down in the stomach of a giant space slug. One again, Lucas has woven into the story the imagery of consumption and of the journey into the belly of the beast. (p. 64/5)

There they are confronted by the small, furry Ewoks, who like all elves, fairies, and other inhabitants of fairy-tale forests, may be either dangerous or helpful. The Ewoks' lush green environment and harmony with nature make a warm contrast to the austere, cold technology of the empire. In fact, while in the Ewok village Leia wears a soft animal-skin dress and lets down her magnificent hair, perhaps reflecting the subtle magic of the Ewoks' connection to the natural world; their creative powers are shown by the fact that they are the only creatures in the trilogy shown with children. (p. 103/5)

This is a bravura performance of interpretation, I think, one which is rich in detail. Campbell's own 'machine' reading of the trilogy could easily be (and was) accused of being reductive, but this more thorough myth reading integrates much that he glossed over in his brief appraisal. When first proposed by Andrew Gordon, of course, the myth reading had only a single film to be mapped across. *The Magic of Myth* projected Campbell's schema across the entire trilogy, making it relevant to many characters. Gordon thought that Luke alone descended into 'the belly of the beast', but the later example of Solo's flying into the space slug finds hero's journeys for all. Even Threepio has developed as a character, the exhibition suggests, contrasting his claim in *A New Hope* – this book can call it that now that we are discussing events after it had been retitled – to be a poor storyteller with his retelling of the saga to date which enraptures the Ewoks in *Jedi* (pp. 29, 105/6).

Whatever criticisms we may lay against it, the myth reading presents certain advantages. It provides the trilogy with a lineage of greater literary values than *Flash Gordon*. 'Until Campbell told us what *Star Wars* meant, started talking about collective memory and cross-cultural shared history we regarded it as a Saturday morning space movie,' said composer John Williams, amply demonstrating the cultural upgrade which myth theory bestowed upon the saga.[18]

While Campbell's view that all human cultures share a common set of symbols is obviously contestable, the argument that the trilogy deploys the symbols which he identified seems unlikely to be wholly refuted. We return, as ever, to the question of the film's success, which, in this view, as in others which we have discussed, is a result of audiences responding, not wholly consciously, to symbolic systems which they did not know they needed. This reading retains the religious aspects of *Star Wars* but substantially recasts them. The wide range of religious systems quoted results in privileging none. Christian references share space with other beliefs. The opposition between good and evil – light and dark – is described as a central tenet of Zoroastrianism. The Christianity which was prominent in late 1970s interpretations made moral claims on Western viewers, but Zoroastrianism was just an abstraction to most. We might find in this shift a liberation (many surely did), but the cost was undoubtedly a retreat from the social world into a spirituality which sat purely in the individual psyche. This did not sit well with everyone.

Critiquing Campbell

By the 1990s, the people who had been young when *Star Wars* was released, and who had thrilled to it, began to make films and to write books and interpretative essays. The full flowering of where this generation found hope in the trilogy is the subject of the next chapter, but the story of those readings begins here because one of the first things they had to do was counter the Lucas-authorised myth version.

One of the first – and most high-profile – members of that generation to incorporate *Star Wars* references into their work was the independent film-maker Kevin Smith. In his debut film *Clerks*, Randal and Dante, two bored twenty-something store clerks, discuss the destruction of the second Death Star in *Return of the Jedi*.

Randal: Well, the thing is, the first Death Star was manned by the Imperial army – storm troopers, dignitaries – the only people onboard were Imperials . . . The second time around, it wasn't even finished yet. They were still under construction.

Dante: So?

Randal: A construction job of that magnitude would require a helluva lot more manpower than the Imperial army had to offer. I'll bet there were independent contractors working on that thing: plumbers, aluminium siders, roofers.

Dante: Not just Imperials, is what you're getting at.

Randal: Exactly. In order to get it built quickly and quietly they'd hire anybody who could do the job. Do you think the average storm trooper knows how to install a toilet main? All they know is killing and white uniforms.

Dante: All right, so even if independent contractors are working on the Death Star, why are you uneasy with its destruction?

Randal: All those innocent contractors hired to do a job were killed – casualties of a war they had nothing to do with. (DANTE DOESN'T GET IT) All right, look – you're a roofer, and some juicy government contract comes your way; you got the wife and kids and the two-story in sub-urbia – this is a government contract, which means all sorts of benefits. All of a sudden these left-wing militants blast you with lasers and wipe out everyone within a three-mile radius. You didn't ask for that. You have no personal politics. You're just trying to scrape out a living.

This is, of course, a ridiculous conversation to have. Smith is dramatising the style of conversation which passes between fans, often with a self-conscious sense of absurdity. The humour (for viewers) in this exchange lies in the juxta-position of the mythic/epic/metaphysical *Star Wars* with the mundane features of working life, a vocabulary with which the saga has never concerned itself (at least not since Luke left his workaday world behind) and which sounds hopelessly mundane in comparison to the good/evil rhetoric of the films. I call it ridiculous because that is how audiences are invited to take it, but humour has its own structures, and Smith's joke only played out in jest what others became serious about: challenging the metaphysical vocabularies of the films by introducing economic and social ideas. In 2007, Carl Silvio and Tony M. Vinci opened a collection of essays on the film by urging analysts to dispense with

> myth-based criticism of *Star Wars* and adopt a cultural studies model that analyses it as a culturally and historically specific phenomenon, that is as a site of ideological investment that both reflects and shapes late twentieth and early twenty-first century global culture.[19]

What they were calling for was the insertion back into the analysis of *Star Wars* of real lived history and the material conditions represented within the film and which were operative during its production/reception. The constructors of the Death Star (those whose physical labour built the Empire's weapons) would certainly feature as a part of that conversation and, indeed, became increasingly visible once feature film production restarted.

That Silvio and Vinci felt obliged to issue such a bold challenge is testament to how strongly they felt that the myth paradigm of criticism remained a central tenet of *Star Wars* criticism. However, the rejection of myth which they called for had been in motion for well over a decade by this point. Campbell's argument had meshed with some of the major intellectual currents of the early and mid-twentieth century, but was far less suited to cultural attitudes in later decades. As the twentieth century became the twenty-first, the cultural climate in the Euro-American West encouraged the celebration not of a unified human psyche but of ethnic and cultural differences. In such an environment, Campbell's theories would be criticised by those who felt that he was projecting a Western male psyche across the whole world; and in 1990, psychotherapist Maureen Murdoch published *The Heroine's Journey: Women's Quest for Wholeness*,[20] a calculated alternative to Campbell's focus on male heroism. A website inspired by the work reads:

> The Heroine Journeys Project is dedicated to gathering, discussing, and analysing literature, film, and life experiences that follow a different path than the conventional story arc referred to as the 'Hero's Journey.' Our goal is to help people of all ages and backgrounds to explore, understand, and give voice to personal experiences and stories that cannot be adequately expressed within the traditional 'Hero's Journey' narrative arc.[21]

This new framework later became (to nobody's surprise, surely) the basis for an essay on Princess Leia.[22]

Campbell was able to declare the patterns he had discovered universal by downplaying the specificities of culture, geography and history ('this is a book about the similarities; and once those are understood the differences will be found to be much less than is popularly (or politically) supposed'). The *Star Wars* trilogy was susceptible to such readings because it can be viewed as being in many ways similar. Its planets are defined by a single environment blown to massive proportions (desert planet, ice world, forest moon) and devoid of large-scale settlement, culture or society. Social development is not an issue here. Conditions are often harsh, ecologically extreme, and settlement is sporadic at best. Nor are these spaces connected in any meaningful way. A map of the universe of the original *Star Wars* trilogy – though they have been produced – is a meaningless exercise, the placement of planets completely random, since there are no linking materials and no central point of orientation. Luke may feel his homeworld marginal, but he can't say in relation to what: 'Well, if there's a bright centre to the universe, you're on the planet it's farthest from.' These ahistorical environments are largely populated by people without individuality. Stormtroopers, Tusken Raiders, Ewoks, Ugnauts and Jawas are visually indistinguishable, functionally interchangeable and, if characterised at all, it is only in generalisations (all Jawas are cowardly).

The same lack of connective tissue is apparent in the treatment of time, which moves at different speeds in different plot strands. Thus, although Biggs's plans to contact the rebels could generously be called *vague* ('My friend has a friend on Bestine who might help us make contact'), when Luke arrives at the rebel base, only three or four days later at most, he is already there, a respected member of the squadron. It makes no more chronological sense than does *The Empire Strikes Back* where Luke spends significant time (weeks, if not months) training with Yoda, while his friends are pursued by Imperial ships in a sequence which clearly takes far less time. Most of all, evil itself is static, singularly devoted to darkness and made physically monstrous by its bad moral choices. Darth Vader takes that part initially, but when the plot demands that he can no longer sustain that sort of characterisation, the Emperor is introduced as a substitute.

As I outline in the next two chapters, *Star Wars* moved to a different aesthetic. Coruscant and Naboo are not static planets but cultures which change in the course of the prequel trilogy. Once the saga had shifted in this way, Campbell's relationship with Lucas was re-evaluated, most notably by the academic John Shelton Lawrence.[23]

Lawrence's phenomenally negative view of Campbell sees the myth theorist as an unrepentant cultural conservative, and he speculates that Lucas's

> admiration likely cooled somewhat after [he] was fully exposed to Campbell's snobbish ignorance of most popular culture and his arrested tastes in high culture, expressed by his refusal to advance past the modernists of the early twentieth century. (p. 22)

Given Campbell's almost total non-engagement with pop culture, Lawrence assumes that his interest in *Star Wars* was polite rather than genuine ('Campbell likely had trouble restraining his flippant indifference at Skywalker Ranch', p. 26), and he finds the mythologist's reading of the saga, in terms of the dilemmas caused by living in a machine society, reductive.

> Almost all of *Star Wars* is omitted in such an account of its mythic significance. where is the valorisation of loyalty to the group? The appeal of torturing power over others? The importance of family recognition and reconciliation? (p. 26)

For Lawrence, the emblematic moment of the original trilogy is the final scene where Luke cremates his father alone while others celebrate, and he takes this to mean that the Campbellian hero is an isolate, one who looks ever inward rather than engaging with the rest of the world. Although he admits that there is no biographical evidence of Lucas making a distinct break with Campbell's thought, Lawrence speculates that the director underwent his own Oedipal struggle, throwing off the influence of his master so that he could do what Campbell made a point of principle about not doing: relating his work to social events.

This is provocative thinking, but the break with Campbell (if, in fact, it ever happened) took time to enact. *The Magic of Myth* exhibition opened in October 1997 and a second exhibition, *The Power of Myth*, toured Europe in the summer of 1999, continuing to mix classical mythology, Campbellian interpretation and *Star Wars* props. When those who had championed Campbell's schema saw *The Phantom Menace*, they continued to detect the mythic outline. Lucas was happy to discuss this for an hour on public television with Bill Moyers, who described his own response to Darth Maul:

> When I saw him, I thought of Satan and Lucifer in 'Paradise Lost.' I thought of the devil in 'Dante's Inferno.' I mean, you've really – have brought from – it seems to me – from way down in our unconsciousness this image of – of – of evil, of the other.[24]

The same year, Lucasfilm was happy to authorise clips from *Star Wars* and pre-existing Lucas interviews for inclusion in a BBC documentary, *Hollywood's Master of Myth: Joseph Campbell*.[25]

There were new readings developing, but it would take time to turn the *Star Wars* juggernaut around.

In this chapter, I have discussed the formation of the trilogy structure and the rhetoric surrounding it which Lucasfilm projected into the public sphere. This, along with a mythological reading of the story, was the company's heavily promoted preferred reading until the turn of the century. It was not only a Campbell-influenced reading of the trilogy itself but also an insistence that the core meanings and narrative outline of the films had been set in stone early in the production process.

In the new millennium, however, things have changed. In the twenty-first century, Lucasfilm released a new range of 'making of' books which used their corporate archive to examine the development of the films in greater detail than ever before. As ideas came and went, often being finalised only during the production process itself, claims of a single intention, planned from the start, became unsustainable. The authors of these books, granted levels of access to the Lucasfilm archive beyond anything which their predecessors had enjoyed, found no trace of the documents outlining nine films, and this was dropped, without fanfare, from the official histories.[26] The documents may be a red herring, of course. As we have seen, Lucas could talk of Vader's backstory in 1977 in ways which are recognisably the climax of *Revenge of the Sith*, released twenty-eight years later.

This chapter has traced how Lucasfilm strongly promoted a certain reading of the original trilogy based on its overall (pre-planned) coherence and the mythological schema outlined by Campbell. Although the company later ceased to promote such a reading, interpretations which have enjoyed large-scale institutional support never wholly die. They may become marginal or even dormant, but they are always still existent, ripe for reference by those influenced by them. Thus, when *Time* magazine issued a special publication to celebrate forty years of the saga, editor Matt Vella would write in his introduction:

> Much has been made of the formative influence Joseph Campbell's work on what human beings seek from their myths had on Star Wars creator George Lucas. His Luke Skywalker is, like Osiris, Prometheus, Moses and Jesus before him, one of those archetypal heroes with a thousand faces.[27]

Moreover, should the institution choose to do so, the reading can always be resurrected, possibly with slightly modified language. As this book is prepared, George Lucas no longer polices the reading of his films. He is, however, building a museum at Exposition Park in Los Angeles. The Lucas Museum of Narrative Art is due to open in 2022. While it will explore 'narrative art' in all its forms, its basis is Lucas's own collection, to which the museum is strategically purchasing additions. Promising great paintings, but also original pages of comic art, it breaks down distinctions between high and low culture, unifying the storytelling process under large psychic and historical claims.

> Narrative art is art that tells – or narrates – a story through imagery. The power of a story is in how and what it makes us feel. Images ignite imagination, evoke emotions and capture universal cultural truths and aspirations. We think you will see a bit of yourself in the collection – even in stories from long ago or depictions of worlds in the distant future . . . Narrative art is as old as humanity. Some of the oldest examples of art tell the stories of heroes, gods, rulers and legends of times past. Storytelling is central to the history of visual art across nearly every culture and time period in human history.[28]

We recognise the language and arguments contained here from Lucas's interviews of the late 1980s and 1990s, and from the Lucasfilm-endorsed publications of those same decades. Lucas has surrendered his control of *Star Wars*, but it, if its promotional literature is to be believed, is hard not to see how his museum (which bears his name, will feature material from the saga among its film exhibits and which seems deliberately designed to look like a spaceship) will implicitly reflect the same contextualisation he promoted so heavily in the 1980s and 1990s, but which has subsequently gone into abeyance. Though shorn of its explicitly Campbellite vocabulary, the reading is the same: stories recur across cultures as a basic human psychological need, and we will recognise parts of ourselves in tales told across diverse societies.

5

The progressives strike back:
Star Wars as liberal text

For something which had been so central to mainstream culture in the late 1970s/ early 1980s – breaking box-office records and dominating toy sales – *Star Wars* was relegated to the margins of public interest surprisingly quickly. Marvel's comic ended in 1986. Fan lore has always maintained that it still sold well, but Lucasfilm's ever-changing requirements and restrictions were a headache which Marvel, now flourishing in a revived comics market, no longer needed. The following year, Lucasfilm wound up *Bantha Tracks*, the magazine of the *Star Wars Fan Club*, membership of which had sunk to 5,000.[1] Some new commercial products were released in 1987, but these, such as a set of collectable coins celebrating the tenth anniversary of the original film, were niche-marketed fan products rather than mass-marketed phenomena. The iconic story of the world's disinterest in the saga is the action of toy company Kenner. Having been awarded, in return for an annual licensing fee, the rights to make *Star Wars* toys 'in perpetuity' (including the action figures which dominated late 1970s Christmas lists) the company handed the rights back to Lucasfilm in 1991, seeing no value in continuing the license.

Commercial disinterest had its equivalent in critical circles. *Alien Zone*, a collection of academic writing on science fiction cinema published in 1990, makes only passing references to the *Star Wars* films, usually as part of lists. Even the essay on 'The Alien Messiah' primarily concerns other films. The essay takes the view that transcendent aliens are used by popular cinema to provide fantasy solutions to the stresses of modern life – *Star Wars* barely features, though it was once crucial in these debates.[2] For left-leaning academics, the trilogy had been thoroughly demystified, and ambitious academics were drawn to other science fiction such as *Blade Runner* (Ridley Scott, 1982) and the *Alien* series (Ridley Scott, 1979; James Cameron, 1986), apparently sophisticated films informed by theories about psychoanalysis, feminism, global capital, social class and postmodernity.

Disinterest in *Star Wars* would not last long, of course. Only ten years separates the winding up of the official fan club and the successful re-release of the films as CGI-enhanced 'Special Editions'. Between these two events lay the emergence of a new view of the *Star Wars* universe, one which was sold through Lucasfilm-endorsed original novels to an audience of fans – and fans was something academia was becoming extremely interested in.

Throughout the 1980s, university film studies, following the lead of media studies and communication studies courses, expanded from analysing the text itself to discussing the ways in which audiences made sense of them. Early studies dissected audiences along traditional demographic lines (class, age, gender), but by the 1990s, media fans were seen as a distinct audience, one which not only interacted with their favoured texts in ways which their originators had not anticipated, but who conveniently produced magazines/artwork and wrote letters to periodicals, giving analysts very physical traces of their activity to discuss.

While academic articles appeared on fans in the second half of the 1980s, the publication in 1992 of Henry Jenkins's *Textual Poachers* brought fan studies to the centre of the expanding discipline of cultural studies by offering a more complex (and sympathetic) analysis and outlining a general theory of fan practice which could be used as a model by other researchers. For Jenkins, fans were 'poachers' who encroached on the intellectual property of media corporates, appropriating characters and imagery to feed their own magazines, jokes, songs and stories. These works circulated through the fan community's networks of magazines and conventions. A calculated attack on the negative images of fans as consumers and corporate dupes, Jenkins's book argued that fans' use of their chosen texts was creative and their readings liberal in politics. In a subsequent volume, he took extended disagreement with those who assumed that the *Star Wars* films produced only conservative political meanings and that fans unquestioningly reproduced these. 'A fan-reading of *Star Wars*,' Jenkins suggested, 'would stress the film's heroic treatment of resistance to totalitarian authority and the need to form alliances across multiple planetary cultures, races and genders.'[3] This constituted a radical shift in emphasis because such a reading would not stress the mysticism of Luke's journey, but the capacity of 'the rebel alliance' to bring together diverse alien races unified under one banner while retaining their cultural specificity.[4]

In the mid-1990s, British critic Will Brooker merged these insights into fandom with *Star Wars*' return to the merchandising mainstream. He noted the presence of products retailing between £50 and £100.[5]

Common now, these products were a new development then. Targeted at what is sometimes called 'the *Star Wars* generation' – those who had seen the films as preteens and had now entered universities or the job market – such items were a significant contrast to the days when *Star Wars* comics cost 12p. Moreover, Brooker cited a range of cultural examples – from indy pop band Ash to Kevin Smith's *Clerks* – to show that this was not just a producer-led merchandise onslaught, but evidence of the trilogy's ongoing importance as a cultural reference point in the lives of that generation, particularly the male half. Comparing the films to a range of mid-1990s cinematic dystopias (science fiction or otherwise), his reading of the trilogy was initially traditional enough:

> *Star Wars* entertains a vision of optimistic possibility . . . this sense of the potential for change, the gaining of purpose and the validity of a struggle based on principles – of new hope, to put it at its simplest – is perhaps why *Star Wars* has retained, or regained, such poignancy among the generation now in their twenties. (p. 105)

Familiar as that was, Brooker's account of the political situation onto which viewers might map the film was surprisingly novel. Like Jenkins, he found the fan reading leaned leftward. The film, he argued is built around a trajectory towards liberation, emancipation and the overthrow of the tyrannical state; a narrative with understandable resonance for a generation which has seen a single government in office for seventeen years, and for whom political change may well seem the stuff of fairy tales.

This continues a shift which we have already seen in action. In the 1970s and early 1980s, leftist critics, primarily based in universities, thought that *Star Wars* represented the values of the Reagan/Thatcher administrations. Later commentators, I demonstrated, remembered the moment of *Star Wars'* release as economically depressed but did not feel the need to project the Reagan/Thatcherite response onto the film's optimism. Brooker found fans for whom the reading reverses completely. For them, the films resonate not with the emergence of the New Right but with the resistance to it. For Brooker 'the Rebellion fosters difference in its own organisation and direction. Its ranks, we see in *Return of the Jedi*, are made up of both humans and alien life forms from a bewildering variety of cultures' (p. 108). This is a somewhat opportunistic and partial reading. It may be true of *Jedi* (his carefully chosen example), but as noted earlier, the rebellion in *Star Wars* itself is largely about white males in military uniform.

What Henry Jenkins asserted, and Will Brooker documented more fully, was the emergence of readings of *Star Wars* which, familiar now, describe its pluralist values. These readings, I would argue, are largely constructed around a series of oppositions.

nature: technology
the marginalised/rubbish: the officially sanctioned
improvisation: top-down planning/authority
indigenous life: occupying forces
small: large

In structuring readings around these oppositions, commentators deploy the assumptions of critical thinking which have often been labelled *postmodernist*. This concept is far too malleable a critical term to allow quick definition. Let us say, however, that postmodern thought is suspicious of universalising claims of progress and nature and, declaring itself to be in opposition to the cultural centre from which such claims are presumed to emanate, it celebrates the marginal, the discarded and that which is, or defines itself as, different or oppressed. The terminology of postmodernism can be oblique, but it declares its ambitions to be populist, priding itself on an agenda of seeking to locate and amplify the voices of those who are silenced by a hegemonic centre. Much of this has passed into the political language of the twenty-first century, shorn of the theory's often oblique terminology.

Laying out the critical debate in these terms underlines the ways in which these questions have lain at the heart of the interpretation of *Star Wars* from 1977 onwards. In the wake of the social upheaval of the 1960s, Frank Allnutt was appalled by the diverse views held by non-Christian Americans – 'fantasies' was his favoured term – and he thought that the success of *Star Wars* lay in its function as a signpost back to the traditional centre. Dan Rubey abhorred what Allnutt celebrated: he argued that the traditional centre of Western society had fragmented beyond reconstruction because people no longer believed in the transcendental claims upon which it had been built. Despite their diametrically opposed positions, both felt the film sought to re-create a spiritual centre to which all Americans were invited. Similarly, Joseph Campbell's theory of the meaning of myth was that a worn-out society could always be redeemed by a hero who ventured far from home to face his own self and returned with a redemptive knowledge for everyone, re-energising the jaded centre once more. Leftist social politics of the twenty-first century would not postulate a cultural centre to which we must all come, but rather would celebrate the fragmented and diverse nature of modern Western society. Projecting this onto the *Star Wars* trilogy would entail engaging with a different, and wider, range of textual cues from the films than the prior generation of critics had used.

Several of the writers who would do this work were a group the like of which we have not yet seen and they used a style of writing which flourished in the 1990s: the guidebook to a fan-favourite franchise which concentrates on textual features and production history but dabbles in biography where it helps build the author's aesthetic argument. Home video allowed articulate fans to write such books, and what they lacked in production values (they rarely had illustrating photographs and, in this respect, recall academic textbooks) they made up for in enthusiasm and detail. As cultural criticism, they could even be published without Lucasfilm's permission. Those who wrote them – overwhelmingly male – often had degrees in film/media and/or backgrounds in fan activities, and they championed the texts they loved as progressive and stylistically sophisticated. James Clarke, writing on Lucas in 2002 as part of the *Pocket Essentials* series, for instance, identifies the smallness of the protagonists as their winning quality.

> Scale is important in the *Star Wars* world. Yoda is the smallest member of the Jedi Council but also the most powerful. Anakin Skywalker is a nine-year-old boy from a backwater planet yet he is labelled The Chosen One who will restore order to the galaxy. Darth Sidious is a frail, hooded man of immense corruption and influence. The Naboo starfighters, small and bright like toys, go up against the mammoth machine of the Trade Federation. The Gungan warriors over-come the Trade Federation army.[6]

He is talking explicitly of *The Phantom Menace* here, but his point can be read across the whole saga: rebel craft of varying sorts (X-Wings, snowspeeders) win against larger Imperial vehicles (the Death Star, AT-AT walkers); Luke is a marginal figure at home; Kenobi is a frail old man, one described as 'crazy'; the Ewoks can triumph against stormtroopers; Jar-Jar is a clumsy outcast, but Queen Amidala must explicitly ask for his help, etc.

Similarly, Clarke builds a significant ecology theme, arguing that the rebels are associated with the natural landscapes of Tatooine or Yavin, while the Empire and its commanders reside on the Death Star (p. 45) and argues that this reaches its fullest expression in *Return of the Jedi* and *Menace* when the nature-based cultures of the Ewoks and the Gungans find their worlds invaded by hi-tech armies.

Lucas' ecological motif runs through the film [*Menace*]. When the Trade Federation H-shaped ships land in the forest Lucas acknowledges and implicitly critiques deforestation. When Qui-Gon runs from the huge machines the statement is plainer still as trees are felled and countless tiny animals flee for cover . . . the intrusion of technology and industry is also referenced when the Queen's ship returns to Naboo towards the end of the film. Watch as the flock of birds rise from the tree canopies. The Gungan race are attuned to nature and have clearly built an impressive culture with it. (p. 52)

If Clarke seizes on the imagery of smallness, academic (but also a fan) Will Brooker prioritises rubbish and decentralisation in his post-millennial analysis. He sees the original trilogy as contrasting a rebellion built on improvising from scrap with the shiny, new technology of the Empire. He argues that 'the rebellion's strength is primarily in its fragmentation, the fact of its being everywhere and nowhere' – and he sees in this 'a progressive community based on small-scale projects and creativity.[7] In a later analysis of *A New Hope*, published in 2009 as part of the British Film Institute's 'Film Classics' series, he argues that informal recycling and improvisation using rejected materials are consistently contrasted with the ordered beauty of the Empire's shiny newness. The heroes must work with what they've got. Solo and Chewie have modified the Falcon beyond its limits, and Luke is used to buying second-hand droids and repairing technology. Forced to improvise, they consistently turn to the Empire's waste channels for ways to fight back, be it losing pursuers via a trash compactor, destroying the Death Star by aiming for its exhaust or, in *Empire*, the escape of the hyperdrive-disabled *Falcon* undercover of the star destroyers' rubbish-dumping procedures. Brooker's reading draws on, and expands upon, an earlier essay by Ian Saunders who calls the Millennium Falcon 'bits and pieces, poorly-resourced but somehow kept going by dint of ingenuity and know-how', and sees Solo as a freewheeling 'bricoleur-poet' who bests Imperial planning through madcap improvisation from available materials.[8]

The imagery of size, and how it was seen to be at work in the *Star Wars*, sharply differentiated this group of writers – though they placed themselves loudly on the side of liberationist politics – from the leftist academics active at the time of the original trilogy's release. That group read the size of the protagonists as an economic allegory. Thus, the cumbersome nature of Imperial technology and the inflexibility of its command structure would be seen to represent the centralised machinery of the Soviet Union, and the triumphant improvisation of the free-thinking heroes stood for capitalism at its most creative. Michael Ryan and Douglas Kellner had understood precisely this economic metaphor to be at work in the imagery of small/large, arguing that 'it is significant, therefore that Han Solo is a small capitalist entrepreneur who outruns the state's police ships' (p. 230). The emergence of a politics which made the subcultural presentation of unusual bodies a dominant motif, regarded pleasure as a political act and saw magic realism as a major form of progressive narrative, was one which made *Star Wars'* imagery and metaphors more acceptable. To a generation of leftists who prided themselves on their rationality and materialist theory, the touchy-feely faith in the Force over targeting computers was religious and technophobic. To their New Age successors, it seems both ecologically sound and admirably suspicious of the 'master narratives' of science.

The analyses of both Brooker and Clarke derived from two decades of enthu-siasm and the sort of close reading made possible by decades of soaking up the films' details enabled by the emergence of home video. Brooker, in his 1997 essay, may have been analysing the emergence of a generation of twenty-somethings who were keen to make reference to the films in their personal lives and cultural products, but – as he'd surely agree – he was also another example of it. In the years since these analyses were printed, the production of readings based on the liberal possibilities which he detected has snowballed. Essays with titles such as 'How the *Star Wars* Saga Evokes the Creative Promise of Homosexual Love', 'Eugenics, Racism and the Jedi Gene Pool' and 'Imperial Plastic, Republican Fiber: Speculating on the Post-Colonial Other' are now common currency. Indeed, the three I name are consecutive chapters now available in just one of the collections of academic writings on the films.[9] If a liberal reading of the *Star Wars* saga was what was required by fans, then the merchandise sold to them would be another site where that reading would be prominent.

The return of *Star Wars* novels

Although *Star Wars* merchandise had vanished from most mainstream shelves in the late 1980s, 1991 saw the franchise return in comics and novels. This was part of the merchandise stream which Brooker discussed. Aimed at those who had loved the films in their youth, it was not primarily aimed at mainstream audiences, nor was it primarily marketed to children (the books were kept in the science fiction sections of bookstores at adult prices, for example). Readers of these books and comics could now enjoy the saga as a story of increasing detail and complexity as it expanded literally by the month.

The new *Star Wars* novels published from 1991 onwards would be produced with Lucasfilm's cooperation. Though initially intended to be released annually – thus retaining the prestige of an event and the value attached to scarcity – they would later be released almost monthly. With the saga rebooted for more regular publication, the universe inhabited by the characters became more recognisably based on human history – where distinct groups trade, fragment, infight or align – rather than on mythology. In 1995, *The Corellian Trilogy* was released: three books written by author Roger MacBride Allen: *Ambush at Corellia, Assault at Selonia*, and *Showdown at Centerpoint*.[10] I shall use these books as my example here as they seem concerned to self-consciously reflect upon how the *Star Wars* universe works, breaking down its monolithic blocks into more diverse identities. In this universe, Luke is paused to reflect upon a more sophisticated topography than the films had ever presented.

> People tended to label a world, and leave it at that, as if it could be all one thing. But that was wrong . . . It was easy to say Coruscant was a city world, or that Mon Calamari was a water world, or that Kashyyk was a jungle world, and leave it at that. But there could be an infinite variety in the forms of a city, or an ocean or a jungle – and it was rare for a world really to be all one thing. The meadow world would have a mountain or two; the volcano world would have its impact craters; the bird planet would have insects.[11] (p. 53)

In this trilogy, Han Solo returns to his homeworld with his family (Leia and their three children) only to find the five-planet system riven by ethnic divides. Ahead of a trade negotiation with the New Republic, of which Leia is now a formal head, someone is stirring up racial hatred between the diverse species of the Corellian system as cover for their own operations. As this concern with trade and ethnicity suggests, the saga has moved out of mythic mode and into something approaching historical storytelling. The two opposing worldviews meet when Han challenges his cousin, Thracken, leader of one of the racist groups, over why the rebellion beat the Empire.

> 'There was more to it than who had the most ships, Thracken. We had other things going for us.'
>
> 'Skywalker you mean.'
>
> 'Well, yes, Luke Skywalker. And maybe the forces of history.'

'I've never believed in fate,' Thracken said, 'I've always made my *own* fate.'[12] (p. 88)

While Han is prepared to entertain the notion of wider historical processes, the villains are not: Thracken doesn't engage with the notion – he turns Solo's argument into a concept of 'fate' which is easily rejected. In this new, more complex universe, events turn, as Han suggested, not just on spaceships and battles (though they are dutifully present) but on social and political arrangements like the story's central focus – a complex trade negotiation which will free the Corellian system from poverty and racism by opening up new economic opportunities via free trade.[13] Within this context, the book can address some historical criticisms of the saga, notably those over Leia's allegedly subservient role. When Luke is called for a meeting by Mon Mothma – the once-head of the new government who has subsequently made way for Leia – he is left in no uncertain terms about which of the Skywalkers will be the most useful. After having had his own relative redundancy pointed out to him, he listens as Mothma explains:

'I have heard it time and time again, from all sorts of people,' she said, somewhat testily. How the two of you are twins, how you each inherited the same potential, but only one of you made use of it, while the other chose to do something else, something less. People say what a shame it is. And always it is Leia Organa Solo, the chief of state of the Republic that they talk about that way. The chief of state, and they whisper that she has not done enough with herself.[14] (p. 47)

In peacetime, Luke's Jedi abilities are seen as less useful than Leia's diplomacy. The book establishes a full parity between the two siblings which many had found missing from the films, while also confounding those who argued that such parity could only be forged by Leia becoming a Jedi like Luke. The sequence in the novel ends with Luke realising that he too has underestimated his sister, and at their next meeting he gifts to her a lightsabre in acknowledgement that she has fought as successfully against evil as he has.

This explicit politicisation of the discourse around *Star Wars* made it easier to answer dangling philosophical questions such as *what was so bad about the Empire, anyway?* The film answers this by showing the slaughters it undertakes to remain in power (most obviously the destruction of Alderaan) but does not show what it uses that power for. How does its commitment to 'the dark side' impact upon the citizens? We do not know from on-screen evidence. We are told nothing of its social and economic policies. The first film implied that the evil of the Empire was its secularity, its denial of the existence of the Force, but that had been subsequently abandoned. Neither are disciples of the dark-side sensual gluttons out to enrich themselves at society's expense. They do not indulge their physical senses in lives of hedonistic revelry or conspicuous personal consumption. Rather, they appear to live the same ascetic life as the Jedi.

What, then, is the Empire's actual agenda? These novels would answer the question in a way which has subsequently become common: the Empire opposes the diversity of the rebel alliance because it is xenophobic. Han reflects that

> the Empire had been notoriously pro-human. It had treated the members of nearly all other species as second-class citizens as best. Han glanced over to where Chewbacca was working. Some species, like Wookies, were made slaves. (p. 151)

This new concern with racism meant that fans and merchandise, alike, would reconsider how they dealt with the various aliens of the *Star Wars* universe. Jawas, Sandpeople and the rest were, after all, now firmly characterised as the foremost victims of the Empire and, sometimes, as a significant part of the rebel alliance. This entailed rethinking about races which had previously been characterised in simple terms. In the first film, Kenobi asserts that 'The Sandpeople are easily startled.' In the ghost-written Lucas novelisation, Jawas are described as 'inherent cowards'. The human population of Tatooine may be many things (settled like Owen, restless like Luke, retired/waiting like Kenobi), but the other races are apparently defined simply by their timidity. These broadstroke characterisations of races and planets infuse the films with an essentialism – the view that all things contain an essence which is an irreducible quality of their being. A Jawa which was not cowardly would, by this argument, no longer be a proper Jawa. Wide swathes of social thought critique this essentialist thinking, arguing that the qualities which it ascribes as natural to environments or people are rarely inherent but are instead socially constructed. They impose easy meanings upon complex and multifaceted identities, deny people(s) their right to self-definition and, by re-enforcing cultural norms, retard cultural progress and sustain existing hierarchies. From the 1990s onwards, the liberal values of the books challenged this.

The non-human characters in the *Star Wars* universe had long been something which Lucasfilm promoted and marketed. In 1979, the creatures from the cantina had been sold as action figures, but had been given 'names' based on the most obviously outlandish features of their physical appearance: Hammerhead,

Snaggletooth, Walrusman, etc. In 1995, these characters were purposefully rebranded in a short-story collection *Tales from the Mos Eisley Cantina*,[15] a book which self-consciously rethinks the logics of living on Tatooine to produce a workable culture for a planet where water is a rarity. In such a geographic and social framework, the patrons of the bar are not bizarre others to be feared, goggled at or labelled by the crudest reference to their physiognomy. Each becomes an individual personality. The duo who picked a fight with Luke in the cantina became Ponda Baba (which is unwieldy, but I think we can agree it has greater dignity than Walrusman) and Dr Evazan; the leader of the band playing there was named Figrin D'an, and the spy who leads stormtroopers to the Millennium Falcon came to be called Garindan. Hammerhead becomes Momaw Nadon, a gifted agrarian who has been exiled from his homeworld where his people can telepathically talk to sentient plants, and religion and ecology are so intertwined that the best agriculturalists are made High Priests. Seeking to atone for the deeds which got him exiled (which themselves were carried out under Imperial duress), Nadon seeks redemption in cultivating plants which might thrive in Tatooine's harsh conditions. Like a number of characters across the book, events lead him to realise that the only way forward is to join the rebellion.

More substantial still is the story of Het Nkik, a courageous and imaginative Jawa who takes mischievous delight in shocking his clanfolk with odd questions about why things need always be the way they are. The book outlines a significant Jawa culture, and aspects of their nature which had previously been treated negatively were instead celebrated as parts of their being.

> Humans and many other sentient creatures loathed the way Jawas smelled, detecting only a stink that made them turn up their noses. But Jawas derived an incredible amount of information from such smells: the health of their companions, when and what they had last eaten, their identity, maturity, status of arousal, excitement or boredom. (p. 219)

When he uses his technical skills to salvage and reprogramme a discarded assassination droid, Nkik is formally reprimanded for stepping outside normal practices, but his smell sense detects that his clan leader is actually impressed by his abilities and initiative, an incident which leads him to question the generalisations about his race ('"Jawas are too small," Wanameeka said "Sand People are too warlike"'). Realising that his people have untapped potential, Nkik acquires a laser weapon and plans to shoot stormtroopers in Mos Eisley, hoping that a martyr's death will inspire others to revolt. His plan gains greater sophistication when his story intersects with the film's main plotline – his clan come across a decimated sandcrawler. Kenobi is there, burying the vehicle's dead while awaiting Luke's return from the home he will find devastated.

This is a moment which is passed over quickly in earlier retellings. The ghost-written 1976 novelisation reflects that the dead Jawas could be left for the planet's scavengers, but that Kenobi 'would consign no one to the bone-gnawers and gravel-maggots, not even a filthy Jawa' (p. 99). Sixteen years later, in the *Cantina* book, we are given more details and a very different perspective. Kenobi's respect for the people on whose planet he has made his home means that he is enacting very specific funeral rites and, when encountering Nkik's clan, he does not require Threepio to translate. He talks freely to the Jawas, having taken time to learn their language and customs. This is a significant shift. In the novelisation, Kenobi buries the Jawas because of his own spiritual dignity. In the *Cantina* book, he does it to acknowledge theirs. Furthermore, while the film clearly implies that the stormtroopers stage the attack on the Sandcrawler in search of the missing droids, Kenobi explains to Nkik that it is also part of a wider Imperial strategy.

> The Imperial occupying Forces would like nothing better than to see a war among Sand People and Jawas and human moisture farmers. You must not allow yourselves to believe their deceptions . . . The Imperial governor will continue to foster turmoil between the Jawas and the Tusken Raiders. Then the human turned and looked directly at Het Nkik. 'The Jawas are not powerless – if they do not wish to be.' (p. 231/2)

In his engagement with the Jawas, Kenobi made cross-cultural understanding seem easy ('I know of your customs because I try to understand the other people who share my desert home', p. 231), but he never tried to change anything. For Ariq Joanson – the human moisture farmer who is the focus of another story in the book – establishing an active common cause with the other people of the planet is difficult. Having situated his moisture farm further out in the desert than anyone has ever farmed before, Joanson becomes aware that his vaporators are not only situated on land once roamed freely by the Sand People, but also that they interfere with the planet's natural processes.

> Before I came, the water collected inside by vaporators would have been their water, distilled out of the air in the morning dew, not pulled out at all hours of the day by a machine. (p. 335)

The contrast of the gentle process of distillation with the violence of being 'pulled' makes it clear that the human moisture farms act outside of the planet's natural cycle. Consequently, Ariq comes to realise that the reticence of the Imperial governor to mapping the planet beyond the moisture farms is not simply due to cost, as claimed, but as a way of keeping humans ignorant of the culture of other races and their relationship with the planet. He attempts to create a map with which he can negotiate a settlement with Jawas and Sand People over rights to territory and water resources.

Ariq's plan meets resistance from other farmers who are fearful of dealings with the Sand People, and a culture war motif enters the story when one of the farmers introduces his bride, Ariela, a native of Alderaan. Like the female schoolteachers from 'back East' in the traditional Western, Ariela speaks cosmopolitan values to frontier culture, supporting the cause of peace to the annoyance of locals who think that this resident of a planet often described as 'blue' has no understanding of desert life. For all his hard work, Joanson's plan is undone by the existing planetary tensions and the interference of the Imperials. Like other characters in the book, he elects to join the rebellion and searches for rumours of its location in the Mos Eisley cantina where, pausing to reflect, he comes to a new understanding of the bar's patrons.

> I sat in the dark corner and watched the people around me – people from all corners of the Empire. Representatives of peoples who had each, in their own way, been oppressed by the Empire. We had all endured it. (p. 360)

What Ariq had offered, of course, was a hope of something better. With whatever degree of self-consciousness, *hope/hopes/hoped* occurs twelve times in the short story in which he features, often being repeated in quick succession for emphasis: 'I hoped for the good, that's what I hoped' (p. 346). It is in this wave of merchandising (the early to mid-1990s) that the word *hope* becomes talismanic, a focus for what the saga is about and a reference to the film which started it all.

If the Corellian trilogy formally rebrands the Empire as racist, *Tales from the Cantina* is the logical flipside of that – the rebellion as liberal diversity. The question of what the rebellion should look like is going to be a major one from now on. The answer had already been revised once. Lucas's original vision was a militaristic one: when the Rebellion was displayed, it was as a uniformed force which stood to attention as medals were awarded. *Return of the Jedi* remade the original film in many ways, but its conclusion could hardly be more different. The rebel celebration is held not with a military ceremony but in a forest with

the indigenous people. In 1997, *The Special Edition* would revise this further, adding CGI scenes of celebrations across the galaxy, and *The Phantom
Menace* would conclude with a street parade for the newly united peoples of
Naboo. All of these celebration sequences may be read as conscious refutations
of the original film's military ceremony. In 1977, in the famous deleted scene,
Luke thought the rebellion was a long way from Tatooine, and Biggs had only
rumours about how to find it, but the *Cantina* book implies a branch which is
local to Mos Eisley. From this point onwards, the rebellion isn't depicted only
as starship pilots heading out from a hanger on Yavin. It is anyone who cares
enough and it is working in the shadows – the rebellion is street politics, and
everyone's invited.

    As I have suggested, Marvel's comic was exploring the pluralist reading of
Star Wars in the late 1970s. In the mid-1990s, Lucasfilm made it central to
its merchandising of the saga through new emphases which include: a focus
on cultural rituals (a human wedding, the rites by which adolescent Sand
People become adults, and Jawa trading traditions and swap meets all feature in the *Cantina* book); an emphasis on 'empowering' (p. 227); the privileging of imaginative characters whose questioning of social roles is both an
individual trait and a wider concern; cartographic and liminal metaphors (the
farm is prominently referred to as being 'on the edge'); the ethics of language
(in attempting to mark out a Jawa territory on his map, Joanson considers
the term 'Jawa Preserve' before rejecting it as somewhat insulting); and being
self-conscious enough about all of these processes to talk about the value of
anthropologists (p. 357).

    Tales from the Mos Eisley Cantina, then, was part of a reinvention not
just the individual cantina patrons but also the social workings of the *Star
Wars* universe itself. This new version of characters and environment would
be promoted across Lucasfilm-licensed products; the numerous character
guidebooks, planet gazetteers and technical manuals which began to appear in
the mid-1990s as well as later novels, games and websites.[16] Each new wave of
publications added further details and complications to the territories and societies described. From the prequel trilogy onwards, Lucasfilm would hire a pro-
fessional archaeologist, David West Reynolds, to compile visual guides to the
saga's films, annotating them with extreme levels of cultural details.[17] It would
be too much to claim that this reimagining of the *Star Wars* universe as a place
of conflicted meaning and more fluid identities was responsible for the many
pluralistic readings produced in the 1990s and since, but the new narrative and

thematic arrangements did create an environment within which those readings could flourish. Essays such as Mara Wood's examination of Leia's character – exploring her childhood and her relationship with her father – could not exist without the embellishments provided in the Expanded Universe, which she cites as evidence, given that the films contain so little relevant information.[18] In these cases, the attraction of the spin-offs from the 1990s onwards is precisely that they bring a cultural complexity to those issues to which the films had assigned an uncontested meaning.

It is not a random choice that Ariela, the wife who hopes for cross-cultural communication on the Tatooine frontier in *Tales from the Mos Eisley Cantina*, came from Alderaan. This is, of course, Princess Leia's peaceful ('We have no weapons') blue world, often depicted within the expanded universe as a bastion of culture and social harmony. Leia acquires importance in the pluralist reading not just because she is the most visible head of this rebellion marked by diversity but because she is the female presence whose role must be reinterpreted if she is not just to be seen as simply a 'damsel in distress'. Those who felt *Star Wars* to be patriarchal had concentrated on plot points such as her capture (thus being in need of rescuing) and remaining as a spectator on Yavin while the men attacked the Death Star. Her famous holographic plea ('Help me Obi-Wan Kenobi, you're my only hope') was seen to emphasise her passivity, and Robin Wood argued, post-*Jedi*, that there 'is never any suggestion that she might inherit the Force, or have the privilege of being trained by Obi One [*sic*] and Yoda.[19]

Just as that argument was being parried in the novels, which acknowledged her equal contribution, it was also being taken apart by criticism. Will Brooker argued that

> an attentive viewer would soon disprove this claim: Leia alone is able to hear Luke's mental plea for help at the end of *The Empire Strikes Back*, and knows, when Han does not, that Luke has escaped the Death Star at the close of *Return of the Jedi*. Indeed, Obi-Wan and Yoda note her potential as a replacement for Luke – 'there is another' – in *The Empire Strikes Back*.[20]

In paragraphs like this – and Brooker anticipates the hundreds of them which have been written in the twenty-first century – we can see how the pluralist reading is constructed out of small details which can be overlooked among the bangs and flashes on a single viewing, but which fans and scholars, conversant with the text from multiple rewatchings over decades, can confidently cite. Jennifer Stuller's 2010 account of Leia, as she overviews pop culture heroines across several decades, made Brooker's defence of the character look positively tentative. Stuller argues that from the moment Luke 'attempts to rescue' her, it is

> immediately clear that she's a leader who is used to calling the shots. Rather than swooning over her rag-tag team of 'saviours', she tells them, 'I don't know who you are or where you've come from, but from now on you'll do as I say, okay?' Her delivery makes it clear that it is a statement, not a question.
>
> She's also resilient; by the time Luke finds her, she's withstood torture without betraying the location of the rebel base. Here Leia is a senator, a spy, and one of the leaders of a political rebellion. She's snappy and savvy, and about business first. Though she has just witnessed the destruction of her home planet, Alderaan, her first concern is not herself . . . Her response to a concerned colleague is brave: 'We have no time for sorrows, Commander. You must use the information in this R-2 unit to help plan the attack – it's our only hope.'[21]

Viewing Leia as a determined and focused heroine in this manner requires certain adjustments to the traditional interpretations. That Luke 'attempts to rescue' Leia would come as a surprise to the first twenty years worth of *Star Wars* interpreters who did not question that Luke and Han actually *did* 'rescue' her. (Diana Dominguez takes a similar tack in a similar essay: discussing the same scene, she puts inverted commas around rescues [i.e. 'rescues'] to make her point[22]). Emphasis is given to moments which are passed over quickly in the film (Leia's torture), and a resilient personality is deduced from thinking about the implications of that. Similarly, long-neglected moments of the film are brought to the fore to support this new view of Leia. If her line 'We have no time for sorrows, commander' is quoted at all in twentieth-century *Star Wars* analysis, I am unaware of it. At the turn of the millennium, I imagine that only the most obsessive of fans would identify the phrase as being from the film. It emerges in more recent years, however, as a much-quoted line, backing up assertions of the princess's emotional maturity and determination to show leadership.

Stuller is honest enough about how the original trilogy played out to be concerned about Leia's degradation when forced into a 'slave bikini' in *Return of the Jedi*. This revealing costume has acquired an iconic place in both *Star Wars* cosplay and wider culture (as evidenced by an episode of the sitcom *Friends* when Ross admits to it as a fantasy, Rachel dutifully obliges). This is not a problem for those who only discuss the first film, including Cass R. Sunstein who views Leia thus:

Created in the 1970s, Leia was way ahead of her time. Sure, Obi-Wan Kenobi was her only hope, but she's no damsel in distress. On the contrary, she's a military leader, the most important of them all, and the person who sets the whole rebellion in motion. For many viewers, she's a feminist icon. A natural commander, she is the smartest, the wisest, the most steadfast, and the bravest. She knows how to shoot, and she doesn't hesitate to do exactly that . . . a lot of women were inspired by what Lucas did.[23]

It is perfectly legitimate to talk only of the first film, to return to that moment when the film was released to such extraordinary impact, but in this instance, it does allow Leia's later sexualisation to be avoided. Sunstein was writing in 2016, and his interpretation of Leia would be repeated incessantly at that year's end when actress Carrie Fisher passed away. On television, her death was marked by news programmes showing film clips of her taking command and grabbing Han's gun in the Death Star corridor and of her acerbic put-downs of the smuggler. After reviewing news footage from all major networks in Britain and the United States, I can see no evidence that the 'You're my only hope' dialogue, crucial to a previous generation of scholars in their understanding of Leia, was ever shown at this time, though in other contexts (such as talking toys) it remained her signature line.

The emergence of a reading stressing the rebellion's credentials as a coming together of diverse equals did not mean that the old complaints about racist stereotypes had gone away. Following the release of *The Phantom Menace*, Jar-Jar Binks was widely seen as an offensive caricature of Afro-Caribbean people.[24] The pluralist reading of *Star Wars* enters into continual dialogue with these arguments, and the films provide evidence for either side of the argument. Is the computer-generated Jar-Jar really the negative caricature he has been branded? Or was he a further progressive attempt to integrate non-humans into the saga's core cast, an agenda which ongoing developments in CGI have now made commonplace? In the same film, the leader of the villainous trade federation was called Nute Gunray. Those who wished to attack the series concentrated on aspects of that character which appeared to be drawn from negative images of Asians. Alternatively, those who preferred to find their own liberal instincts reflected in the film concentrate on the character's name, finding in it allusions to right-wing politicians Newt Gingrich and Ronald Reagan. Moreover, the military march-past which concludes *Attack of the Clones* reinflects fascist imagery as the obvious reference point not of the Republic/Rebel Alliance but of the emerging Empire. It takes a real film buff to spot allusions to Leni Riefenstahl in the original film, but this later imagery is obvious to all but the youngest viewers. Consequently, the prequel trilogy seems designed to refute certain of the political critiques made of the original trilogy. How can *Star Wars* be fascist, when fascism is so clearly what it fights? How can it be part of the New Right when free traders and corporate capital themselves are the villains?

Retelling the original trilogy

A book like *Tales from the Mos Eisley Cantina* existed at one step removed from the main action of *A New Hope*. It, and other works in the Expanded Universe, sought to explore viewpoints, characters and cultures which passed fleetingly through the films or which had been dealt with in broad – some would say stereotypical – terms. The return of *Star Wars* to the centre of popular culture by the late 1990s created a market larger than the fan-centred one which emerged at the start of the decade. This would include a stream of narrative retellings of the original trilogy across a range of target audiences, formats and price points. In 2015, Disney/Lucasfilm released new novelisations of the films for young adult audiences. These incorporated the new political sensibilities not into spin-off stories but to the core narrative itself. In 2017 – the saga's fortieth anniversary – another series of novelisations was released, this time targeting preteen readers, while *Star Wars from a Certain Point of View*, marketed to adults, retold the original film from the perspectives of forty minor characters.

While the early novelisations had struggled to find language to capture Lucas's imagery (particularly that which was still in ILM's workshop as publishers' deadlines loomed), twenty-first-century retellings for primary school readers required a zippy prose which deftly captured long-familiar images. Thus, *A New Hope* begins: 'Bursts of laserfire streaked after the consular starship *Tantive IV*, which was racing for the planet Tatooine. The ship was fleeing from the *Devastator*, an immense Imperial star destroyer that was firing nearly all its turbolasers at its elusive target' (p. 3). While much is edited out of these books as the story rushes through at pace, those sequences regarded as central to the story's themes continue to accrete new material. We learn, in the volume for *A New Hope*, that the Mos Eisley barman has a droid detector fitted at the entrance, and it chimes as Artoo and Threepio enter (p. 67), and the rebellion's collective identity ('The Alliance to Restore the Republic – commonly known as the Rebel Alliance'[25]) is emphasised on its first page. The prologue to *The Force Awakens* continues the theme, imagining the rebellion in terms far removed from anything seen in 1977: 'At first it was a ragtag alliance of defiant freethinkers, maverick artists, enlightened nobles and restless youths. It began its fight against the Empire unorganised, small and weak.'[26] There is a lot to identify with there for fans who don't fancy themselves standing rigidly to attention in rows while Leia hands out medals to the chosen few.

In these new books, the diverse creatures of the universe are described briefly but never disparagingly. The Tuskens' appearance is contextualised within their harsh environment ('The figure was clothed in a gauzy robe, and his head was masked by bandages, distinctive eye-protection lenses and a metal-plated breath filter', p. 43), while the description of the Jawa sandcrawler emphasises the technical skills needed to return scavenged equipment to a saleable state:

> The sandcrawler was large enough to serve as a mobile home for an entire clan of Jawas. It was also an autonomous mineral-processing facility, equipped with ore crushers, a superheated smelter, and metal compactors. (p. 22)

The Jawas are no longer mere scavengers, selling what they happen to find, but technicians and skilled craftsmen. Psychologically, they are recurrently described as 'shy', a significantly less judgemental interpretation of their on-screen behaviour than the description of them as 'inherently cowards' in the original novelisation. Threepio's line about how 'disgusting' he thinks the Jawas are is retained, but that comment has always told us more about him than them. Away from Tatooine, these books find new creatures to redeem. *From a Certain Point of View* retells part of the original film from the seemingly unpromising viewpoint of the trash compactor monster, here reimagined as a fully sentient female being, but one without understanding or language to communicate with Luke, Han, etc. when they enter her world. Taken forcibly from her swamp home, she is another exile, a person displaced by the Empire and making a life by improvising within Imperial refuse.[27]

The trash creature is an extreme example of what is common across these books – their emphasis on the agency and initiative of those whom the late 1970s critics regarded as being passive in the face of the white males. Thus, Leia who is imprisoned on the Death Star, and facing up to the possibility of her homeworld's destruction, can still plan:

> Leia trembled against Vader. There are billions of people on Alderaan. What can I do to save them? She gazed past Tarkin's shoulder to look again at Alderaan in the viewport. 'Dantooine,' she said, 'They're on Dantooine.' (p. 91)

Later, Chewbacca and Han exchanged amazed glances. 'Neither had expected the princess to be so resourceful' (p. 123). This is very much the post-millennial Leia in a world of post-millennial political questions – one where Luke, lost on Dagobah in *The Empire Strikes Back*, is forced to confront his own gender-based assumptions: 'For the first time, Luke realised he'd been assuming Yoda was male, when in fact he didn't have any idea' (p. 91). This is typical of the ways in which these retellings of the familiar story reimagine the first encounters between the central characters and those around them. In the 1980s, Robin Wood had no doubt that the rebels' encounter with the Ewoks replayed the narrative tropes of (pun unintended) Imperialist fiction, seeking to reinstate the old thrills of exploration stories along with, if per-haps unconsciously, its racial hierarchies. Later critics took issue with that, seeing the creatures as Endor's indigenous lifeform who, in defeating the stormtroopers who guard the shield generator, rise against their colonisers, another brick in the diverse wall of the rebel alliance. Caleb Grimes, writing in 2007, saw them thus:

> The Empire ignores the Ewoks, who play a major role in defeating the Empire's base on Endor . . . This is a wonderful story and an excellent example of a victory by the insignificant underdog. The rebels actually take time to get to know the Ewoks. Han and Luke and the whole gang do not need to allow themselves to be taken prisoner by the Ewoks. They could just as easily shoot them or escape and go on with their vitally important mission. Luke steadies Han and simply remains observant to what happens during their capture. He interferes just a little at just the right moment, and the result is they find Leia, obtain supplies, and gain the aid of an unexpectedly resilient tribe of allies.[28]

This shift in the critical understanding of the Ewoks is, again, reflected in the new novelisations. James Khan's original, issued in 1983, had revealed the creatures through Leia's point of view. Having been knocked unconscious in a fight with an Imperial scout, she awakens, and an entire page is given over to her growing realisation of the sounds and sensations around her before we are told 'slowly, she saw the Ewok. A strange, small, furry creature, he stood three feet from Leia's face and no more than three feet tall' (p. 93). Ryder Wyndam's 2017 volume adopts a wholly different strategy. The seventh chapter follows Leia's narrative until she passes out, then the narrative switches location to follow with Luke and Han, worried for her safety. Chapter 8 opens with an Ewok walking in the forest, his entry to the narrative unmediated by any of the humans:

A small, fur-covered figure had been travelling through the woods, using his stone-tipped spear as a walking stick, when he'd heard the sound of speeder bikes moving at high speed. A native of Endor's forest moon, he was aware of the presence of white-armoured invaders on his world . . .

The native didn't know the origin of the white-armoured invaders, but he knew they weren't friendly. Because of what they'd been doing on his world – cutting down trees, erecting large metal structures, racing around on noisy machines – he neither liked nor welcomed them.

The furry creature was an Ewok and his name was Wicket.[29]

A still further radical rearrangement of the narrative and the perspectives from which key moments are seen had been published in 2015. Aimed at young adults and written by YA novelist Alexandra Bracken, *The Princess, The Scoundrel and the Farm Boy* retold the story of the original film from the perspectives of Leia, Solo and Luke, the title itself making clear Leia's priority as first among equals in the story's triad of heroes. The first third deals with her capture on the rebel ship and detention on the Death Star; the second section follows Han from the cantina through to the escape from the Imperial station; and the final third retells the rest of the story from Luke's viewpoint.[30]

As we might expect in a young adult-targeted novel, there is much emphasis on the emotions of the young characters as they experience new things. On Yavin Luke encounters his first tree, something he had previously only seen on holovids. The most substantially reimagined character, however, is Leia. While other interpretations of Leia as active and dominant in the story take her adult leadership qualities for granted, Bracken's novel finds much narrative material in her youth and inexperience. No less then Luke, she is now the person who comes of age on her first adventure. After the traditional prologue about the fall of the republic, the story begins thus:

Leia wasn't the girl they thought she was.

That girl might have seen this plan through successfully. The crew of the Tantive IV thought Senator Leia Organa would be able to get them untangled from the net she'd flown them straight into. But her plan had gone wrong – so, so wrong. There wasn't any way out, any way to save them. She had let them down, and now there was only one hope for completing her mission.

Leia had never been inside the access corridors on the ship. They were meant for droids and technicians to get around without being trampled underfoot by crew. (p. 7)

This is a Leia stepping out of her comfort zone, improvising in areas she has never ventured into before. Those analysts who denied that Leia was a 'damsel in distress' had been required to place large emphasis on a very small number of actions. They would find much more to work with here. This is a Leia whose mind is always in motion, always planning. In wholly new narrative additions, she escapes from her cell on the Tantive IV, only to be recaptured in the shuttle bay, and later plots escape from her prison on the Death Star. Once captured by the Imperials, she is given a number and stripped of all royal privileges. We understand this as a humiliation. She resists by asserting that royal identity – speaking with authority, expectation and dignity to the nervous stormtroopers who guard her – but breaking with her role as princess is also something which she herself is attempting.

> Leia hadn't served long on the senate, but she'd spent years fighting to be trained for the role. She'd let herself shape her future around that dream, the way it would open up her world beyond the quiet, dull, strangely powerless existence of being a princess. (p. 45)

The cliché role of a passive princess is one which this Leia is actively fighting, culminating in a casual relinquishing of her title at the book's conclusion when the hero(in)es are reunited after the destruction of the Death Star.

> 'I knew there was more to you than money,' she said.
>
> 'Don't tell anyone,' he said with a wink.
>
> 'Wouldn't want to ruin the surprise, your worship.'
>
> '*Leia*,' she insisted, rolling her eyes. 'Just Leia.'

By this point we have viewed Leia not just through the story of her own experience but Solo's too. He thinks of her as both 'a tiny wisp of a girl with the bite of an acklay. She must have had Vader cowering in fear' (p. 172) and as a 'thermal detonator in a white dress' (p. 177) whose 'swearing scorched even his ears' (p. 183).

It would be churlish to deny the genuine pluralist intentions in rewriting the original trilogy from these new perspectives – but, equally, it would be naive not to understand the commercial factors in play. While the *Star Wars* saga stretches across decades, the most commercially successfully part of the story is the first film.[31] Amplifying Leia's voice in the story legitimately adds to the narrative of *Episode IV*, but it is also a reason for Lucasfilm to return, once more, to its prime asset, repackaging the story of the original film for, in the books surveyed here, multiple audiences.

The pluralist reading of *Star Wars* was not something which merely concerned academics or fan debate. It was publicly enacted on a number of prominent occasions from 1997 onwards. At that year's MTV awards, the Lifetime Achievement Award, always a tongue-in-cheek moment, was given to Chewbacca. With Peter Mayhew in costume, the Wookie walked towards the podium where Carrie Fisher placed around his neck the medal which had been so conspicuously absent twenty years earlier. In Britain, a general election held on the first of May in the same year returned an independent candidate, Martin Bell, who had stood in opposition to what he saw as declining standards in public life. Among the other political business of his acceptance speech, he reflected, 'There was a time, when I received the endorsement of Sir Alec Guinness, that I thought the Force was with us.' If the MTV awards played out the new account of the Alliance as a community in which all races were granted equal respect, Martin Bell's reference (topical because *Return of the Jedi: Special Edition* had opened in Britain the previous Friday) played out, in a highly visible polit- ical contest, Will Brooker's view that, by the 1990s, people might associate the Empire with an apparently entrenched Conservative government. Decades later, these moments seem mere preludes to the invariable presence of people dressed in *Star Wars* costumes, or otherwise referencing the films, at Pride festivals or celebrations/marches for other liberal causes. In Britain in 2016, a group of MPs who were opposed to the government's implementation of the result of that year's public referendum on membership of the European Union dubbed them- selves 'the rebel alliance'.[32] This linguistic traffic travelled both ways. The twenty- first century had seen vastly increased use of the word 'resistance' to describe the actions of minority activists fighting a perceived hegemonic centre, and the word would enter prominently into *The Force Awakens* (2015) where it, rather than *rebellion*, is used as the title of the hero(ine)s' alliance.

Like the mythological reading, these new concerns were incarnated in the form of an exhibition of props, costumes and design artwork – *Star Wars Identities* – opening at London's O2 Arena in October 2016. Unlike *The Magic of Myth*, however, the exhibits were not contextualised by an authoritative explan- ation of the relation of the films to a pre-existing schema. Rather, the exhibition required attendees to engage with questions of identity. Visitors wore digital bracelets which allowed them to construct their own in-universe character by making choices when faced with a series of questions: What were you born with? How were you raised? Which experiences have made you? The exhibition treated the two trilogies as equals, beginning from the premise that Anakin and Luke had both been brought up on the same planet but became very different people because of their contrasting experiences and choices. Striking promotional artwork depicted the saga's central characters – their images constructed from hundreds of smaller pictures (Dagobah's green foliage for Yoda, harder metal starships for Vader) to imply that identity is constructed from multiple determinants and, since the images frayed at the edges, not wholly stable. While showing off Lucasfilm's ingenuity with models and costumes from its archive, the exhibition displayed the diversity of life and life choices in the *Star Wars* universe. It was unfortunate, then, that when attendees booked their tickets online, they were met with a dialogue box familiar from such transactions. Innocent enough on most occasions, the box, which required a response, read: *We don't like bots so please verify that you're human.*[33] In this clear prejudice against droids, the spirit of Mos Eisley's bartender lives on.

6

New twists on old hopes: Prequels and sequels

The imposition of a subtitle (*Episode IV: A New Hope*) upon a film previously known as *Star Wars* suddenly changed the nature of that film. While *Star Wars* may be taken to be incomplete (the villain escapes, no romantic couple is formed), the dangling plot threads pointed to the narrative future. The announcement of three missing episodes opened an even greater sense of incompleteness, but one which looked backwards. Narrative information which had seemed to viewers, in 1977, to be nothing more than backstory (the Clone Wars, the fall of the Republic, the death of Luke's father) was now implied to be narrative of an equal standing with that which we had seen. Eighteen years after *Return of the Jedi*, a new *Star Wars* trilogy brought that narrative to life. In 2012, Lucasfilm was sold to Disney who commenced production on a new trilogy set thirty years after *Jedi* and 'Star Wars anthology films' in which major characters or events were spun off from the main saga into stories of their own. Lucas, in his prequels, and Disney would take distinctly different attitudes towards the original films.

The prequel trilogy

The Phantom Menace (1999), *Attack of the Clones* (2002), *Revenge of the Sith* (2005), all directed by George Lucas

By the time of the prequel trilogy, the novels had established a form of narrative, and a view of how the *Star Wars* universe worked, which was far removed from the original trilogy. This historical mode of storytelling, with planets and their cultures understood as the result of specific social and geographic conditions and political roles being seen as important and dramatic, is evoked from the start of *The Phantom Menace*. The opening narration, discussing the way a 'trade federation' opposes the Senate's taxation laws, clearly places us in a vastly different understanding of human community than the one which Joseph Campbell, or the original trilogy, had explored. Naboo has two distinct cultures, one on land, one beneath the water, and Tatooine's spaceport settlement is granted an economic culture of free trade and gambling, one which the heroes must consider the workings of ('These junkdealers must have a weakness,' muses Amidala) in order to gain an advantage. Cultures aren't just fought with weapons. Rather, as Amidala demonstrates, they can be analysed and manipulated from within. Such thinking necessarily changes the nature of the storytelling. The original trilogy runs breathlessly from place to place, rarely looking back (Yavin, Hoth and Bespin are never revisited), but the prequels depict a complex plot around Naboo and Coruscent, with an Anakin subplot tied to Tatooine, and the characters are in constant movement between these locations. Naboo is the first planet of the *Star Wars* films to undergo social development. Initially split between the Naboo people, who live on land, and the Gungans, who reside beneath the seas, *Phantom*'s conclusion demands that they unite against a common invader, and when we return to the planet in *Clones*, the city of Theed is fully integrated. Moreover, the prequels insist that the original films play by their revised historicist rules. Everything that was once expected to stand as a self-evident fact now has a complex origin. No one in *Star Wars* ever asked where the Death Star came from, and the second was similarly born at a stroke for *Return of the Jedi*. What Kevin Smith had once treated as a ludicrous joke (who built the Death Star?) would become a major plot point. *Clones* has an early holographic blueprint, taking us into a history of the station's production which will find even greater exploration over a decade later in *Rogue One*.

This disjunction in the vocabularies of the two trilogies met varied responses at the time of the prequels' releases. Some were simply dismissive of the new focus, unable to reconcile the more material concerns of the new films with the excitement generated by the heightened metaphysical language of the originals. In 2003, Ryan Gilbey, in his book on 1970s cinema, would recall laughter at *Menace*'s press screening.

> The cause of amusement and apprehension could be traced to the film's prosaic opening credit crawl. It read: 'Turmoil has engulfed the Galactic Republic. The taxation of trade routes to outlying star systems is in dispute' . . . could there be a less enticing sentence with which to begin a movie – any movie, let alone a flight of fantasy designed to stimulate the daydreams in schoolboy skulls?[1]

We might wonder if the event really happened as described, or whether Gilbey is playing to the by-then-established theme of *Menace* being an almighty disappointment. Regardless of historical accuracy, four years after the film's debut, he was prepared to raise the new trilogy's engagement with political processes as antithetical to the traditional values of *Star Wars*.

This attitude would not last. While *Phantom* was widely criticised, the later films in the trilogy coincided with the War of Terror – the US administration's response to the attacks of 9/11. For some, these films' narrative, in which the Republic's senior politician engineered a conflict abroad in order to boost military spending and pass draconian legislation at home, acted as a critique of the policies of President George W. Bush, a reading which cemented *Star Wars*' reputation as a liberal text. Once secretary-of-state Dick Cheney asserted that 'We also have to work, though, sort of the dark side.'[2] *Star Wars*-related readings of the administration's policy were probably inevitable. Lucas himself walked a tightrope, acknowledging the parallels with the contemporary situation, while also paying lip service to his long-held assertion that the saga had all been planned out in the 1970s. 'The parallels between what we did in Vietnam and what we're doing in Iraq now are unbelievable,' he reflected at the 2005 Cannes Film Festival.[3] This vision of the series was so strong that it would sustain an animated series (*The Clone Wars* 2008–14) which considered combat, terrorism and the home front from varying perspectives.[4]

The existence of the prequels actively rewrote the meaning of the original trilogy. Readings about hope had often turned upon Luke Skywalker's journey. By the turn of the century, however, Lucasfilm, promoting the prequels, would instead present Anakin/Vader firmly as the focus of the films: 'His son comes back and redeems him,' Lucas told the Los Angeles Press, 'That's the real story. It's always about the redemption of Anakin Skywalker. It's just that it's always been told from his son's point of view.'[5] A number of critics were happy to follow this new orthodoxy. In 1997, John Seabrook would write in *The New Yorker* that the new films would 'make it clear that *Star Wars*, taken as a whole story and viewed in chronological order, is not really the story of Luke at all but the story of Luke's father, Anakin'. 'The *Star Wars* saga is Anakin Skywalker's story,' wrote academic critic Christopher Deis in 2007. In 2016, Cass Sunstein suggested that

> the first two trilogies – Lucas' half dozen – should be called 'The redemption of Anakin Skywalker'. The redemption occurs as a result of intense attachment, otherwise known as love . . . he can't bear to see his son die.[6]

This new reading necessarily shifted viewer's understanding of where the emotional drama lay in *Return of the Jedi*'s conclusion. There was little which could be done to read that back into the physical film itself, though an anguished cry of 'Noooo' was added to the moment where Vader kills the Emperor to reflect the increased emphasis on his mental state and psychic journey. It was mostly left, however, to the revised novelisations subsequently published by the Disney regime to properly mine the sequence for its full dramatic impact, and tie the six films together.

> Beside the Emperor, Darth Vader continued to stand and watch. He looked at the Emperor again, then back to Luke.
>
> And then, in a moment, something changed. Perhaps he remembered something heard in his youth a long time ago: an ancient prophecy of the Chosen One who would bring balance to the force. Perhaps the vague outlines of someone named Shmi and a Jedi named Qui-Gon struggled to the surface of his consciousness. The most powerful, the most repressed thought of all could have emerged from the darkness: Padme . . . and her undying love for someone he once knew well. And despite all the terrible, unspeakable things he'd done in his life, he suddenly realised he could not stand by and allow the Emperor to kill their son. And in that moment, he was no longer Darth Vader.
>
> He was Anakin Skywalker.[7]

Some fans resisted this development. Questions of the priority of Luke over Anakin, or vice versa, became inevitably tied to the relative strengths of the trilogies and the now-vexed question of what order they should be viewed in: should the story be watched in chronological or production order? Lucasfilm insisted that *The Phantom Menace* should be the point of entry to the saga, and used its ownership of the films to promote this. When the films were first released in the Blu-ray format in September 2011, it was as a box-set containing all six, clearly marked and packaged in the company's preferred order. Lucasfilm had already announced that all six films would be re-released in 3D in episode order, and the stereo-converted *Menace* duly appeared in February 2012, the only film to do so since the 3D programme was subsequently abandoned.

Fans could resist this new reading. 'Vader is silent in the original version and that's how I'm going to remember it,' wrote Alex Langley.[8] Reports circulated of those who loved the original trilogy but refused to allow the prequels in their homes. In 2011 there was much online coverage of 'the Machete Order'. Named for the website upon which it was proposed, this is the idea that the films are best watched in the order: *A New Hope, The Empire Strikes Back, Attack of the Clones, Revenge of the Sith* and, finally, *Return of the Jedi*. This viewing order includes two of the prequels (the author regards *The Phantom Menace* as narratively redundant) but places them as an extended flashback inside the original films. Creator Rod Hilton, explaining his arrangement, said, 'The purpose of Machete Order was and always will be to refocus the story of the Original and Prequel Trilogies to be about Luke's journey.' In this way, The Machete Order was an act of fan resistance, one which asserted, against Lucasfilm's insistence, that the centre of meaning in the *Star Wars* saga would always lie in Luke and in the original films.[9]

For those prepared to engage with the saga in Lucasfilm's preferred order, readings became possible because of the contradictions and mismatches. In the light of the prequels, the original films could be pushed into giving up meanings which they cannot possibly have held at the time of their original release. Knowing the perversity of doing so, Elizabeth Sandifer read the trilogy from *Menace* onwards, allowing her to find that *Episode I*'s problems with racial representation were finally resolved in *Jedi* by the Ewoks.

> It's easy to make too much of this; the Ewoks are, like R2-D2 and Chewbacca, left untranslated, which makes it difficult to ascribe much depth to anything they do. But the fact that the Empire's climactic downfall is fundamentally down to a subaltern indigenous population rising up against oppression is valuable – a significant statement that makes editing Naboo into the closing montage sensible in spite of the fact that we've not spent any significant time there since *Attack of the Clones*.[10]

Sandifer pulls off a number of such reversals, seeing in Han Solo not an energy and cocky glibness which was missing from the prequels (having already been present in the original films), but a whirlwind which enters halfway through the saga to rewrite the possibilities: 'he represents a fundamentally new idea. And it's one that finds a close cousin in the other new idea the film introduces: the Rebellion.'[11]

Sandifer's engagement with the new anarchic possibilities offered by Solo is escalated by her dismissal of the Jedi. Disinterested in the slavery existing on Tatooine and emotionally sterile, she regards them as completely at fault in turning Anakin from an idealistic ten-year-old who dreams that he frees slaves into someone so warped as to become easy prey for Palpatine. Sandifer wants us to understand the Jedi as faded and implicated in both the Republic's malaise and, consequently, their own destruction, though she concludes (as we so often must when discussing the prequels) that it is 'not even remotely clear how much of this is intended'.[12] Expressed in this way, we can push things a little further than Sandifer is prepared to. Since the first three films have shown the Jedi to be ineffective against evil, perhaps the new hope of the subtitle is not Luke's rediscovery of the Force, but the engaging smuggler.

This returns us to a recurrent question in this study: are the Jedi an introverted elite or a force for and of the people? If we are prepared to take Lucasfilm at its word, read the films from *Episodes I–IV*, and find resonances in *Return of the Jedi* which couldn't possibly have been present in 1983, then a neat reading presents itself. The prequels show the Jedi as denying themselves family relationships and seemingly friends outside of the order. When Luke Skywalker disagrees with his mentors, it is precisely over this issue. In *The Empire Strikes Back*, he receives a vision of his friends in pain on Cloud City and, though Yoda and Obi-Wan urge him to ignore their plight and remain in training, he leaves to free them. In *Jedi*, Luke and Obi-Wan disagree over how Luke must deal with Vader. Obi-Wan, for all the comparisons to Jesus which were made in the late 1970s, can see no redemption for the person he surely must still think of as Anakin and feels he must be killed.

> *Luke:*   I can't kill my own father.
>
> *Obi-Wan:* Then the Emperor has already won.

Travis Langley points out that 'Luke succeeds each time through hope, faith, loyalty and compassion'.[13] He achieves that success in the Emperor's throne room when he casts aside his lightsabre and declares, 'I am a Jedi like my father before me.' In 1983, the moment meant several things. It was both Luke's definitive statement that he will not join the Dark Side and an appeal to what remains of his father inside Darth Vader. Cass Sunstein sees the line as an affirmation of the importance of the love between parents and children, and ascribes it such importance in decoding the saga as it makes it the triumphant last line of his book.[14]

These are perfectly plausible readings in both 1983 and today. The creation of the prequel trilogy, however, charges the line with a more potent meaning for, with the Jedi forbidden to form families, Luke's sentence ought to be unutterable. Luke Skywalker shouldn't have been born as the son of a Jedi, or if he were, it should be a subject of shame, an embarrassing disgrace, like the unacknowledged offspring of an eighteenth-century plantation owner and his female slave. In this light, 'I am a Jedi like my father before me' is a near-blasphemous statement in which Luke triumphs over Palpatine, Vader, Obi-Wan and Yoda by asserting that he no longer acknowledges their traditional rules. Viewed in this way, though it is a long time since anyone cared to ask, the final piece of a Campbellian reading falls into place. The hero of Campbell's theory does not simply save the present by restoring the past but takes the insight/energy he has acquired and builds from it something new. Luke's improved version must be a Force-consciousness which has not distanced itself from common humanity. This is, in fact, exactly what he does in the 'Expanded Universe' novels of the 1990s and 2000s, building a new order of knights who are not bound by the old codes of limited relationships. The knights he trains have relationships and chil-dren. He himself has a son, and in this re-alignment of the relationship between Jedi, Force, emotional openness and general populace, he may have resolved the problem we have spent so much time probing in this book.

Dealing with bad *Star Wars*: Redeeming the prequels

The notion that the prequel trilogy is poor, a disappointment, is widespread. Any google search of the relevant terms produces evidence of this. Before we consider this, it should be said that this is the response of a certain type of fan (Will Brooker's '*Star Wars* generation') who brought to the prequel trilogy exten-sive experience of the original films. Younger fans from the twenty-first century, who discovered the films under different circumstances and quite possibly in a different order, will have a contrasting view. Nevertheless, the notion of disap-pointment features prominently in much discourse surrounding the prequels.

The readings considered so far in this book take the largely traditional form of lengthy pieces of writing by people with training in the production of lit-erary readings. The release of the prequels, however, coincided with the spread of digital technology in the form of DVDs, the internet and social media. Technology allowed people to upload clips from the film, often highlighting minor details which even the most devoted of fans might not be able to recall. While re-edited videos – humorous or serious – had previously circulated in fandom on tapes, the availability of sophisticated editing tools took the com-plexity of unofficial videos to new levels, while the internet offered a whole new level of exposure. Moreover, the entire tone of internet postings was substan-tially different from that of traditional media. On the printed page, the inter-pretation of *Star Wars* remained largely a serious affair. Those who published books or articles needed to make their way through a number of editorial and marketing gatekeepers. Academics were bound by their own practices, and official licence holders continued to work under Lucasfilm's oversight. The internet offered a way around all of this and encouraged the generation of meanings which were hyperbolic, flippant, scatological or, in other ways, unlikely to get a printed hearing. The website alluded to in Chapter 1 – which discussed Luke's Jedi training as a case of a directionless young orphan being indoctrinated by religious extremists who lie to him – is one example. The most widely circulated case, however, was surely the theory that Jar-Jar Binks is a Sith Lord. Google the words *Jar-Jar Sith Lord*, and hundreds of sites promoting or examining this idea are revealed.

The theory argues that Jar-Jar is actually a Force-sensitive master of evil manipulating the events of *The Phantom Menace* without anyone knowing it. This is a calculated assault on the common understanding of the character as immature and naïve. It proceeds, however, through standard interpretive procedures. Jar-Jar's apparently innocent character is taken to be an act, and his 'true' nature is deduced from a consideration of textual evidence. His ability to dive athletically into the seas of Naboo is understood not as the obvious natural talent of an amphibious race, but likened to the leaps and bounds of the Jedi. The waggling of his limbs, normally taken to be signs of his lack of self-control and coordination, is reread as his working of Jedi powers, and these are related to events around him. In an example of how the use of digital clips on websites can be used to illustrate even the smallest of details, and the depth of analysis that modern *Star Wars* interpretation is capable of, many of these sites encourage us to compare a shot where a number of characters leap from a balcony on Naboo with the subsequent shot in which they land on the ground. The position in which Jar-Jar lands, so this argument goes, is incompatible with the one from which he started. He must, therefore, have pulled off one of his Jedi stunts in whatever space exists between two consecutive shots. Such detailed analyses as this show off the interpreter's mastery of the text – we might even say his/her superiority over it – as they pull it apart to create a new story which no one had ever thought existed before. From an analysis of the text itself, the theory moves through knowledge of the film's making. Since Jar-Jar is a wholly animated character, we cannot ascribe any of his movements or poses to the random events which might afflict an actor. Every detail is the way it is because Lucasfilm's digital artists crafted it that way

Ingenious though this undoubtedly is, the reading eventually hits an obvious brick wall. Jar-Jar Binks is not a Sith Lord. There are only ever two of them, and both positions are accounted for. When evil ascends to power, Jar-Jar does not join them to take the spoils, but is, instead, last seen among the mourners at Padme Amidala's funeral. Unable to sustain itself with reference to the films themselves. the reading shifts to extratextual material, arguing that negative public reaction to the character caused George Lucas to change tack, create a new dark lord for *Clones* and downgrade Jar-Jar's role.

This is audacious speculation, but it varies from other interpretive practices only by degree. I have argued throughout this book that joke interpretations (be it the idea that Luke is radicalised by antisocial extremist or the fate of the Death Star contractors) pursue the same processes as interpretation which does not seek to be humorous. Here we reach the logical end-point of that: a rigorously argued, but wholly counterintuitive, interpretation which it is difficult to gauge the status of: is it presented in seriousness, or as a complex piece of self-consciousness daftness?

There are stakes in this question. Underlying the theory of Jar-Jar as Sith Lord is a redemptive reading of *The Phantom Menace*, for the theory that Jar-Jar was originally intended as a Sith Lord asks us to look again at some of the most heavily criticised moments in the film and see them in a new light. The theory foresees a scene, somewhere in *Episode II* or *III*, where the childish/racist persona which viewers found so annoying is thrown instantly aside, shown to be a red herring, and the real character revealed. Retrospective viewings of *Menace* would no longer be dominated by a dislike of Jar-Jar's childishness but by a knowledge of his duplicity and play-acting. If this whole narrative development was cast aside, as this theory suggests, then the blame for the failure of the prequel trilogy shifts. Lucas didn't fail us by making poor films. Rather, we viewers failed him by not allowing him to stay the course. His vision would have been validated had we trusted – shown faith – and stopped complaining before the full pattern emerged. Instead, our outrage caused him to change his plan, wrecking who knows how much other damage on the story in the process.

In its attempts to find a better version of *The Phantom Menace* than the one we know, the Jar-Jar theory has much in common with other attempts by fans to find a way of liking it. With the original trilogy held in high regard by most, dealing with bad *Star Wars* was a new experience. The 'prequels as critique of the war on terror' reading would finally become the central plank of such redemption, but that possibility was not open until the third instalment and did little to redeem the first film of the trilogy. In his book *Using the Force,* Will Brooker gives examples of the ways in which disappointed fans sought to redeem *The Phantom Menace,* a film in which they had a heavy emotional investment but didn't necessarily enjoy very much. He quotes one female *Star Wars* fan suggesting that 'People like me, who enjoyed *The Phantom Menace* more on repeated viewings, did so because we began to tune out Jar-Jar.' That comment was taken up by a subsequent commentator, Tom Shone, who found it heart-breaking in its mixture of disappointment (with the film) and hope (that it might one day become wholly enjoyable if she can just watch it enough).[15]

Others returned to the film after immersing themselves in fan fiction and speculation. This had prioritised the elements that fans found interesting (the noble but not humourless Jedi knights, for instance), and this additional knowledge created interests for adults to read back into the film, enough to give the interesting elements a priority over the annoying slapstick moments.[16]

If screening out Jar-Jar weren't enough, Emily Asher-Perrin has written of blanking out the entire soundtrack by watching the prequels with the sound muted.[17] She calls her viewing 'an experiment'. As we might expect, blocking out the audio makes her more receptive to visual qualities, and while she finds little return for her viewing of *The Phantom Menace,* the prequels reward her more as she progresses through them: 'people turning to each other and away again, smiling and touching, arguing and pleading. The costume changes for Padmé again let us know so much about her – when she's feeling flirtatious, whimsical, or sexual.' This is a reading of scenes from *Attack of the Clones,* surely among the most positive notices that that film's love story has ever received. Her piece is illustrated with film stills. Reproduced in hi-definition at 2.35:1, and often depicting small figures against impressive CGI backgrounds, they look like paintings. That comparison was not uncommon during the period of the prequels' production and release, though it has been rarely discussed since, probably because no director has followed Lucas so wholly down the route of artificial backdrops. It remains, however, a reasonable basis for analysis, a new location in which to locate positive qualities within the films.

Having posted the results of her experiment online, Asher-Perrin received a number of responses. Some were simply dismissive ('Let me just say: You don't have to turn the sound off to appreciate the visual beauty of *Lawrence of Arabia*'). Others, however, recorded their own unusual viewing experiences of the prequels. One, who prioritised sound design, took the exact opposite tack: 'I went and saw *Episode II* twice in the theatres, and closed my eyes for the entirety of the second screening, just to listen to it.' Others talked of watching their DVDs/Blu-rays with the soundtracks switched to foreign languages which they did not understand. This drained the words of any communication content and turned them into abstract sound effects. These readings are attempts to locate the small experimental films that Lucas always said he was going to make by finding them buried within the *Star Wars* movies.

These were people stretching their viewing patterns to maintain an enthusiastic (or, at least, meaningful) relationship with films which they initially struggled to like. We can enjoy all of the cleverness on display here, the straining to find aesthetic value where none was obviously apparent. However, another set of redemptive readings worked precisely by switching the focus away from *The Phantom Menace* itself and towards the moment of its release. Writer/actor Todd Hanson attempts to defend *Menace* in a fairly half-hearted manner before finally finding a reason to love the film and a genuine legacy which it gave us. He recalls being in the cinema queue when at some point the local news showed up.

> Because I was wearing a costume, a reporter singled me out and asked, 'why are you wearing that?' I was speechless. I had no real answer prepared . . . So after a brief pause, I said 'Why do you think? Because I'm a big freakin' geek? This is our day. Geek nation!', and then I turned around to the people standing behind me and yelled, 'Geek nation!', and they all started yelling it too. I don't think the reporter understood what we were trying to say.[18] (p. 201)

From there, Hanson enters the cinema for the prequel trilogy's greatest moment: the collective experience as the opening credits began to role and 1,700 people – he saw it in an extremely large theatre – cheered the familiar icons (the Lucasfilm credit, the saga logo, 'A long time ago. . .') and 'went absolutely apeshit' (p. 202).

The anticipation and fan-bonding which Hanson writes about are dramatised in the low-budget indie movie *Fanboys* (Kyle Newman, 2009). Set in November 1998, the film concerns four young men who were inseparable *Star Wars* fans in their youth. Three – Linus, Hutch and Windows – have kept the geek faith, working in a comic store, but Eric Bottler has been estranged from them for three years, having taken a job at his father's chain of car dealerships. He is a talented artist who once dreamed of a comics career but has, presumably, bottled it. Through Bottler is worked out a theme of redemption which is clearly drawn from the original trilogy itself. He is an ex-fan who has sold out, a man without hope. 'I did what I had to. I grew up,' is how he rationalises it. Even in social situations, he has invariably come 'straight from work' and thus wears a shirt and tie, while those around him dress casually for relaxation. His elder brother teases him relentlessly over his geeky past and is assumed to be the heir apparent, but it is Eric whom their father asks to take over the company. Likened in a dream sequence to Vader's inviting his son to join him, it is clear that this is a further step away from his suppressed fan identity and if Eric takes it, he will not be able to return. The metaphor is an obvious one: geeky fankids are the rebellion. Careerism is the Dark Side.

When he is made aware by his friends that Linus is dying of cancer and will not live to see the release of *The Phantom Menace*, Bottler reluctantly joins them on a road trip from Ohio to California, there to break into Skywalker Ranch and view a rough cut of the film. On the journey, Bottler's authentic identity as a fan reasserts itself, rendered visible by his switching to a Dark Side t-shirt and by his willingness to get into an argument with Trekkies. The film's final scenes, a Linus-less coda, celebrates the day of the film's release, depicting costumed fans in queues. Even Eric's bullying brother has a ticket: 'Hey, it's the *Wars*, bro.' They enter the theatre, smaller than the one Hanson visited but just as crowded with fans. 'What if the movie sucks?' asks a worried Eric. It's a good joke (an acknowledgement that many people indeed thought that it did), but the wisdom of the film was a line he spoke earlier: 'This was never about the movie. It was about all of us.'

This is a very different vision of the release of *The Phantom Menace* than Ryan Gilbey gave us at this chapter's opening. Hanson's essay and Newman's film both locate the film's value in the moments before anyone saw it (both end as the film starts to roll). They enact the pluralist reading of the film, but apply it to fans who publicly out themselves as media-fixated geeks in an atmosphere where such behaviour, often mocked in the 1990s, was made acceptable by the film's release. Neither contextualises that moment within a wider history, but we could. If we accepted the claims being made at face value (and didn't investigate whether both texts were guilty of retrospectively mythologising the moment), we would place it within a history which extends through the 1990s and into the twenty-first century whereby media fandom, once ridiculed, became socially accepted. I am not at all convinced that *The Phantom Menace* had much to do with that trajectory, but as a way of redeeming a film that most fans don't enjoy, mythologising it as central to the process might well be the best available option.

The Disney trilogy: *The Force Awakens* (J. J. Abrams, 2015), *The Last Jedi* (Rian Johnson, 2017) and *The Rise of Skywalker* (J. J. Abrams, 2019)

More so than the prequel trilogy, Disney's new films took their bearings from the ways in which *Star Wars* was discussed and perceived publically. The films positioned themselves in relation to these debates so much of this section discusses how new entries in a film series (re)interpret the episodes which preceded them. In doing this, the company took its bearings from a position which I have discussed already in this chapter: the idea that the prequels were a disappointment.

To counter this disappointment, Disney looked back to 1977, to the first film and the moment of its release, and the symbol of that was the word *hope*. The word features eleven times in *The Last Jedi*, every instance being by a major character as a statement of what the galaxy needs. In *Rogue One*, hope is the last, conclusive word of dialogue, and the film was promoted with the slogan *Rebellions are built on hope* (also a line in the film). In these instances, the word had taken on self-reflexive qualities, aligning the new films with *Episode IV*, the saga's originating text, the glories of which the new instalments would seek to re-attain. Consequently, the protagonists of these new films would be obliged to endlessly play out the actions of hope and its spiritual opposite, despair.

Like *Episode IV*, the new trilogy begins after a sustained period of galactic crisis. *The Force Awakens* offers us new hope because its first spoken line (after the opening crawl and some dialogue-free scenes) is 'This will begin to make things right.' What has gone wrong is not just a resurgence of the dark side but – worse than that! – *Star Wars* itself is in ruins. Han and Leia's marriage has collapsed and the former has returned, with Chewie, to the freelance smuggling life which they lived before his redemption. Artoo Detoo has fallen silent ('He may never be his old self again'); Luke has gone missing; the Millennium Falcon has finally been sent to the junkyard that people were always comparing it to ('This ship hasn't flown in years'); Threepio has lost an arm; and, if the title is to make any sense, even the Force has fallen asleep on the job.

In such a context, it is unsurprising that the new heroine, Rey, lives a life of desert scavenging on Jakku, a planet littered with the detritus of the classic trilogy. Crashed star destroyers litter the skyline, and Rey herself lives in the remains of an Imperial walker along with a doll representing an X-Wing pilot. Just as the Jedi were a legend by Luke's time, so the events of the original trilogy have passed into myth now. An orphan, Rey lives in hope of her parents' return, just as fans await the return of the *Star Wars* of their youth. 'Don't give up hope,' she urges the droid BB-8, 'He might still show up, whoever you're waiting for . . . I know all about waiting.'

Rey's life on a world littered with wreckage renders literal the reading about rubbish which had grown up in the twenty-first century. She defines herself as someone who wants more than just to break things down, and wishes her scavenging to be about more than spare parts. When BB-8 flees into the desert, he comes across two scavengers, Rey and an alien called Teevo. They presumably have equal salvage rights to the droid, and, given the staging of the scene, Teevo might reasonably argue that he found it first, but Rey fights him off, legitimating her claim to BB-8 on the ground that she will retain his wholeness: 'That's just Teevo. He wants you for parts.'

What has been torn into parts most of all is *Star Wars*, so this is what Rey must put back together. Metatextually, she begins by getting involved in a remake of the original film's plot. In-world, her appropriation of the Millennium Falcon from a junkyard initiates the reconstruction, bringing her into contact with its previous owners who confirm everything she has heard about the past, but who does so with sadness in his voice. 'You're Han Solo?!' she exclaims. 'I used to be,' he says. 'I knew Luke.' His statements are all in the past tense, and he is unable to re-create the heroic version of himself. Han, like the other heroes of the original trilogy, has lost his real identity. The speaker of the film's opening dialogue ('This will begin to make things right'), however, remembers them. Supplementary materials call him Lor San Tekka, but he is only called 'an old ally' on-screen, and he has the knowledge of the heroes' past identities required to make them whole again. When Leia is referred to as a general, he asserts the primacy of the title by which she was known in the original trilogy: 'General? To me she's royalty.' What he has which will make things better is a map to find Luke Skywalker, and when the map passes into Rey's hands, she uncovers the truth of the original trilogy sufficiently that when Han dies, he does so having been regenerated into the man he was when the original trilogy ended in 1983. Artoo is re-activated and, in the film's final sequence, Luke is found.

Rey, like any internet blogger, has forged her own *Star Wars* from the multiple options around her, but all the technology which litters her home comes from *Episodes IV–VI*. Rey's specific task is to repair the original trilogy. The original film of 1977 offered us a quest to rediscover a lost secret. Now that film itself is that which has been lost. Extratextually, the reason why the *Star Wars* universe has fallen upon hard times is the existence of the disappointing prequels, and it is noticeable that Rey resurrects almost nothing from these films.

Viewers were cued to make this reading by trailers for the film where dialogue, though minimal, pointed towards a resurrection ('There has been an awakening' – the opening of the first trailer) and a return ('Chewie, we're home' – Han Solo at the end of the second). In playing out this plotline of resurrection at such length, the film differed only in degree from the procedures of other returning franchises of the same period. In *The Muppets* (James Bobbin, 2011), two men who loved the old television series in their youth must locate the muppets, now dispersed across America, and save the theatre in which they once performed. In *Blade Runner 2049* (Denis Villeneuve, 2017), Harrison Ford is once again the lost treasure of the original franchise which must be located by the new, younger lead. In all of these films, the same ideas play out – the characters of the original version have been lost over the years, their skills rusted and their true identities neglected. The efforts of young followers (metatextually: viewers, fans) will restore them. If *Star Wars* makes a bigger noise about the procedure than these other examples, that is not just because the franchise is always the biggest but because *Blade Runner* had merely ceased production. *The Force Awakens* speaks to that generation of fans who felt that the franchise had not only vanished but had been actually wounded by disappointing prequels. To all possible complaints about its content, originality or aesthetic worth, *Awakens* responds that it is not so much a film as a collective act of resurrection.

While liberal interpreters had applauded the Jedi of the prequel trilogy for the diversity to be found among their ranks, it is with Disney that the films become fully conscious of the pluralist reading. What would the resistance look like? The original film offered us religious faith and a military force standing to attention at a medal-giving ceremony. The young person's adaptation of *The Force Awakens* described 'a ragtag alliance of defiant freethinkers, maverick artists, enlightened nobles and restless youths'. *The Force Awakens* engages with the question in the most literal terms during the first meeting of Rey and Finn.

Rey: I've never met a resistance fighter before.
Finn: Well, this is what we look like. Some of us. Others look different.

With a female lead, a wealth of non-Caucasian heroes and heroines, and a discreet same-sex kiss in *The Rise of Skywalker*, the Disney trilogy casts the rebellion in line with left-liberal visions of how it draws from diverse identities to form an alliance against fascism. In the original trilogy, Luke's trajectory had led him constantly away from non-Force users to spend his time with Yoda, Vader, etc. Rey, by contrast, is more completely integrated into the Resistance. Although she is dispatched on Force-related assignments of her own, she always returns to the camp and, in *The Rise of Skywalker*, takes non-Force users with her – acknowledgement that resistance requires diverse talents. Luke himself continues his isolation from others, residing in self-imposed exile in a hidden location.

The word *hope* had not featured prominently in *The Force Awakens*. Rather, that film acted out the saga's redemption. It falls to *The Last Jedi* to once again play out the question of who or what might be the hope which the galaxy needs. The opening crawl tells us that the Resistance is 'certain that Jedi master Luke Skywalker will return to restore a spark of hope to the fight'. Rey tells Luke that 'Leia sent me with hope', and Supreme Leader Snoke asserts that 'Skywalker lives . . . as long as he does, hope will live in the galaxy'. Leia reflects that in 'every corner of the galaxy, the downtrodden and oppressed know our symbol and they put their hope in it'. Late in the film, as Luke fails to return to the front lines, the resistance – its forces decimated – send out a signal to unspecified 'allies', whom they believe to reside at the edges of the galaxy. When there is no response, Leia reflects that 'the galaxy has lost all its hope'. I have asserted that the rebellion reached its lowest ebb in the space above the fourth moon of Yavin in *A New Hope*. Then, all seemed lost because the Death Star was preparing to destroy the moon, Han had absented himself from the battle, and Luke had not yet found his faith. Although *The Last Jedi* replays narrative moments from *Empire* and *Return of the Jedi*, its primary borrowing from the original film is this moment of despair, and the moment is evoked/repeated even more blatantly in *The Rise of Skywalker*. In this film, the same strategy is attempted. While Poe Dameron leads the rebel ships against the resurrected Emperor's battlefleet, he sends Lando and Chewie in the Millennium Falcon to send a rallying signal: 'We've got friends out there. They'll come if they know there's hope.' As battle is engaged, and the rebels' cause appears to be lost, he loses faith and apologises to those he has misguidedly led: 'I'm sorry. I felt we had a shot but there are too many of them.' Like Luke above the Death Star, he is saved by the appearance of the Millennium Falcon, this time leading a motley armada of the galaxy's citizens, rising up. 'But there are more of us, Poe. There are more of us.'

This moment is the trilogy's fullest enactment of the 'alliance' theme of the saga: the rebellion is everyone and, at the crucial juncture, they finally show up to save the day. Elsewhere, the films play out the question of a redeeming

Force-empowered saviour. While Leia declares hope dead in *Last Jedi*, other characters are debating who might incarnate it. Luke declines the role, casually discarding the lightsabre which Rey presented to him with such expectation. He cannot, however, escape the role. Even Artoo pressures him, replaying – from his memory banks – Leia's original holographic plea ('Help me Obi-Wan Kenobi, you're my only hope') with the implication that Luke himself is now the retired Jedi who must come to her aid. As he remains unresponsive, Rey considers other options, declaring Ben Solo to be 'our only hope'. In the throne room, Supreme Leader Snope casts Rey in the role. He doesn't use the H-word, but clearly has these themes in mind when he declares that Ben's rising in darkness would be balanced by the appearance of a similar figure to stand for the light.

Whatever the viability of these candidates as the incarnation of hope, the logic of these films, and the expectations of the audience, insists that Luke must finally step forward and claim the title that has been his ever since George Lucas first appended it to the original film. Leia's talk of all hope dying is his cue to re-enter the fray, taking on First Order Forces in a delaying battle which buys the princess's forces time to escape and regroup. 'The rebellion is reborn today', he declares, a triumphant claim, not least because, by shucking off the name of Resistance and returning to its original title, the saga's reconstruction of the world of the original trilogy is complete.

Prior to this triumphant return, Luke has hidden himself on 'the most unfindable place in the galaxy'. It is a lonely island with a sacred tree, an underground cavern seemingly in touch with the dark side, and structures 'built a thousand generations ago' to house the only copies of the original Jedi texts. The saga will not be returning to its Campbellite themes, but there is an echo of them here in this most mythic of locations. Luke, however, has not come here to access the primal energies of the cosmos (which do seem to be present). He has gone into hiding because of his perceived failure.

The nature of that failure requires probing. Luke declares that he will never train a new generation of Jedi. There are two possible reasons for this, and the film is unable to either decide between them or merge them into a coherent whole. The common sense interpretation – because of the narrative emphasis placed on it – is that Luke's reluctance stems from his failure to keep Ben Solo from going to the dark side and his own moment of weakness: in direct contrast to his refusal to countenance killing Vader a generation earlier, he thought for a moment that slaughtering the young man might be the only answer – a moment which was instrumental in driving him towards evil. By this reading, Luke will not train Jedi because he feels himself incapable of doing the job properly.

An alternative explanation is also in the film. When Luke asks Rey what she thinks the Force is, she gives a debased answer which lacks spirituality and which concerns only privilege and power.

> *Rey:*   It's a power that Jedi have that lets them control people and make things . . . float.
>
> *Luke:*   Every word in that sentence was wrong . . . The Force is not a power you have. It's not about lifting rocks. It's the energy between all things . . . a balance that binds the universe together.

He subsequently asserts, 'The Force does not belong to the Jedi. To say that *if the Jedi die, the light dies* is vanity.' From this perspective, Luke has indeed learnt something from his time on the island. He originally led his Jedi recruits to an isolated spot and sought to train them there. That led to disaster just as the old strategy of isolating them in a temple did. Luke has subsequently learnt that separating the Force from the general populace and isolating it in the hands of a privileged few is a self-defeating move.

The fact that *Last Jedi* features two explanations for why Luke has isolated himself from humanity, and cannot reconcile them in a coherent narrative, reflects the new trilogy's wider inability to decide if the Force is the province of a select few, or if it does, indeed, belong to everyone. Something of an outlier in the Disney trilogy, *Last Jedi* is heavily invested in the notion that the Force lives among the general populace. At the film's conclusion, a small stable lad apparently moves a broom through the power of the Force, and this child, as surely as the seed-planting girl from the Marvel comic decades earlier, is metaphorically a hope for future growth. Such a belief is also central to the way that *Last Jedi* plays out the question of Rey's parentage.

The mystery of Rey's parents is central to the trilogy, and it plays out the different answers. They left her on the planet Jakku for reasons unknown, and she spent years awaiting their return. Online speculation was rife, but although the answers were notionally varied (Luke's daughter, Obi-Wan's great-grand-daughter, etc.), they all assumed that she was the offspring of a powerful Force-user. In *The Rise of Skywalker*, Disney gave an answer in the same vein: Rey was the descendent of the Emperor himself. *Last Jedi* had asserted otherwise, telling us that her parents 'were nobody'. Ben Solo, affirming her insight, declares, 'You have no place in this story. You come from nothing. You're nothing – but not to me.' The story which Rey had no part of was the one where Force-consciousness is a special trait, often inherited. For all his faults and confusions, Ben Solo offers her a place in a better story where there are no bloodline qualifications for being Force-sensitive. I would have preferred the saga to end this way rather than with the later revelation.

We might say that, like the original film, *The Last Jedi* shows the passing of the torch of hope to a new generation, and *Skywalker* displays what they do with it. That, however, would be a post-millennial reading. There is no evidence that *Star Wars* was understood in generational terms in 1977. The malaise under which the galaxy groaned was not a generational matter. No one argued that Luke specifically redeemed the sins of his parents' generation. There are obvious reasons for this: in 1977, Luke's father was presumed to be among the dead, and Kenobi looked like his grandfather. Forty years later, as the Disney films introduced a third cohort of heroes/heroines, and explicitly dealt with the passing of the ageing original characters, generational conflict was seen as a major axis for understanding the new films. The following titles are just a selection of the online pieces written in the wake of *Last Jedi*: *A New, New Hope: Luke Skywalker and the Soul of Baby Boomer Men*; *Yes, Star Wars The Last Jedi Is an Open Letter to the Millennial Generation*; *The Last Jedi: Loser Boomers & a New Hope from Millennials*; *Millennials Strike Back: An Esoteric Reading of the Last Jedi*; *'Star Wars: The Last Jedi' Has a Message for Baby Boomers: Trust*.[19] The arguments in these pieces diagnose a wealth of contemporary ills: Millennials don't like the film because the constant setbacks suffered by the heroes don't fit their worldview; the baby boomers, as represented by Snope and Luke, don't trust their young disciples to make the right decisions with their inheritance.

In making arguments like this, the pieces cited situate *Star Wars* films at the centre of contemporary political debate. This was somewhere that Disney was frequently not keen to place them, though it was hardly rigorous in policing this. Perhaps the sequence which most evoked twenty-first-century society was the Canto Bight casino in *The Last Jedi*. In this vision of the fabulously rich at play in an exclusive casino, the sequence affiliates itself with concerns about modern Western economies which produce spectacular inequalities of wealth. The fact that many of the wealthy seen here acquired their wealth by supplying arms to the First Order returns us to the question of where the villains get their weaponry from. The answer here is that they buy it from arms dealers who grow wealthy in the process. Again, *Last Jedi* was something of an outlier in the trilogy, for *Rise of Skywalker* returned us to dark locations far divorced from the political centre and economic reflections. That may have been a calculated ploy to forestall arguments about political relevance, debates about which had been central to a number of 'anthology' films – stories which told what iconic *Star Wars* characters did or how significant moments occurred before they entered the saga proper. These included more explicitly political material, and debates were rife.

Star Wars anthology films:*Solo* (Ron Howard, 2018) and *Rogue One* (Gareth Edwards, 2016)

Divorced from the main centres of galactic history, the anthology films take place on desolate planets amidst enslaved or degraded populations. Conditions are often harsh, subsistence living is rife, and the films reflect that desperation in muted shades of grey and brown. Imperial installations, when we see them, are hi-tech oases amidst seas of rural poverty, and the Empire is recurrently characterised as rapacious in its need for raw materials to fuel its conquests (again, we return to how the Empire builds its war machine). The endlessly poverty-stricken worlds of the anthology movies may be suggesting that the Empire deliberately impoverishes people to keep them from rising up. This would generally be regarded as a liberal reading, though we should remember that the first person to suggest that the Empire practiced economic warfare upon its subjects was Frank Allnut in *The Force of Star Wars*. Alternatively, Disney, forever rehashing the original film, may simply think that every planet must have Tatooine's subsistence economy. That the anthology films consistently seek new viewpoints on *A New Hope* returns us to the happy coincidence discovered in the last chapter; the liberal impulse to incorporate those who were barred from an heroic role first time round entails returning to the most profitable part of the narrative. *Rogue One* tells us how the rebels attained the Death Star plans, while *Solo* shows how the young Han became the man he is when first encountered at the Mos Eisley cantina. It is this film I discuss first.

The transition from the world of the saga's main episodes to the bleaker galaxy of *Solo* is enacted at the very beginning. It begins with the traditional invocation – 'A long time ago in a galaxy far far away' – but then moves to a second statement in the same blue lettering against the same black background: 'It is a Lawless Time.' This second notion of time supplants the first and brings the story into the present tense, rather than a mythic past, and shears it of the fairy tale qualities often ascribed to the usual opening. Given this shift, we should not be surprised that *Solo* is the first *Star Wars* film not to mention the Force (aside from whatever associations are brought to the film by a pseudo-lightsabre fight with a laser knife at the film's climax and a cameo by Darth Maul) which necessarily reduces everyone's horizons and denies the characters the franchise's traditional route to a higher calling and a better life. Consequently, things are grim. Young Han and his girlfriend Qi'ra escape the criminal environment of Corellia, but there is nowhere to run to. Han spends three years in the Imperial Forces, while Qi'ra rises to the top of a different planet's crime cartel.

Set on poverty-stricken frontier planets, the film plays out the Western tropes with which Han was associated when he first entered the saga (and, with the film dispensing with so many of saga's most famous trappings, it is easier than usual to notice the structures of traditional genres). The plot concerns shipments of coaxium, an unstable element required for travel through hyperspace. Escaping Imperial duties by joining a criminal gang led by Tobias Beckett, Han fails in an initial train heist, thus indebting himself to the gangs and requiring that an even-riskier theft be attempted in order to pay off the debt. Their operations are complicated by the presence of 'Marauders', another criminal gang who themselves pursue the coaxium. They return at the end, just as Han and his partners have acquired the element, and seek to take it for themselves. When the possibility of an arrangement which doesn't involve killing is proposed, Beckett laughs, arguing that 'They're Marauders . . . all they know how to do is kill.' In response, the leader, Enfys Nest, removes her helmet and reveals herself. The antithesis of traditional images of a killer, she is a young woman, red-haired and freckled. If Anne of Green Gables became a space pirate, she'd look like this. Nest makes the film's longest speech.

> My mother once told me about a band of mercenaries that came to a peaceful planet. They had a resource there that these men coveted, so they took it. They kept coming back, taking more, but finally the people resisted. When they came back, demanding their tribute, the people shouted back in one voice 'No more.' The mercenaries didn't like the sound of that, so the cut off the tongues of every last man, woman and child. Do you know what that pack of animals became?

Actions make it clear that the mercenaries became the crime syndicates which have committed crimes across the galaxy in league with the Empire. Beckett remains cynical. 'Says you!' he exclaims, seeking to marginalise Nest's claims as self-justifying and lacking in authority. 'No,' she replies, 'Says them' and signals that the other Marauders remove their masks, revealing a wealth of races, each of which has had their planet 'brutalised' by the criminals. 'We're not Marauders – we're allies, and the war's just begun.'

We have heard this story, or something like it, before. I discussed it in Chapter 3. In 1977, Marvel comics, requiring a follow-up story to their adaptation of the original film, similarly turned to Han Solo's Western tropes and sent him to Aduba-3 where an agricultural village hired him to form a surrogate Magnificent Seven to fight off the outlaws who pillaged their crops each year. Marvel's story, however, was one of saviour heroes. The villagers turned to Han, and he succeeded by wielding a lightsabre and savouring, briefly, 'what it's like – to be a Jedi Knight'. *Solo* tells us a similar story, but shorn of mysticism and saviours. The villagers do not turn to outside help but rise up themselves. Modern metaphors – of *speaking out, finding a voice, raising that voice* and being *silenced* – are all replayed in the story of the villagers who declared 'No more' and lost their tongues as a consequence. However, if the criminal gang became the Empire and its underworld, then this small group of Marauders may also transform into something larger. If they possess the coaxium, it will become 'the blood which brings life to something more . . . a rebellion'. In this latest iteration of *what the rebellion might look like*, *Solo* offers us its origins lying with the oppressed (largely female) rising up to say 'No more'. In this secular vision of Lucas's galaxy, devoid of Force references, redemption must lie in the banding together of victims.

Many perhaps welcomed a thoroughly secularised *Star Wars* film. However, the film's box-office failure brought to a halt the ongoing programme of anthology films which Disney/Lucasfilm had announced. There might be any number of reasons for that (including the development of streaming television services, a priority platform for Disney, which meant that *Star Wars* content was developed for use there), but *Solo*'s failure contrasted with the commercial and critical success of the previous anthology film *Rogue One*. *Rogue One* offered a more complex interweaving of the saga's diverse tropes than *Solo* managed, presenting itself – both on-screen and in its spin-off narratives – as both a tale of faith and a culture war narrative. It was tied closely to the original trilogy because its plot concerned the rebellion's appropriation of the Death Star data. Released a year after *The Force Awakens*, it continued Disney's return to the themes of 1977, reintroducing much of the imagery of the Christian readings of the first film by presenting a Force which is not only open to all but which may be actively worshipped in a religious manner. It also envisaged the Death Star as being devised and constructed by Imperial officers/employees – a rejection of the imagery of free-market arms traders in favour of something more consistent with 1977. Released at the end of 2016 – a year which had seen a number of large political shocks for the left, culminating in the election of Donald Trump as president – *Rogue One* was drawn into the heated political debates of the period. I will consider the film in these two lights: as the return to a more clearly religious *Star Wars*, and as a film received and interpreted in light of the culture war politics of the moment.

Shortly before the film opened, *Rogue One*'s screenwriter Chris Weitz had tweeted, 'Please note that the Empire is a white supremacist (human) organization opposed by a multi-cultural group led by brave women.'[20] Though deleted only days later, the tweet generated a twitter campaign #DumpStarWars and, apparently, an alt-right boycott of the film, though the financial impact of this would appear to have been negligible. Trump supporter Jack Posobiec subsequently tweeted, '*Star Wars* writers rewrote and reshot *Rogue One* to add in Anti-Trump scenes calling him a racist.'[21] Given how little credibility Trump's campaign was given right until the moment he was elected, and the matter of weeks between the election and the film's release, this seems almost literally impossible. Weitz subsequently denied that the film had been amended in this way, and Bob Iger, head of Disney, played down anti-Trump interpretations which circulated at the time of its release. 'This is a film that the world should enjoy. It is not a film that is, in any way, a political film. There are no political statements in it, at all,' he said, undercutting his own argument by adding that the film 'has one of the greatest and most diverse casts of any film we have ever made and we are very proud of that, and that is not a political statement, at all.'[22]

While Disney's attempt to position the film apolitically fits a long industry tradition, some fans insisted on political interpretations. Teresa Jusino, writing for themarysue.com, clearly felt that anyone taking a meaning from the saga other than a liberal one was simply misreading.

> As *Rogue One: A Star Wars Story* approaches, there is apparently a group of alleged *Star Wars* fans (I say 'alleged' because they seem to thoroughly misunderstand everything the franchise is about) trying to urge people to #DumpStarWars, because they're apparently surprised that the franchise is about fighting an oppressive power that takes people's rights away.[23]

Similar writing could be found across social media and the internet. Noah Poling wrote: 'BREAKING NEWS: Movie series that has always had an antifascism theme criticizes a fascist wannabe. In other news, water is wet #DumpStarWars.' SanMartin Garcia added: '#DumpStarWars because it took the right wing almost 40 years to figure out what an allegory is.' OhNoSheTwitnt said: 'Love that it took racist idiots nearly 4 decades and a KKK-endorsed POTUS to figure out what *Star Wars* is about. #DumpStarWars.'[24]

The political moment of its release aside, *Rogue One* generated considerably more politically oriented reviews and interpretations than *The Force Awakens.* The film's imagery of expensively equipped stormtroopers patrolling a desert town while struggling to keep an insurgency under control was ripe for 'war on terror' readings. Ian Doescher – who had playfully translated the first six films into Elizabethan English for a series of books presenting the scripts in Shakespearean style – argued that 'This is *Star Wars*, yes, but it could also describe American combat in the middle East',[25] while pop culture website *The Gryphoin* struck a more historical note:

> Jyn expresses in the film that if she accepts silently her pseudo-enslavement to the Empire, then a satisfactory existence is possible. This is the life of a citizen under a despotic dictatorship; the life many will have experienced in the countries carved from the Sykes-Picot agreement.[26]

The desert setting of the film, and the images of occupation, provoked a wealth of readings. In many contexts, both promoting the film at its release and in discussion afterwards, director Gareth Edwards would frequently reflect on the saga's multiple generic borrowings and include biblical epic in the list.[27] If *The Last Jedi* emphasised that the Force was open to everyone, *Rogue One* returns us to a religious notion of its existence. In so doing, it used a number of ideas which had featured in the original film's earliest drafts but been abandoned. The Kaiburr Crystal makes its big-screen debut, having been discarded at draft stage in the mid-1970s, resurrected for the first *Star Wars* novel *Splinter of the Minds Eye* (1978), and used in the cartoon television series *The Clone Wars*. Now spelt Kyber, it is revealed as the jewel that powers all lightsabres and which will, once collected in massive quantities, now arm the Death Star's laser. *The Book of the Wills*, a (possibly) religious text within which the whole saga was, at one point, going to be contained, had been similarly abandoned after the first novelisation, but *Rogue One* introduces us to the Guardians of the Whills, a special position within a temple given over to the worship of the Force.[28] The Whills are now a religious position/order, residing on the holy planet of Jedha (the name serves to denote both a planet and its major city). This is a place of pilgrimage for those who love and trust the Force. Pilgrims and priests line its streets, but it is under Imperial occupation, an image resonant not only of today's Middle East but also the Roman occupation of New Testament Judea. Any exact link between the Holy planet and the emerging rebel alliance is kept vague, but rebel 'extremist' Saw Gerrera has made his base here, and when the Empire tests the Death Star weapon systems by destroying the city, their immediate motivation may be to seal an information leakage, but it also fits neatly with the first film's vision of the Empire as eroding the Force worship which is so offensive to its secular technocracy. Orson Krennic, overseer of the Death Star's completion, explicitly makes the link when he gloats about what has been destroyed: 'Jedha, Saw Gerrera , his band of fanatics, their holy city, the last reminder of the Jedi.'

Fanatics? Holy? Elsewhere in *Rogue One* we find *miracle*. The religious vocabulary of the original film is back along with statements deriding the faithful: 'dreamers like this fool'. Like the original, *Rogue* is a film about the persistence of faith, here played out through three characters. Baze Malbus and Chirrut Imwe once worked in the Temple as Guardians of the Whills, until the Empire ransacked it and threw everyone out. Neither can manipulate the Force Jedi-style, but Imwe remains a believer in its powers, and he and his friend play out familiar arguments. When locked in a cell, Baze mocks his friend for praying that the door will spring up. 'It bothers him because he knows it's possible,' his friend cheekily responds, 'Baze Malbus was once the most devoted guardian of us all.'

Thrust into this world is the film's protagonist, Jyn Urso, a typical *Star Wars* orphan. Jyn's mother, Lyra, is dead, and her father has been taken away by Imperials to a destiny unknown. He is a gifted scientist, while his deceased wife is characterised by her faith in the Force. We see Lyra only briefly. Though not a Jedi, she wears brown and white robes which visually recall them, and around her neck hangs a Kyber crystal pendant. She passes it to the preteen Jyn with the instructions to 'Trust the Force'.

As the offspring of such parents, Jyn potentially embodies the fusion of both science and spirituality. However, her early years offer little opportunity to develop any skills save those required for minor larceny. When the rebels break her out of a low-level Imperial penal colony, they have no expectations of her abilities or commitment – they simply need her to vouch for them with Saw Gerrera, the anti-Imperial 'extremist' who raised her after the death/capture of her parents. Pursuing this aim, Jyn receives a message from her father: the Death Star has a design flaw and can be destroyed. This information, and proof of her father's good faith, is Jyn's initial redemption. She reports eagerly to a meeting of the rebel hierarchy that the station's full technical details can be retrieved from the security vault on the planet Scarif.

In a similar sequence from a film later in the saga's timeline – say, the tactical meeting in *Return of the Jedi*, also chaired by Mon Mothma – we know how this would play out. The threat would be explained, a plan outlined, and a team put together to execute it. This is not yet the rebellion as we know it in the saga, however. Indeed, it barely knows what it is. When Jyn says 'The Alliance, the rebels, whatever it is you're calling yourself these days,' she is being deliberately dismissive, distancing herself from a cause which she knows she could easily be pulled into, but she captures well the rebellion's lack of identity at this point. Any alliance is in name only, and, faced with the threat of the Death Star, the component parts disagree on strategy and begin to depart the rebel base without a plan.

I have said that the rebellion's lowest point was played out in the original *Star Wars* film, occurring when – on top of the day's other losses – the Death Star seems about to destroy Yavin, and that Disney's films frequently seek to dramatise equivalent moments. This is another one: the rebellion fragmenting before it has begun, all hope lost. There are, perhaps, too many agendas. Mon Mothma seeks political solutions (the Death Star might be halted by Senate hearings), Gerrera advocates violence, and others stand on the wide spectrum between them. Neither has what is required. Gerrera's war has been dehumanising (largely mechanical now, his mechanically enhanced breathing recalls Darth Vader), and viewers know that Mothma's Senate is only days from disillusion. What Jyn and, subsequently, Luke Skywalker, between them, demonstrate is an effective course of resistance. We have seen that for some modern commentators it is important that the rebellion is actually an *alliance*. *Rogue One* dramatises the moment at which that alliance between the diverse people that the Empire dispossessed was forged. For those who find the medal-awarding ending of *Star Wars* too overtly militaristic or individualistic, a new reading presents itself: that ceremony is the Alliance celebrating its own coming together as a coherent force over the course of the Scarif operation and the subsequent destruction of the Death Star.

Before that can happen, Jyn must complete her mission. With the alliance in disarray, a handful of its members form a team to infiltrate Scarif. This is a mission thrown together in the traditional *Star Wars* way, improvised from hastily-assembled resources. 'It won't be comfortable. It'd be cramped but we'd all fit,' is the judgement on the stolen Imperial shuttle they will use to infiltrate Scarif. 'Grab anything that's not nailed down,' is the order to equip it. While most of the team find their salvation simply in sacrificing their lives for a rebel action which will actually achieve something, Jyn's redemption also lies in her coming to a faith in the Force. 'I'm the daughter of Galen Urso,' is how she introduces herself early on, but the film is about her learning to be more than that. As the mission gets underway, she speaks a collective version of the saga's iconic line, 'May the Force be with us.' Like Han Solo, her redemption is in being able to say that. As the pilot seeks to guide their stolen Imperial shuttle past the Empire's security, we see her silent praying or meditating (the novelisation goes with the former[29]); and in the final confrontation with Krennic, she declares, 'I'm Jyn Urso – the daughter of Galen and Lyra.' By embracing her mother's faith, Jyn has become both soldier and believer, exactly that which the rebellion needs for success.

It is no casual thing that the novelisation refers to Jyn's moment of contemplation as *praying*. The religious vocabulary is one which explodes across the pages of the spin-off texts. The novel *Guardians of the Whills*, aimed at younger readers, includes the following religious terms: *prayers, disciple,* sage, *devotions, worship, pilgrimage, faith, holy, grace, deliverance, enlightenment, profane, sect, litany, beatific, belief, spiritual, soul, religious, mantra, blessing, shroud, priestess* and *order* (as in 'a holy order'). Whatever readers make of this, it is the stunning return to prominence of a vocabulary which the saga had seemed to leave behind in 1980.[30] Thematically, the book offers religious reflection, thus these passages:

> 'The Force is with me, and I am one with the Force,' Chirrut told Althin. 'And I fear nothing, for all is as the Force wills it.'
>
> Althin stayed still in his arms, silent once again.
>
> And why does the Force take a child's parents? Chirrut found himself wondering. (p. 170)
>
> His faith held him to a moral code, but that morality was the same regardless of any faith in the Force. One did not need to believe in the Force to know right from wrong. Many who held no faith in the Force acted righteously, and he had known more than one sentient who had acted selfishly, even cruelly, and used belief to justify doing so. (p. 172)

This writing introduces no original sociological or theological positions (these are well-worn reflections, though they may be new to younger readers), but the franchise's rehearsing them in this way returns us to the days when Kenobi and

Solo would trade similarly familiar arguments. Alternatively, if religious themes were not your favourite, the novels reflect on the culture war politics with which the films are now securely enmeshed for some. Culture, of course, is a word which barely registers in 1980s *Star Wars* texts, but it becomes crucial to the twenty-first-century ones as cultural diversity – belief systems, lifestyles, ways of living – is seen to be exactly what the monolithic Empire suppresses. *Guardians of the Whills* contains this reflection:

> 'Onderon remains.' Baze took another sip. The sting was softer this time, but the warmth more intense.
>
> The planet, yes. But our way of life is gone, our culture is gone, our beliefs are gone. That's what the Empire does. We were a republic that celebrated our differences, thousands and thousands of worlds, peoples, lifestyles. Not anymore. There is one Empire. Either you are part of it, or you are destroyed. (p. 147/8)

Similarly, an adult novel, *Rebel Rising*, also published in 2017, features a younger, pre-film Jyn Urso visiting the planet Inusagi where a festival celebrating the planet's distinctive flora is taking place.

> 'We welcome you all as we celebrate the beautiful festival of sakoola blossoms,' the chieftess said. She glanced behind her at the statue made of flowers.
>
> 'Yes, thank you,' someone said before the chieftess could continue. An Imperial officer stepped forward, and the microphone shifted toward him. 'We are pleased to share this festive day with an event equally joyous: the installation of Inusagi's first Imperial governor!' . . .
>
> Jyn made her way to the back of the crowd. It was clear what this little party was really about – a show of power and prestige from the Empire. It seemed almost like a mockery to turn a festival in honor of the planet's beauty into an excuse to showcase an Imperial governor.[31]

If much of this, and the last chapter, concerned the rethinking of what the rebellion looked like and worked, this is a similar moment in the depiction of the Empire – portraying it as exercising power not just through star destroyers and troops on the ground but through the manipulation of a conquered culture.

To a significant degree, the novels I have discussed here are business as usual. This book is premised on the notion that merchandise – particularly narrative merchandise – enacts interpretation. The shift in the twenty-first century is towards a coordinated transmedia approach whereby a film such as *Rogue One* contains vocabularies and themes which are more explicitly explored in a text released within months of the film's release. Consumers can choose the spin-off merchandise which most closely explores their own interests and readings of the film. The longer-term implications of Lucasfilm so consistently producing their own interpretations of the movies (under the cover of tie-in products) will only become apparent in the years to come.

In this book I have discussed the journey which *Star Wars* has made in the public consciousness from its first appearance, through years of neglect, to a triumphant second act as an omnipresent part of contemporary pop culture. I have used academic essays, spin-off merchandise, fan reaction and other materials to follow this journey. There is, however, one more way to tell it. If you believe the biographies, it wasn't just *Star Wars* that made that journey into darkness and out again. It was its creator, George Lucas. A good amount has been written about him, including several full-length well-researched biographies. This is a body of literature which is distinct from *Star Wars* criticism, but is clearly linked to it. Moreover, we can map the critical fortunes of the films against the readings of the man, and that is the work of my conclusion.

Conclusion: The many lives of George Lucas

The debates which we have been following through responses to the *Star Wars* films also found expression in the biographies of George Lucas which have been published at regular intervals since 1983. This conclusion overviews the historical debates which I have discussed and asks how they were refracted through the lens of directorial biography.

As a man seen to have revolutionised American film, for good or ill, Lucas was an obvious source of interest for biographers. These works naturally grounded their interpretation of *Star Wars* in Lucas's life/personal psychology and sought continuities across his work. Thus, his teenage years spent tinkering with and racing in cars were seen as the essential backdrop not only to the hot-rod movie *American Graffiti* (1973) but also Luke's love of racing down Beggar's Canyon.

Is this legitimate interpretation? Are the films best seen as Lucas's own self-expression, or should analysis of them be subsumed beneath the sort of cultural forces explored in Chapter 2? In interviews, Lucas has cast himself as a perfectionist creator on several occasions. 'I have an overwhelming drive,' he told *Film Quarterly* in 1974, 'To get that great shot of the two spaceships, one firing at the other as they drive through the space fortress.'[1] We see his quest to get this image on-screen first in *A New Hope* (the Death Star trench is an unlikely architectural and narrative feature, but it makes perfect sense in this context) and attempted again in *Jedi* where the incomplete nature of the second Death Star's outer shell allows starships access to its superstructure. Whether this makes Lucas a serious artist will depend on what value we attach to the image of two ships duelling in the bowels of a space station. Lucas, however, was clearly searching to create the picture he had in his head as early as 1974. His need to recurrently attempt to match the images on-screen with those perfect ones in his head reached its controversial zenith in 1997 when the original trilogy was re-released as digitally enhanced 'special editions' with CGI deployed to show things that were not possible twenty years earlier. When fans who valued the films as they were originally released expressed their dislike of such amending of the films, Lucas would consistently assert his right as the creator of *Star Wars* to use improved tech-nology to bring the compromised originals in line with his vision.

Counterbalancing these arguments about Lucas as a creator of unique, personal imagery are arguments against his being original. For his critics, he is complicit in the process whereby American cinema turned away from the director-led films which it was producing (however imperfectly) in the 1970s towards a focus on tentpole blockbusters based around recurrent characters and established genres upon which individual production crew could be rapidly changed. Similarly, Lucas's acknowledgement of how he mined both the pop culture of his youth and the world's mythologies makes the origin of the films' meaning a complex question relating to the artist's innovative use of an inherited tradition. At one extreme, it could mean that he has deferred his own creativity to the meanings created by prior generations of culture.

There are issues here to feed biographers for generations to come. The first was Dale Pollock's *Skywalking*, published in 1983, the year of *Return of the Jedi* (the author visits the set while filming, but the book concludes before it is released).[2] For Pollock, Lucas is a 'natural born filmmaker with an intuitive grasp of what audiences want to see' (p. 1), and his amazing sensibility is affirmed by many of his co-workers. *Intuitive, instinctive* or variations thereof recur across the book. Pollock sees Lucas as an auteur, if not a wholly conscious one, noting that his years at film school coincided with the arrival of auteur theory in American uni-versities (p. 46).[3]

Pollock's book is not explicitly religious but is wholly compatible with the vague Christianity surrounding the film in its earliest years. A prologue to the book is set in June 1962 when a teenaged Lucas wrapped his car around a tree and was freakishly lucky not to have been killed. The young man's resolution upon recovering – to commit himself to some serious study and make some-thing of his life – sets up the book's major themes: an Horatio Alger-type parable of hardwork paying off and as a Damascene turnaround, actually referred to as a 'religious conversion' on page 140. The book takes its cues from the spiritual readings of *Star Wars* as it retells Lucas's life. The Christian vocabulary which had by this point vanished from the films, but was still viable in interpretive merchandise, is rarely far from the surface of the biography. Lucas's gifts are 'God-given' (p. 51); he shares with then-wife Marcia 'a moral sense of right and wrong' (p. 66); and this ethical worldview is frequently attested by his friends. 'Lucas thinks he was put here for a purpose,' we are told on page 277. While later books would ascribe his dislike of the Hollywood studios to creative issues,

Pollock again finds a religious angle. 'I've never had the confidence that I was strong enough to resist all the temptations,' the director tells him (p. 246). A major event for Pollock was Lucas's precocious spiritual crisis.

> At age six, he had a mystical experience whose effects still linger with him: It centred around God, what is God, but more than that, what is reality? What is this? It's as if you reach a point and suddenly you say, 'Wait a second, what is the world? Where are we? What am I?' (p. 19)

This religious questioning might have led anywhere, but Pollock constructs Lucas's life and work in Christian terms in a way that later biographers do not. Consulting early versions of *Star Wars*, he alights on a draft where the Force's good side was called Ashla and finds this 'reminiscent of Aslan, the lion and Christ symbol in author C. S. Lewis's famous *Narnia* books' (p. 145), and his most explicit statement of the film's meaning is this: 'The message of *Star Wars* is religious: God isn't dead, he's there if you want him to be' (p. 139). The caveat 'if you want' takes us some way from Frank Allnutt, perhaps, but this is the central reading of the films presented in the first biography, one with which Lucas cooperated and which, although not formally Lucasfilm-endorsed, follows the company's view of history (the holiday special isn't mentioned). Pollock glosses *The Empire Strikes Back* this way:

> Lucas also wanted his version of the Christ story in *Empire*. Luke beheads Vader in an underground cave, only to find his own head inside Vader's black helmet – it is the equivalent of Jesus' temptation in the desert. (p. 211)

As the book draws to a close, Pollock summarises Lucas's cinema thus, mixing his take on Lucas's religious themes with his view of the director as an artist uniquely in touch with his audience: 'Lucas is dealing with the big issues here, God and the Devil, good and evil, and the ways he illustrates them resonate in moviegoers' minds' (p. 272).

As an intuitive artist and a man tackling the big questions, there can be no doubt that Pollock regards Lucas as a man with a distinct vision, one which flows from his moral character. He easily finds parallels with the heroic rebel alliance in Lucas's own life: at USC, 'Lucas enjoyed being a campus outcast; he was fond of his image as a rebel against the academic empire' (p. 50). Later, he 'was a brave warrior fighting an empire (Hollywood) that threatened to stifle his vision and soul' (p. 189). 'Hollywood is the Death Star, and Lucas is the eternal rebel' (p. 247).

Commentators of all types have pointed to the likeness of the names Luke and Lucas, using the link to project the character's traits onto the man who created him: young, idealistic, innocent in a tarnished world. In Pollock's book, however, Lucas plays every heroic part in the saga. When just starting out, he is Luke to the roguish Francis Coppola's Han Solo (p. 73 – a theme common across several books on Lucas, not least because Coppola called him 'Kid'), then plays Solo himself to Mark Hamill (p. 164 – whom he called 'Kid') before finally becoming respectable and taking on corporate responsibilities (like Lando Calrissian, p. 250).

Skywalking (the title itself evokes the film's most transcendent language) can be relentlessly upbeat because it was published before the sobering disappointments of films such as *Howard the Duck* (Willard Huyck, 1986) and *The Phantom Menace* – some would include *Return of the Jedi* – and before Lucas's seeming retreat from filmmaking. By the end of the millennium, he represented not the success story which Pollock celebrated but an enigma – 'A complex man who would have us believe that he stumbled into commercial movie making and that in his heart he would sooner make art-house movies for a small audience' – runs the back-cover blurb of one millennial study.[4] Why did the man who apparently had so much creative and financial freedom never achieve this oft-stated ambition? Any book, save those officially licensed, published within the years, either side of the millennium, probes the paradoxes, often critically.

In John Baxter's *George Lucas*, published in 2002,[5] Pollock's 'natural film-maker' is replaced by its polar opposite: 'Nothing in his character fits him to make films. The process irritates and bores him, and even makes him physically ill' (p. 17). Pollock's book had been produced when the Christian reading of *Star Wars* was still (just about) current, and the director he describes was a religiously committed man telling a coherent tale about our relation to, and need for, the higher power. Baxter, faced with more films and diverse interpretations, finds no such commitment in Lucas's life, arguing that the college courses he took (astronomy, sociology, speech and art history) were precisely 'those traditionally chosen by adolescents who, having rejected religion, are looking for a new belief system based on rationalism' (p. 43). Baxter's characterising Lucas as a searcher in this manner necessarily means that his account of the *Star Wars* films offers little in the way of a coherent spiritual vision.

If Pollock was writing well within Lucasfilm's preferred areas of interpretation, Baxter is aware that, by the turn of the century, he is writing against an ingrained official version from which he wishes to dissent at crucial points. Sometimes this will be biographical details. He disputes the official version of how and when Lucas met Haskell Wrexler and the exact reasons why Lucas was turned down for service in Vietnam. They aren't our worry here except to note that, in spinning a version of these events, Lucasfilm demonstrated a need to control even the most minute details of its founder's history. Moving to interpretive matters, Baxter frequently attacks the bedrock upon which the myth reading stands. These are perhaps the most prominent examples.

> Although he has been credited, retrospectively, with a near-lifelong interest in cultural studies and science fiction which blossomed in the *Star Wars* films, nobody can remember him being interested in anything but television and cars until long after he left Modesto. (p. 43)
>
> Someone told him about *The Hero with a Thousand Faces*, by anthropologist Joseph Campbell, though apparently Lucas never read it, but heard some extracts on an audiotape in his car. (p. 164)
>
> Just as *Howard The Duck* shows no sign that Lucas either likes or understand comic books, *Willow* reveals, despite supposed years of study and intense, intimate association with Joseph Campbell, an acknowledged master in the field, a woeful ignorance of mythology. (p. 363/4)

Disbelieving that the trilogy sets out a coherent vision of mythology, Baxter is sent back to the less-reputable culture which were discussed as the source texts for *Star Wars* in the late 1970s. Like all biographers, he pays attention to the art cinema which circulated through the USC film department, but in all of Lucas-literature it is here, in the chapter on his university days, that we get the best picture of Donald Glut, USC's lowbrow rebel, the man who screened 1930s serials for fellow students and who was nearly thrown out for continually making genre pastiches and superhero movies. While Lucas went to Hollywood, Glut wrote comics and Saturday-morning cartoons – the perfect grounding for *Star Wars*, apparently, because Lucas offered him the chance to write the original film's novelisation. He presumably regretted passing up the opportunity as he did do the one for *Empire*.

Baxter's dissent from the idea that Lucas engages with the deep meaning of myth results not only from his biographical researches but also from his insistence that mythology is not just a style of storytelling or a collective experience for a crowd who are putty in the hands of a talented storyteller. Baxter views mythology as a gift to the community, something which the teller literally gives to their audience, handing the myth over to public ownership and losing control of it as they do so because the myth belongs to everyone. By this argument, naming the Strategic Defence Initiative 'Star Wars' was a perfectly legitimate use of a real myth – everyone understood the link, even if it did make the weapon-isation of space sound far too attractive; but Lucas's deployment of lawsuits to stop it, and the countless other usages of which he didn't approve, simply denied audiences the opportunity to deploy the films' imagery in their everyday lives. 'He hadn't given us a mythology,' Baxter writes ruefully, 'We could only rent it' (p. 245).

Lucas's zealous protection of his corporate property and, by the 1990s, his seeming seclusion in Skywalker Ranch, working only with a selected few, created the space for a particularly tragic reversal of meaning between Pollock's book and Baxter's – the complete inversion of how *Star Wars* itself was meta-phorically mapped onto the director's life. Pollock had called one chapter about Lucas's success, 'Ruling the Empire', but that was joke because the text made it clear that that wasn't who he was. Baxter is a lot less sure, recurrently using the word 'empire' to describe Lucas's vast influence, and quoting others doing so, with full knowledge of the dark implications. His book begins with a chapter titled 'The Emperor of the West' and describes a corporate event at Skywalker Ranch with crowds gathered for a rare view of their boss who keeps his distance, apparently mingling only with his closest friends. If this empire is not evil, we understand, it is at least some sort of ironic tragedy. Perhaps the saddest example is the way that the metaphor permeates another book, Will Brooker's 2002 account of *Star Wars* fans. Writing of corporate attempts to regulate their activity, Brooker argues that 'these chapters raise the spectre of Lucasfilm as a tyrannical empire, stamping out rogue interpretations where it fails to assimilate them, and by extension constructing the fan creators as a rebel alliance'.[6]

With all pretentions to myth demolished, Baxter wonders what the director's cinema is really about. 'Perhaps,' he suggests (p. 403), 'what Lucas really believes in is the *idea* of story. He seems convinced that narrative, even innocent of con-tent, is worthwhile in itself.' The emblematic image of Lucas in Dale Pollock's book was the one at the beginning – the young man who turned his life around after nearly dying in a car wreck; but Baxter saves his for the end – a vision of the cinema auditorium fading out, replaced by a crowded souk where a skilled story-teller, faced with a crowd, takes a moment to enjoy his audience before begin-ning 'Once Upon a Time. . .' Although he had been terribly critical of Lucas, it is an uplifting image, one which does lead Baxter, to affirm, more completely than his previous criticism might lead us to expect – many of the things which Lucas claims for his saga. Here, after all, we have both the power of a story to bind a community and the necessity of cultural transmission across the generations. Of the films themselves, Baxter concludes:

> The *Star Wars* cycle, for all its lack of originality, is stirring. It reaffirms the best in us, celebrating heroism, dignifying our worthier emotions by crowding every alien creature and technological creation under the often leaky umbrella of human nature. (p. 403)

The problems which Baxter agonises over simply dissolve for James Clarke in his volume in the 'Pocket Essentials' series, also titled *George Lucas* and published in the same year. As extracts quoted in Chapter 5 suggest, this is an enthusiastic and unapologetic auteur study of a filmmaker whom the author clearly admires greatly.[7] He opens his work this way:

> A wide-eyed kid gazes longingly at the suns setting. A wide-eyed kid gazes long-ingly at his mother as she leaves her. A wide-eyed archaeologist grins with the satisfaction of discovery and understanding. An escaped future man stands against the sunrise. A wide-eyed teenager realises that everything changes. (p. 7)

Clarke uses a repetitious sentence structure to emphasise what he sees as the repetitions within Lucas's films. He takes it as read that the themes of those films (he suggests that they are 'community, self-belief and the realisation of potential, respect for an established system and tradition, and the good and bad voice of the past' (p. 20) along with 'strong women' and 'speed' (p. 21)) are the signs of an authorial signature rather than, as might be argued, the common currency of Hollywood cinema in the period. For Clarke, that latter suggestion is a misreading because Lucas is tied intrinsically to his own ideas. Unlike other directors of his generation, he has never adapted a novel or directed a film that he did not at least co-write (p. 7), and his long absence from directing simply makes him a man with two legacies to modern cinema – the films he made, and the visions he enabled others to provide by his relentless improvement of cinema technology (p. 87). For films like *Empire*, which Lucas oversaw but did not direct, Clarke finds context in the history of auteur producers – people who were more responsible for the films they produced than the hired hand directors. Taking his cue from a piece of *Empire* promotional art which echoed *Gone with the Wind* (where Han and Leia ape the famous pose of Rhett and Scarlet), he uses David Selznick as an example (p. 67). He is happy to list Lucas's endless sources, but finds in his researches not the plagiarism some have accused him of but real artistic work:

Lucas is a story archaeologist who gathers and works storytelling forms and narrative devices from other films, TV serials, mythological tales, comic books and old rock and roll songs. He dusts them down and represents them to contemporary audiences like a modern Brothers Grimm. (p. 8)

For Clarke there is no high art–pop culture divide to work through. Mythology and comic books sit in the same list, apparently equal. He even manages to locate the avant-garde films which were famously never made, or at least their seeds, arguing that Lucas has found an outlet for his dialogueless sequences of pure speed, light and motion in the special-effects shots which his company, Industrial Light and Magic, produced for *Star Wars* films and numerous others (p. 18). Beyond this, he sees Lucas as recurrently turning to themes of ecology and the heroism of the small and threatened.

In all of these ways, Clarke sets an agenda which others have followed. John Baxter felt Lucas had himself become terribly isolated from his audience, but Clarke – and later analysts such as Chris Taylor and Brian Jay Jones[8] – would portray him more positively. His educational organisations could be celebrated; his formation of a computer animation division, which became Pixar, could be emphasised (even if he had shown little interest in its narrative possibilities and sold it off long before it assumed that name or conceived any of the films for which it is now celebrated); and his company's multitude of technical innovations (from theatre specifications to maximise sound quality to editing software) had transformed the experience of both making and viewing films. In his personal life, Lucas's marriage to Obama fundraiser and successful businesswoman Mellody Hobson underlined his liberal credentials; and this, along with his successfully having raised three children as a single parent, undercuts accusations that he was a lonely isolate. In public appearances in recent years, he appeared to be a man finally comfortable with his life. Even the lawsuits were gone. The Pentagon continues, at the time of this writing, with its cloud-based initiative, the Joint Enterprise Defense Infrastructure (or JEDI for short), without fear of prosecution for trademark violation. *Star Wars* fans, more publically visible than ever, similarly pursue their own activities largely unbothered by Lucasfilm lawsuits. Indeed, rather than imposing a single version of the saga, a central plank of Lucasfilm's current marketing strategy is the aggressive production of hybrid versions in which *Star Wars* imagery is merged with that of other popular products: LEGO, Angry Birds and Mr Potato Head, to name but three. Could it be that – contra Baxter – Lucas had actually gifted, rather than just rented, the world a mythology, even if that world has consistently embraced it on different terms than he ever imagined?

What next for *Star Wars*? The box-office failure of *Solo* and the conclusion of the Luke/Han/Leia story mean we perhaps enter a period of negotiation between producers and viewers over what the saga's parameters are. There can be no question, however, that such negotiations take place in a context where *Star Wars* is loved and many of those criticisms which I have revived and analysed here have largely retreated. An essay, 'No Time for Sorrows', published in 2013 by Nicholas J. Cull and James Chapman, is indicative of the current trends in *Star Wars* criticism and culture in many respects.[9]

The piece wears its contemporary credentials on this sleeve, taking its very title from a line of dialogue which was ignored for decades before the rehabilitation of Leia as a strong woman of action made it quotable. The sorrows which it discusses are those of 1970s America, and it reads the film as nostalgic for a 1950s America, an innocent time before the political splits of the 1960s. This is not a new theme. Dan Rubey, Robin Wood and others pursued it decades earlier. Cull and Chapman, however, write without the same political urgency and outrage. If the original film's nostalgia for pre-1960s America was a precursor to the Reagan revolution, they don't condemn it for that. Similarly, they argue that 'the giant worm skeleton seen in the desert of Tatooine was a tribute to Frank Herbert's *Dune*' (p. 165). This sentence transforms the question of the relation between Lucas's film and Herbert's novel away from arguments about plagiarism or the contrasting eco-credentials of the two texts. The moment becomes just another of the film's myriad collection of references. Cull and Chapman explore traditional questions about the film and its impact, but the polemics of the late 1970s/early 1980s soften and fade away.

Star Wars, by this reading, exploded into contemporary pop culture in 1977, and it went through Hell, but it came out the other side, happier and shinier, liberal and diverse, ready to speak to us all (no translation droids needed). It will, no doubt, continue to do so in future years. A braver soul than I might conclude this book with a prediction about what form that dialogue between the films and their viewers might take, but a wise being – Yoda – once declared that 'impossible to see the future is' and that impossibility seems heightened as I write. The final draft of this book was concluded under lockdown conditions during the Coronavirus pandemic of 2020 – a shock to the world system which has put the very future itself up for grabs. Newspapers and the internet are rife with pundits declaring what new society must or might emerge from the experience. I will wager, however, that under any new social conditions which do evolve, Lucas's saga will continue to speak to us, yielding meanings and facets which no one could have imagined in 1977. I do believe this. And I have hope.

Notes

The content of all webpages remains as quoted in March 2020 except where noted.

Introduction: Possibilities of interpretation

1 Cass R. Sunstein, *The World According to Star Wars* (New York: HarperCollins), 2016, p. 41.
2 John Baxter, *George Lucas: A Biography* (London: HarperCollins), 1999, p. 243.
3 Original review in *Time*, 30 May 1977, reprinted in *Star Wars: Forty Years of the Force* (New York: Time Books), 2017, p. 62.
4 David Thomson, *The Whole Equation: A History of Hollywood* (London: Little, Brown), 2004, p. 371.
5 Robin Wood, *Hollywood from Vietnam to Reagan* (New York: Columbia University Press), 1986, p. 163. Further page references are given in the text.
6 Henry Jenkins, *Textual Poachers: Television Fans & Participatory Culture* (London, New York: Routledge), 1992. This and the quotation in the following paragraph are from page 31.
7 https://dictionary.cambridge.org/dictionary/english/interpretation
8 There are many histories of American and British society in this period. On American specificities and their impact across a wide range of American films, see Michael Ryan and Douglas Kellner, *Camera Politica: The Politics and Ideology of Contemporary Hollywood Cinema* (Bloomington: Indiana University Press), 1990. This work is discussed later in relation to the *Star Wars* trilogy.
9 Michael Pye and Linda Myles, *The Movie Brats* (London: Faber and Faber), 1979, p. 133.
10 Jonathan Rosenbaum, 'The Solitary Pleasures of *Star Wars*', originally published 1977, collected in Jonathan Rosenbaum, *Movies as Politics* (Berkeley: University of California Press), 1997, p. 105.
11 *Newsweek*'s review of *Star Wars*, https://www.newsweek.com/star-wars-george-lucas-40-years-carrie-fisher-anniversary-614373; *Time*'s review of *Star Wars*, 30 May 1977, and *Empire*, 19 May 1980. Both reprinted in *Star Wars: Forty Years of The Force*, pp. 66, 68. A. D. Murphy, review of *Star Wars*, *Variety*, 25

May 1977, reprinted in Chris Salewicz, *George Lucas: The Making of His Movies* (London: Orion), 1998, p. 124.

12	Robin Wood, *Hollywood from Vietnam to Reagan* (New York: Columbia University Press), 1986; and Ryan Gilbey, *It Don't Worry Me* (London: Faber and Faber), 2003, are just two of the books which celebrate the 'golden age' of 1970s Hollywood. The same view runs through many works not just on the period but on the individual directors active in this period (Robert Altman, Frances Ford Coppola, Martin Scorsese). Both Wood and Gilbey contrast the aesthetic richness of the 1970s with the following decades, and their views on *Star Wars* films are discussed later in this book. Much of this mythologising of the period has been subsequently questioned, not least by George Lucas, who, when asked in the 1990s about the alleged superiority of American cinema in the ten years before *Star Wars*, stated that 'I grew up in that era and it's a complete myth', suggesting that he had a staff-compiled folder of films exhibited in America over the decades which empirically backed up this personal memory. Jack Mathews, 'Saber Rattler', *Los Angeles Times*, 17 January 1999, reprinted in Sally Kline (ed.), *George Lucas Interviews* (Jackson: University Press of Mississippi), 1999, p. 230.

13	Terry Eagleton, *Hope without Optimism* (New Haven/London: Yale University Press), 2015.

14	The word is used on a number of occasions with less thematic import (e.g. 'And hope they don't have blasters'). In all, it appears seven times in dialogue in *Star Wars* (counting 'Help me, Obi-Wan. . .' as a single instance, six in *Empire* and five in *Jedi*). Leia herself produces a variant reading when, upon her arrival at the rebel base in the Yavin system, she uses the term 'hope' to refer not to any individual but to the Death Star blueprints contained within Artoo-Detoo. This is a usage which she repeats at the conclusion of *Rogue One* (2016).

1 *Star Wars* versus secularity

1	W. J. Rinzler, *The Making of Star Wars* (New York: London: Ebury Press), 2007, p. 8/9

2	Robin Wood, *Hollywood from Vietnam to Reagan* (New York: Columbia University Press), 1986, p. 169.

3	Dan Rubey, 'Not So Long Ago, Not So Far Away', *Jump Cut*, No. 41 (May 1997): 9.

4	Robert E. A. Lee, 'The Lutheran', 13 July 1977. Quoted in Robert Jewett, *Saint Paul at the Movies: The Apostle's Dialogue with American Culture* (Louisville: Westminster/John Knox Press), 1993, p. 164.

5   Alan Arnold, *Once Upon a Galaxy: A Journal of the Making of The Empire Strikes Back* (London: Sphere), 1980, p. 227.

6   John Baxter, *George Lucas, a Biography* (London: HarperCollins), 1999, p. 210/11.

7   Frank Allnutt, *The Force of Star Wars* (Van Nuys: Bible Voice), 1977. Although hard copies continue to circulate, the easiest way to view it today is in a revised version on the author's website (http://www.frankallnutt.com/). I concentrate on the cultural context of Allnutt's essay, but he had a personal interest in *Star Wars* as well because he had previously worked for the publicity department of Disney, and Lucas's film reminded him of the family films he worked to promote (though he does not say why). This might pass as an incidental detail, but it links his writing with a more widespread analysis of *Star Wars* where references to Disney abounded in the late 1970s and early 1980s when that company was seen as underperforming, while Lucas and Steven Spielberg (the two of them conjoined in many analyses) appeared to be the ones who would take up the unclaimed mantle of providers of quality family entertainment. For some discussion of this, see Peter Krämer, 'The Best Disney Film Disney Never Made': Children's Films and the Family Audience in American Cinema since the 1960s', in Steve Neale (ed.), *Genre and Contemporary Hollywood* (London: British Film Institute), 2002, pp. 185–6.

8   Allnutt is not wrong to ask about the economics of scarcity in the *Star Wars* universe. Arguably, there is a completely undeveloped opposition which appears only occasionally (and never in the sequels) contrasting the poverty of Tatooine with spice, the food flavourings/preservatives long associated by Europeans with luxury. Threepio's concern, early in the film, is that the Empire, having boarded the rebel blockade runner, will send them all 'to the spice mines of Kessel'. It is, of course, Solo's boast that the Millennium Falcon 'made the Kessel Run in less then twelve par-secs', and this may be a hint that spice is what he smuggles. The apocryphal texts of the novel and comic strip confirm this in the famously deleted scene where Han confronts Jabba The Hutt. Spice is not subsequently mentioned in the original trilogy, possibly because it seemed to indicate some creative smuggling of its own – from Frank Herbert's *Dune* books, which have several points of connection with *Star Wars* and where spice is a prominent commodity. In the real world, spices are grown. Lucas's counter-intuitive assertion that they are mined, and to simply assert this without explanation, is typical of his style (at least at this point).

9   http://www.frankallnutt.com/FS.17.07.25.HiddenForce.html.

10 Quoted in Chris Salewicz, *George Lucas: The Making of His Movies* (London: Orion Books), 1998, p. 47 (and numerous other sources).

11 Alan, *Once Upon a Galaxy*, p. 228.

12 James Clarke, *George Lucas* (Harpenden, UK: Pocket Essentials), 2002.

13 Lucasfilm, *Star Wars: The Power of Myth* (London: Dorling Kindersley), 1999, p. 32.

14 Mary Henderson, *Star Wars: The Magic of Myth* (New York: Bantam Books), 1997.

15 Jewett, *Saint Paul*, pp. 19–30; Edward McNulty, *Praying the Movies: Daily Meditations from Classic Films* (Louisville: Geneva Press), 2001, pp. 62–6. Jewett's translation of the verse from *Romans* is 'the author's own' and is eccentric – if not outright opportunistic in its use of the word 'Force'. The original Greek term used at this point – *dunamis* – is rendered in the major translations as 'power'.

16 Phil Phillips, *Turmoil in the Toybox* (Lancaster: Starburst Publishers), 1986, p. 140.

17 Caleb Grimes, *Star Wars Jesus: A Spiritual Commentary on the Reality of the Force* (Enumclaw: Winepress Publishing), 2007. All page references are given in the text.

18 While the United States are still a more religious society than Europe, polling in the twenty-first century consistently records a drop in church membership and attendance and an increase in those without religious affiliation. An extensive Gallup poll, published in 2019, is representative of surveys in its finding that the number of Americans declaring themselves to have 'no religion' more than doubled from 8 to 19 per cent since the turn of the century (https://news.gallup.com/poll/248837/church-membership-down-sharply-past-two-decades.aspx).

19 Roger MacBride Allen, *Star Wars: Ambush at Corellia* (London, New York: Bantam Books), 1994. For more discussion on this book, see Chapter 4.

20 Drew Karpyshyn, *Darth Bane: Rule of Two* (London: Century), 2008, p. 97/8.

21 Comfortably Smug, 'The Radicalisation of Luke Skywalker', http://decider.com/2015/12/11/the-radicalization-of-luke-skywalker-a-jedis-path-to-jihad/.

22 Grimes, *Star Wars*, p. xxi.

23 John C. McDowell, *The Gospel According to Star Wars: Faith, Hope and the Force* (Louisville: Westminster John Knox Press), 2007.

24 One can also find a good number of websites declaring Qui-Gon Jinn to be Jesus. As the spiritual coherence of the saga fragments, Jesus can be found in many places though the thematic import of doing so has vastly reduced.

25 The book opens: '*Star Wars* created soldiers. It created psychologists, Christians and artists.' We might, of course, question this. Did *Star Wars* actually create Christians – did it, in fact, cause conversions – rather than being something which people who were already Christians responded to? I am not convinced. Will Brooker, *BFI Film Classics: Star Wars* (London: Palgrave MacMillan), 2009, p. 7.

26 Cass R. Sunstein, *The World according to Star Wars* (New York: HarperCollins), 2016, p. 178.

27 Chris Taylor, *How Star Wars Conquered the Universe* (London: Head of Zeus), 2015, p. 60

28 Lucasfilm, *Star Wars Year by Year: A Visual History* (London: Dorling Kindersley), 2016 (3rd edn), p. 61.

2 *Star Wars* and the Reagan revolution

1 Glenn Kenny, *A Galaxy Not So Far Away: Writers and Artists on 25 Years of Star Wars* (London: Alison & Busby), 2003; Peter W. Lee (ed.), *A Galaxy Here and Now: Historical and Cultural Readings of Star Wars* (Jefferson, NC: McFarland), 2016; Dan Rubey, 'Not So Long Ago, Not So Far Away', *Jump Cut*, No. 41 (May 1997). That is the source I quote from. The article was originally printed in *Jump Cut*, No. 18 (1978). The 1997 reprint – done to coincide with the re-release of the films as Special Editions – contains some short reflections by Rubey on his writing of the piece and is most easily accessible now on the journal's website. Page references that I give in the text relate to the 1997 reprint.

2 With the excision of the sequence, little remains in the way of explicit Cold War allegory, though Threepio's concern that the Empire might punish the rebel crew by sending them to spice mines connotes a famous Soviet punishment for its dissidents.

3 SEFT Manchester Discussion Group, 'Star Wars: Some Notes', *Framework*, No. 9 (Winter 1978/9), published by the University of Warwick Arts Foundation; Jonathan Rosenbaum, 'The Solitary Pleasures of *Star Wars*', originally published 1977, collected in Jonathan Rosenbaum, *Movies as Politics* (Berkeley: University of California Press), 1997, pp. 105–9. Rubey, 'Not So Long Ago. . .'. Page references when citing these articles are given in the main body of the text.

4 Will Brooker, *Using the Force: Creativity, Community and Star Wars Fans* (New York: Continuum), 2002, p. 52.

5 *Star Wars*' conflict between young American agrarians and an Empire manned largely by British character actors could be seen to reflect America's War of Independence. Robin Wood was among those who saw such a theme, but he found it only marginally present and, like others, did not investigate far. Had the film met its original release date – in December 1976 – it would have been shown at the tail end of America's bicentennial year, and this reading may have felt stronger and been more widely commented upon.

6 There is a large literature on Riefenstahl in both English and German. Steven Bach, *Leni: The Life and Work of Leni Riefenstahl* (New York: Alfred A. Knopf), 2007, combines biography with film analysis.

7 The footage can be found easily online, along with numerous re-editings where the two sequences are intercut and/or John Williams's score is played atop Riefenstahl's footage.

8 http://www.weirdworm.com/the-five-most-racist-star-wars-characters/

9 SEFT Manchester Discussion Group, 'Star Wars: Some Notes'. Page references are given in the main body of the text.

10 The alliance forged between economic liberals and religious social conservatives in the late 1970s has been the subject of sometimes lurid analysis almost since it was forged, often by those unsympathetic to it. Ryan and Kellner's work *Camera Politica*, discussed elsewhere in this chapter for their analysis of the *Star Wars* films, contains much background and was written and published during the Reagan presidency. A detailed account, with the benefit of hindsight and a wider range of sources, is Steven P. Miller, *The Age of Evangelicalism: America's Born-Again Years* (Oxford: Oxford University Press), 2014.

11 Ryan and Kellner, *Camera Politica*, p. 229.

12 Robin Wood, *Hollywood from Vietnam to Reagan* (New York: Columbia University Press), 1986, pp. 162–88.

13 Paul Charbel, 'Deconstructing the Desert: The Bedouin Ideal and the True Children of Tatooine', in Peter W. Lee (ed.), *A Galaxy Here and Now: Historical and Cultural Readings of Star Wars* (Jefferson: McFarland), 2016, pp. 138–61.

14 Peter Krämer, 'Star Wars', in David W. Ellwood (ed.), *The Movies as History: Visions of the Twentieth Century* (Stroud: Sutton Mill), 2000, pp. 44–53. All Reagan quotes are extracted from this essay. The article originally appeared in *History Today*, March 1999. Debate continues about whether a space-borne defense system is required and, in the twenty-first century, the saga's phraseology has continued to feature within them. See, for instance, Matthew Jarvis, 'The Phantom Menace: Ballistic Missile Defence in Congress', a working paper for Department of Political Science, University of California, Berkeley (http://citeseerx.ist.psu.edu/viewdoc/download?doi=10.1.1.92.4318&rep=rep1&type=pdf).

15 Find the speech now at http://www.presidentreagan.info/speeches/empire.cfm

16 McDowell, *The Gospel According. . .*, p. 26.

17 The '*Star Wars* as Vietnam' argument was often backed up with reference to Lucas's history as a filmmaker. While developing *Star Wars*, he also worked with Francis Ford Coppola on what became *Apocalypse Now* (Coppola, 1979). Lucas's involvement is acknowledged in the film purely through the namepatch (Col. G. Lucas) of the otherwise unnamed American military commander played by Harrison Ford.

18 James Kahn, *Star Wars: Return of the Jedi* (London: Futura), 1983. All page references are given in the text. The claim that the book was a bestseller of 1983 is made in *Star Wars Year by Year: A Visual History* (London: Dorling Kindersley), 2016 (3rd edn), p. 110. No author is credited with this text, though Lucasfilm is credited as a partner.

19 Peter Biskind, 'The Last Crusade', reprinted in Peter Biskind, *Gods and Monsters: Thirty Years of Writing on Film and Culture* (London: Bloomsbury), 2005, p. 116/17.

20 Cass R. Sunstein, *The World according to Star Wars* (New York: HarperCollins), p. 41. For similar British accounts in which the release of *Star Wars* is seen as a release from the agonies of the 1970s but without being implicated in the politics which followed, see Brian Blessed, *Absolute Pandemonium* (London: PanMacMillan), 2015, p. 301/2, and Stephen P. McVeigh, 'The Galactic Way of Warfare', in Matthew Wilhelm Kapell and John Shelton Lawrence (eds), *Finding the Force of the Star Wars Franchise: Fans, Merchandise & Critics* (New York: Peter Lang), 2006, p. 55.

3 The first interpreters

1 Many *Star Wars* promotional posters, including those discussed here, are reproduced and contextualised at https://displate.com/blog/ star-wars-posters-evolution.

2 https://en.wikipedia.org/wiki/Tom_Jung (and repeated across the internet from this source).

3 Quoted in Ryder Windham and Peter Vilmur, *Star Wars: The Complete Vader* (London/New York: Lucas Books/Simon & Schuster, 2009, p. 10.

4 See the following among many others: Garry Jenkins, *Empire Building: The Remarkable Real Life Story of Star Wars* (London: Simon & Schuster), 1997, p. 81; John Baxter, *George Lucas: A Biography* (London: HarperCollins), 1999, pp. 223–4; Sean Howe, *Marvel Comics: The Untold Story* (New York: Harper Perennial), 2012, p. 193.

5 The use of the word *adaptation* may be problematised. It may be argued that what these texts adapt is not the finished film (which was not then available) but the screenplay or, at best, a rough cut. It is certainly true, for example, that, because of Lucasfilm's provision of photographs of costumes and models, the visual icons of *Star Wars* survive intact into the comic, but the *mise-en-scène* (the poses of the characters and their arrangement in the locations) varies markedly from the film, and reading it now is to watch the familiar story unfold in a wholly different visual manner. However, these texts were presented to the public as adaptations of the film, and reviewed as such, so it is in that sense that I consider them here.

6 An edited transcript of this meeting (between Lucas, Lippincott, Chaykin and Thomas) was published in *Star Wars Insider*, No. 122 (December 2010): 44–50. Find it online at http://therealcharleslippincott.blogspot.co.uk/2015/03/marvel-meeting.html.

7 *Star Wars Year by Year* gives 8 March 1977 as the release date of issue 1 with issue 2 following on 12 April and issue 3 on 10 May. Writer/editor Roy Thomas, in his definitive account of the comic's launch, manages to assert both that the first issue

went on sale in March and that 'two issues . . . had gone on sale before the opening'. Roy Thomas, '*Star Wars*: The Comic Book That Saved Marvel!', *Alter Ego*, Vol. 3, No. 68 (May 2007): 63–78. The title of the piece refers to the oft-reported story that the comic's huge sales kept the company afloat at a point when the comics industry was in recession, and Marvel employees feared for the company's continuation.

8   'Marvel's *Star Wars* adaptations are not only despicable, but also dangerous and detrimental to the industry. The writing is condescending, padded with needless explanations and changed dialogue never uttered in the original and often inconsistent with the characters . . . someone may pick up a *Star Wars* comic and think that nothing significant has happened in comics' history, that comics are still pretty crappy and juvenile. In fact, anyone who grew up reading The Atomic Knights or Space Museum in *Strange Adventures*, or Adam Strange in *Mystery In Space* . . . would probably think that comics books have deteriorated over the years.' Alexandre Koehn, 'DC Comics: TKO', *The Comics Journal*, No. 39 (April 1978): 47.

9   The comic's impact on Marvel is discussed by that company's editor-in-chief (1978–87) at http://jimshooter.com/2011/07/roy-thomas-saved-marve.html. Sales of the *Star Wars* novel are taken from Peter Biskind, *Easy Riders, Raging Bulls* (London: Bloomsbury), 1998, p. 340. The claim for *Jedi* is made in *Star Wars Year by Year: A Visual History* (London: Dorling Kindersley), 2016, p. 110.

10 Dialogue consistently avoids naming the planet. Luke refers to 'this rock', and when Threepio asks what planet he and Artoo are on, he only answers 'Well, if there's a bright centre to the universe, you're on the planet that it's farthest from.' The Death Star Imperials later reported that the Millennium Falcon 'blasted out of Mos Eisley'. In 1981, when not naming the planet would have seemed bizarre, the NPOR radio adaptation would rewrite the lines with the name in: 'Well, if there's a bright centre to the universe, you're on the planet it's farthest from . . . Tatooine.'

11 Joe Johnston, *The Star Wars Sketchbook* (New York: Ballantine Books), 1977.

12 Peter Biskind, 'The Last Crusade', p. 116/17.

13 Although rendered largely redundant by VHS/DVD, novelisations have a decades-long history and flourished particularly in the period immediately following *Star Wars*. The style of cinema which the film did so much to encourage in the decade which followed it (*Indiana Jones, ET, Gremlins, Back to the Future, Ghostbusters* and many, many more) was released with paperback tie-in books. Though often derided as a low form of literature, the existence en masse of these books may be used to refute the arguments of those critics who suggested that the films were all visual spectacle and kinetic trickery, and that narrative suffered accordingly. For a significant number of people, these clearly were films with a narrative, one worth re-following in written form.

14 George Lucas, *Star Wars* (London: Sphere), 1977. The novel was actually written by science fiction novelist Alan Dean Foster, but is credited to Lucas. Further page references are given in the text.

15 Thomas, '*Star Wars*: The Comic Book That Saved Marvel', p. 70.

16 I have made a point in Chapter 1 of emphasising that the Force appears to be simply a mental power in the original film, and is not used for levitating objects, as would later become routine. However, the idea was clearly apparent in early drafts of the screenplay since both Marvel and Foster have Vader manipulating a cup during the meeting with Imperial officers, though neither gives space or emphasis to the moment. Foster writes a single sentence ('A huge metal-clad hand gestured slightly, and one of the filled cups on the table drifted responsively into it', p. 41), while Marvel devoted a single panel to the cup hanging, unexplained, in the air.

17 Alan Dean Foster, *Splinter of the Mind's Eye* (London: Sphere), 1978. Further page references are given in the text.

18 Ford in 1983, quoted in *Star Wars: The Official Magazine*, Vol. 1, No. 40 (November/December 2002): 41.

19 Chris Taylor, How Star Wars *Conquered the Universe* (London: Head of Zeus), 2015, p. 286.

20 Ibid., p. 287.

21 *The Ingenious Gentleman Don Quixote of La Mancha* (Spanish: *El ingenioso hidalgo don Quijote de la Mancha*) was published in Spain in two volumes in 1605 and 1615 by Miguel de Cervantes Saavedra. Its central character, Don Quixote, has read so much about chivalry and knights that he imagines himself to be one and sets out to return lost, archaic values to the world.

22 *FOOM*, Vol. 1, No. 21 (Spring 1978): 32.

23 Thomas, '*Star Wars*: The Comic That Saved Marvel', p. 76.

24 In *The Phantom Menace*, gambling is a major part of the culture which allows the Hutts to control so much of Tatooine's economy; *Attack of the Clones* uses a casino to stage a sequence which shows how divorced the Jedi have become from a populace that's so decadent it's no longer interested in them; *The Last Jedi* shows a luxurious gambling palace as the natural playground of those who grow wealthy off conflict; and *Solo* links a wealthy criminal class to Darth Maul, thus implying that the Empire runs both sides of the law. Against this relentlessly negative view of gambling, which has been institutionalised by crime or the power system, the films celebrate the reckless gambling of Han and Lando, using it to characterise them as loveable rogues, economically marginal and as people who, in combat, will bluff or improvise wildly even when the odds are against them.

4 The trilogy and the myth reading

1　Analysing what these manuals take from *Star Wars* might be another way of gauging what it is taken to mean, albeit within a very niche context. Since a large part of the target audience for such books is aspirant scriptwriters, part of the film's role in them is to hold out the possibility of blockbuster success.

2　Arnold, *Once Upon a Galaxy*, p. 247/8.

3　Paul Scanlon, 'George Lucas: The Wizard of "Star Wars"', Rolling Stone, 25 August 1977. Find it now at https://www.rollingstone.com/movies/movie-news/george-lucas-the-wiz.

4　Taylor, *How Star Wars. . .*, p. 345. Pollock did not talk about what he supposedly saw.

5　Elvis Mitchell, 'Works Every Time', in Glenn Kenny (ed.), *A Galaxy Not So Far Away: Writers and Artists on 25 Years of Star Wars* (London: Alison & Busby), 2003, p. 79.

6　As ever, supplementary texts allow us to glimpse earlier versions. Both Marvel's adaptation of *Empire* and the film's novelisation open with Luke riding a Tauntaun on Hoth as was the original intention for the film.

7　An alternative reading might emphasise the fact that it is the villains who make declarations about 'your' power, etc., and Luke neither assents or denies the assertion. In *Jedi*, the Emperor declares that 'Everything that has transpired has done so according to my design,' which is a sign of hubris. He should not design events. That should be left to the Force, and what is evil about the dark side is precisely that it sets individuals up in the place where the Force should be. This interpretation retains something of the Christian reading because many of the most dramatic sins recorded in the Bible result from people attempting to acquire for themselves the knowledge/duties/worship that is appropriate to God alone. It is hard to see that this was intended, however.

8　Dale Pollock, *Skywalking: The Life and Films of George Lucas* (London: Elm Tree Books/Hamish Hamilton), 1983, p. 270. Travis Langley (ed.), *Dark Side of the Mind: Star Wars Psychology* (New York: Sterling), 2015.

9　Roland Barthes, *Mythologies* (London: Paladin), 1973, p. 101 (original French publication 1857).

10　Michael Pye and Linda Myles, *The Movie Brats* (London: Faber and Faber), 1979, p. 133.

11　Todd H. Sammons, '*Return of the Jedi*: Epic Graffiti', *Science Fiction Studies*, Vol. 14 (1987): 355–71.

12　Some of the information below is taken from Stephen Larsen and Robin Larsen, *A Fire in the Mind: The Life of Joseph Campbell* (New York: Doubleday), 1991.

13 JosephCampbell, *The Hero with a Thousand Faces* (London: Fontana Press), 1993, p. viii. All further page references are given in the text.

14 Gordon, 'Star Wars: A Myth for Our Time'. The essay was originally published in *Literature/Film Quarterly*. I quote from a reprint in Joel W. Martin and Conrad E. Ostwalt Jr (eds), *Screening the Sacred: Religion, Myth and Ideology in Popular American Film* (Boulder: Westview Press), 1995. Page references given in the text are to this edition.

15 Brian Jay Jones, *George Lucas: A Life* (London: Headline), 2016, p. 263.

16 Taylor, *How Star Wars. . .*, p. 278.

17 Joseph Campbell and Bill Moyers, *The Power of Myth* (New York: Doubleday), 1988; Mary Henderson, *Star Wars: The Magic of Myth* (New York: Bantam Spectra), 1997; Lucasfilm, *Star Wars: The Power of Myth* (London: Dorling Kindersley), 1999.

18 Tom Shone, *Blockbuster: How the Jaws and Jedi Generation Turned Hollywood into a Boomtown* (London: Simon& Schuster), 2005, p. 47.

19 Carl Silvio and Tony M. Vinci, *Cultures, Identities and Technology in the Star Wars Films: Essays on the Two Trilogies* (Jefferson: McFarland), 2007, p. 3.

20 Maureen Murdock, *The Heroine's Journey: Women's Quest for Wholeness* (Boston: Shambhala), 1990.

21 https://heroinejourneys.com/heroines-journey/

22 Mara Wood, 'A Distressing Damsel: Leia's Heroic Journey', in Travis Langley (ed.), *Dark Side of the Mind: Star Wars Psychology* (New York: Sterling), 2015, pp. 134–47.

23 John Shelton Lawrence, 'Joseph Campbell, George Lucas and the Monomyth', in Matthew Wilhelm Kapell and John Shelton Lawrence (eds), *Finding the Force of the Star Wars Franchise: Fans, Merchandise & Critics* (New York: Peter Lang), 2006. Page references are given in the main body of the text.

24 A full transcription of the discussion can be found on Moyers's website: http://billmoyers.com/content/mythology-of-star-wars-george-lucas/

25 *Hollywood's Master of Myth – Joseph Campbell*, BBC 1999, Director/Writer David Kerr.

26 J. W. Rinzler, *The Making of Star Wars* (New York: Ebury Press), 2007, was the first of a series of books examining the production of the original trilogy. Marcus Hearn, *The Cinema of George Lucas* (New York: Abrams), 2005.

27 Matt Vella, 'Introduction', in *Star Wars: 40 Years of the Force* (New York: Time Books), 2017, p. 4.

28 https://lucasmuseum.org/about/what-is-narrative-art (accessed 26 January 2019). The museum's website has subsequently (as at March 2020) removed this paragraph.

5 The progressives strike back: *Star Wars* as liberal text

1 *Star Wars Year by Year: A Visual History* (London: Dorling Kindersley), 2016, p. 134.

2 Hugh Ruppersberg, 'The Alien Messiah', in Annette Kuhn (ed.), *Alien Zone: Cultural Theory and Contemporary Science Fiction Cinema* (London, New York: Verso), 1990. Ruppersberg cites a number of similar studies which shows how routine this interpretation had become. For a more positive view of how and what we invest in charismatic aliens, see Caron Schwartz Ellis, 'With Eyes Uplifted: Space Aliens as Sky Gods', in Joel W. Martin and Conrad E. Ostwalt Jr. (eds), *Screening the Sacred: Religion, Myth and Ideology in Popular American Film* (Oxford/Boulder: Westview Press), 1995.

3 John Tulloch and Henry Jenkins, *Science Fiction Audiences: Watching Doctor Who and Star Trek* (London, New York: Routledge), 1995, p. 39.

4 While this chapter concentrates on the reinterpretation of the trilogy's narrative components, the shift away from a psychoanalytic model of viewership, such as that used by Robin Wood, reopened all the questions of the relationship between viewer and text. In a series of articles, Peter Krämer embraced Lucasfilm's preferred description of the film as 'family' entertainment, as well as the director's own use of children as an audience, and explored the way in which the trilogy, and other blockbusters, addressed different parts of the viewing demographic and how this was a crucial part of Hollywood's economic strategies. Peter Krämer, 'Would You Take Your Child to See This film?', in Steve Neale and Murray Smith (eds), *Contemporary Hollywood Cinema* (London: Routledge), 1998, pp. 294–311. Peter Krämer, 'The Best Disney Film Disney Never Made: Children's Films and the Family Audience in American Cinema since the 1960s', in Steve Neale (ed.), *Genre and Contemporary Hollywood* (London: British Film Institute), 2002. Peter Krämer, 'It's Aimed at Kids: The Kid in Everybody: George Lucas, *Star Wars* and Children's Entertainment', in Yvonne Tasker (ed.), *Action and Adventure Cinema* (London: Routledge), 2004, pp. 358–70.

5 Will Brooker, 'New Hope: The Postmodern Project of *Star Wars*', in Peter Brooker and Will Brooker (eds), *Postmodern After-Images: A Reader in Film, Television and Video* (London: Hodder Headline), 1997, pp. 101–12. All further page references are given in the main body of the text.

6 James Clarke, *George Lucas* (Harpenden: Pocket Essentials), 2002, p. 54.

7 Ibid., pp. 107, 108.

8 Ian Saunders, 'Richard Rorty and *Star Wars*: On the Nature of Pragmatism's Narrative', *Textual Practice*, Vol. 8, No. 3 (Winter 1994): 438–9.

9 Roger Kaufman, 'How the Star Wars Saga Evokes the Creative Promise of Homosexual Love: A Gay-Centred Psychological Perspective; Matthew Wilhelm

Kapell, 'Eugenics, Racism and the Jedi Gene Pool'; Stephanie J. Wilhelm, 'Imperial Plastic, Republican Fiber: Speculating on the Post-Colonial Other', all in Matthew Wilhelm Kapell and John Shelton Lawrence (eds), *Finding the Force of the Star Wars Franchise: Fans, Merchandise & Critics* (New York: Peter Lang), 2006, pp. 131–56, 159–73 and 175–83, respectively.

10 All published by Bantam Books, 1995. Page references are given in the main body of the text.

11 Roger MacBride Allen, *Star Wars: Showdown at Centerpoint* (London, New York: Bantam Books), 1995.

12 Roger MacBride Allen, *Star Wars: Assault at Selonia* (London, New York: Bantam Books), 1995.

13 This vision of *Star Wars* is routinely celebrated by many of those on the political left, but other responses are possible. The social liberalism of the revamped *Star Wars* universe co-exists with liberalised economic regulations, free trade across planetary boundaries being seen as wealth-creating. Multi-planet science fiction defaults to such implicit globalisation in its vision of characters, ships and cargos speeding between star systems with minimal red tape and currencies which seem to work everywhere. The presence, as in the *Star Wars* universe, of smugglers may be used to modify this, because that implies that there are legal restrictions on trade, or tariffs to be paid, which some attempt to avoid, but in practice the economic implications of this are rarely explored in science fiction, where planets which enforce strong border controls are frequently regarded as obstructive, inward-looking and, consequently, economically underdeveloped. *Star Wars* might have been seeking to disassociate itself from Reaganism, but it retained a taste for deregulated trade and global capital. Left-wing critiques could be developed along these lines. Douglas Kellner points to this argument, without exploring it further, when he declares it possible to view Lucas as 'part of a progressive high-tech liberal capitalist wing of the of the Silicon Valley California ideology'. Douglas Kellner, *Cinema Wars: Hollywood Film and Politics in the Bush-Cheney Era* (Malden/Oxford: Wiley-Blackwell), 2010, p. 182.

14 Roger MacBride Allen, *Star Wars: Ambush at Corellia* (London, New York: Bantam Books), 1994.

15 Kevin J. Anderson (ed.), *Tales from the Mos Eisley Cantina* (London: Bantam Books), 1995. Page references are given in the main body of the text.

16 Andy Mangels, *Star Wars: The Essential Guide to Characters* (New York: Del Ray), 1995, kicked off a series of 'Essential Guide[s]' (to *Droids, Planets, Vehicles*, etc.). In the same year, the environments and culture of eight major planets were described at length in Kevin J. Anderson, *The Illustrated Star Wars Universe* (New York: Bantam Spectra), 1995, while Shane Johnson, *Star Wars Technical*

Journal (London: Boxtree), 1995, largely focusing on technology, contained an extensive examination of the geography, climate and social conditions of Tatooine.

17   https://davidwestreynolds.com/about

18   Wood, 'A Distressing Damsel. . .'

19   Ibid., p. 173.

20   Brooker, 'New Hope', p. 111.

21   Jennifer K. Stuller, *Ink-Stained Amazons and Cinematic Warriors: Superwomen in Modern Mythology* (London: I.B. Tauris), 2010, p. 54/5.

22   Diana Dominguex, 'Feminism and the Force: Empowerment and Disillusionment in a Galaxy Far, Far Away', in Donald E. Palumbo and C. W. Sullivan III (eds), *Culture, Identities and Technology in the STAR WARS Films* (Jefferson: McFarland), 2007, p. 113.

23   Sunstein, *The World according to Star Wars*, p. 70.

24   Eric Harrison, 'A Galaxy Far, Far Off Racial Mark', *Los Angeles Times*, 26 May 1999. The piece records early responses in a debate which has never gone away. Find it now at https://www.latimes.com/archives/la-xpm-1999-may-26-ca- 40965-story. html.

25   Ryder Windham, *Star Wars: A New Hope* (London: Egmont), 2017, p. 1.

26   Michael Kogge, *Star Wars: The Force Awakens* (London: Egmont), 2017, p. 2.

27   Disney/Lucasfilm (no individual author credited), *Star Wars from a Certain Point of View* (London: Century), 2017.

28   Grimes, *Star Wars Jesus*, p. 162.

29   Windham Ryder, *Star Wars: Return of the Jedi* (London: Egmont), 2017, p. 99.

30   Alexandra Bracken, *The Princess, the Scoundrel, and the Farm Boy* (Los Angeles: Disney Lucasfilm Press), 2015. All page references are given in the main body of the text.

31   https://www.boxofficemojo.com/chart/top_lifetime_gross_adjusted/?adjust_gross _to=2020&ref_=bo_cso_ac. This list of inflation-adjusted box-office takings finds *Star Wars* (1977) at number two. *The Force Awakens* is the second best-grossing *Star Wars* film at number eleven and *The Empire Strikes Back* at thirteen.

32   theguardian.com/politics/2019/aug/28/cross-party-rebel-alliance-gears- up-for-brexit-clash-with-johnson; https://www.thetimes.co.uk/article/ rebel-alliance-of-mps-summon-the-force-to-fight-a-hard-brexit-z8brlvsjg

33   https://tickets.axs.com/eventShopperV3UK.html?wr=GEN-ed6e-4507-8d84- b2c 79985369f&skin=starwars&CalendarView=1&addData=LON&addData=LON, nfb (accessed 24 March 2017). The exhibition having finished, this link is no longer active.

6 New twists on old hopes: Prequels and sequels

1 Ryan Gilbey, *It Don't Worry Me* (London: Faber and Faber), 2003, p. 29. The idea that the prequels are a disappointment permeates much discourse on them. This chapter largely deals with the views and actions of those who, having loved the original trilogy, were unenthusiastic about *Episodes I–III*. It should be remembered, however, that the films sold millions of tickets worldwide and were enjoyed by many of those who watched it.

2 Speaking on *Meet the Press*, 16 September 2001, quoted in Derek R. Sweet, *STAR WARS in the Public Square: The Clone Wars as Political Dialogue* (Jefferson: McFarland), 2016, p. 39.

3 Douglas Kellner, *Cinema Wars: Hollywood Film and Politics in the Bush-Cheney Era* (Malden/Oxford: Wiley-Blackwell), 2010. The quotation from Lucas is on page 177. Kellner analyses the prequel trilogy in pages 173–83. In the mid-1980s Kellner had been critical of the films as symptomatic of the right-wing Reagan administration. His 2010 reading acknowledges the films' potential for multiple interpretations (including his own liberal one); a neat index of how academia's relation to the saga had shifted in the intervening decades.

4 That series is discussed in Sweet, *STAR WARS in the Public Square*.

5 Quoted in Kline, *George Lucas Interviews*, p. 219.

6 John Seabrook, 'Letter from Skywalker Ranch: Why Is the Force Still with Us?', originally printed in *The New Yorker*, 6 January 1997, reprinted in Kline, *George Lucas Interviews*, pp. 190–215. The quotation is from p. 203. Christopher Deis, 'May the Force (Not) Be with You: "Race Critical" Readings and the *Star Wars* Universe', in Donald E. Palumbo and C. W. Sullivan III (eds), *Culture, Identities and Technology in the STAR WARS Films* (Jefferson: McFarland), 2007, p. 99. Sunstein, 'The World according to . . .', p. 96.

7 Windham, *Return of the Jedi*, p. 126.

8 Alex Langley, 'These Archetypes You're Looking for', in Langley, *Star Wars Psychology*, p. 120.

9 The subsequent release of *Episodes VII–IX* reopens the question of viewing order. My eighteen-year-old son proposes 'Double Machete' order: 'We start with *The Force Awakens* where the plot revolves around the resistance's search for Luke Skywalker, who throughout the film is surrounded by a mythic aura, and finally finding him. We then cut to Luke's story – with the machete order: the original trilogy, with the prequels in the middle (a flashback within a flashback) showcasing Anakin's fall. The end of *Return of the Jedi* shows the galaxy celebrating the fall of the Empire, and Luke at the height of his power. Moving from here to *The Last Jedi* makes the film's core themes hit that much harder – a new Empire is on the rise,

and we see how far Luke has fallen from his ideals, before moving on through the conclusion of the saga.'

10 http://www.eruditorumpress.com/blog/an-increasingly-inaccurately-named-trilogy-episode-vi-return-of-the-jedi/

11 http://www.eruditorumpress.com/blog/an-increasingly-inaccurately-named-trilogy-episode-iv-a-new-hope/

12 http://www.eruditorumpress.com/blog/an-increasingly-inaccurately-named-trilogy-episode-ii-attack-of-the-clones/

13 Travis Langley, 'The Good, the Bad and the Scruffy: Can We Define Good and Evil?', in Travis Langley (ed.), *Star Wars Psychology*, p. 14.

14 Sunstein, *The World according to . . .*, p. 180.

15 Shone, *Blockbuster. . .*, p. 284.

16 Will Brooker, *Using the Force: Creativity, Community and Star War Fans* (New York, London: Continuum), 2002. Pages 79–101 deal with fan disappointment over *The Phantom Menace.*

17 https://www.tor.com/2013/01/16/watching-the-star-wars-prequels-muted-an-experiment/

18 Todd Hanson, 'A Big Dumb Movie about Space Wizards', in Glenn Kenny (ed.), *A Galaxy Not So Far Away: Writers and Artists on 25 Years of Star Wars* (London: Allison & Busby), 2002. Page references are given in the main body of the text.

19 https://medium.com/@zaron3/a-new-new-hope-luke-skywalker-and-the-soul-of-baby-boomer-men-966e6bae061e; https://www.inc.com/john-brandon/yes-star-wars-last-jedi-is-an-open-letter-to-millennial-generation.html; https://fabiusmaximus.com/2017/12/18/loser-boomers-super-millennials-in-the-last-jedi; https://www.firstthings.com/web-exclusives/2018/01/millennials-strike-back-an-esoteric-reading-of-the-last-jedi; http://fandom.wikia.com/articles/star-wars-the-last-jedi-baby-boomers-millennials

20 https://www.theatlantic.com/entertainment/archive/2016/11/the-inevitable-politicization-of-star-wars-rogue-one/508358/

21 https://www.bbc.co.uk/news/world-us-canada-38259838

22 https://www.goliath.com/movies/disney-ceo-rogue-one-is-not-a-political-film/

23 https://www.themarysue.com/bob-iger-says-rogue-one-isnt-political/

24 https://metro.co.uk/2016/12/09/trump-supporters-call-for-boycott-of-rogue-one-a-star-wars-story-with-dumpstarwars-6311782/; https://www.thepoke.co.uk/2016/12/09/alt-right-wants-people-boycott-star-wars-just-realised-theyre-galactic-empire/; https://www.popbuzz.com/news/star-wars-boycott/. All of these pages offer numerous comments in the same vein.

25 http://www.politico.com/magazine/story/2016/12/politics-of-rogue-one-214549

26 http://www.thegryphon.co.uk/2017/01/03/
    rogue-one-and-the-crisis-in-the-middle-east-an-analysis/
27 Originally speaking on Reddit, the quote is archived at http://www.pajiba.com/
    web_culture/gareth-edwards-talks-rogue-one-shooting-details-in-his-reddit-ama.
    php
28 In some sequences, the Force is referred to – as it was in early drafts of *Star Wars*
    but never on-screen before – as 'The Force of Others'. Add this to the Kaiburr
    Crystal, the *Book of the Whills* and the fact that Vader now resides in an almighty
    castle of the sort which was considered but rejected for *The Empire Strikes Back*,
    and *Rogue One* could be seen as returning to the late 1970s narrative practice of
    resurrecting ideas from the abandoned drafts of the first film. Arguably, *Rogue One*
    is the *Star Wars* we might have had if a few decisions had been made differently in
    the 1970s.
29 Alexander Freed, *Rogue One: A Star Wars Story* (London: Century), 2016, p. 217.
30 Greg Rucka, *Star Wars: Guardians of the Whills* (London: Egmont), 2017.
31 Beth Revis, *Rebel Rising* (London: Egmont UK), 2017, p. 134.

Conclusion: The many lives of George Lucas

1 Stephen Farber, 'George Lucas: The Stinky Kid Hits the Big Time', *Film Quarterly*,
   Vol. 27, No. 3 (Spring 1974), quoted in Sally Kline (ed.), *George Lucas Interviews*
   (Jackson: University Press of Mississippi), 1999, p. 44.
2 Dale Pollock, *Skywalking: The Life and Films of George Lucas* (London: Elm Tree
   Books/Hamish Hamilton), 1983. All page references are given in the text.
3 The auteur theory – *des politiques des auteurs*, in French – was the first critical
   working through of how directors could be thought of as the primary creators of
   even films made under the production line conditions of Hollywood.
4 Chris Salewicz, *George Lucas: The Making of His Movies* (London: Orion), 1998.
5 John Baxter, *George Lucas: A Biography* (London: HarperCollins), 1999.
6 Brooker, *Using the Force*, p. xviii.
7 James Clarke, *George Lucas* (Harpenden: Pocket Essentials), 2002. All page
   references are given in the text.
8 Taylor, *How Star Wars. . .*; Jones, *George Lucas: A Life*.
9 James Chapman and Nicholas J. Cull, *Projecting Tomorrow: Science Fiction and
   Popular Cinema* (London: I.B. Tauris), 2013, pp. 161–80.

Bibliography

Non-fiction

Allnutt, Frank, *The Force of Star Wars*, Van Nuys: Bible Voice, 1977.

Anderson, Kevin J., *The Illustrated Star Wars Universe*, New York: Bantam Spectra, 1995.

Arnold, Alan, *Once Upon a Galaxy: A Journal of the Making of The Empire Strikes Back*, London: Sphere, 1980.

Bach, Steven, *Leni: The Life and Work of Leni Riefenstahl*, New York: Alfred A. Knopf, 2007.

Barthes, Roland, *Mythologies*, London: Paladin, 1973, p. 10 (original French publication 1957).

Baxter, John, *George Lucas: A Biography*, London: HarperCollins, 1999.

Biskind, Peter, 'Blockbuster: The Last Crusade', in Mark Crispin Miller (ed.), Seeing through Movies, New York: Pantheon, 1990.

Biskind, Peter, *Easy Riders, Raging Bulls*, London: Bloomsbury, 1998.

Biskind, Peter, *Gods and Monsters: Thirty Years of Writing on Film and Culture*, London: Bloomsbury, 2005.

Blessed, Brian, *Absolute Pandemonium*, London: Pan MacMillan, 2015.

Bowen, Jonathan L. and Wagner, Rachel, ' "Hokey Religions and Ancient Weapons": The Force of spirituality', in Matthew Wilhelm Kapell and John Shelton Lawrence (eds), *Finding the Force of the Star Wars Franchise: Fans, Merchandise & Critics*, New York: Peter Lang, 2006.

Brooker, Peter and Brooker, Will (eds), *Postmodern After-images: A Reader in Film, Television and Video*, London: Hodder, 1997.

Brooker, Will, *BFI Film Classics: Star Wars*, London: Palgrave MacMillan, 2009.

Brooker, Will, 'New Hope: The Postmodern Project of Star Wars', in Peter Brooker and Will Brooker (eds), *Postmodern After-images: A Reader in Film, Television and Video*, London: Hodder, 1997.

Brooker, Will, *Using the Force: Creativity, Community and Star Wars Fans*, New York: Continuum, 2002.

Campbell, Joseph, *The Hero with a Thousand Faces*, London: Fontana Press, 1993.

Campbell, Joseph and Moyers, Bill, *The Power of Myth*, New York: Doubleday, 1988.

Chapman, James and Cull, Nicholas J., *Projecting Tomorrow: Science Fiction and Popular Cinema*, London: I.B. Tauris, 2013.

Charbel, Paul, 'Deconstructing the Desert: The Bedouin Ideal and the True Children of Tatooine', in Peter W. Lee (ed.), *A Galaxy Here and Now: Historical and Cultural Readings of Star Wars*, Jefferson: McFarland, 2016.

Clarke, James, *George Lucas*, Harpenden: Pocket Essentials, 2002.

Deis, Christopher, 'May the Force (Not) Be with You: "Race Critical" Readings and the Star Wars Universe', in Donald E. Palumbo and C. W. Sullivan III (eds), *Culture, Identities and Technology in the STAR WARS films*, Jefferson: McFarland, 2007.

Dominguex, Diana, 'Feminism and the Force: Empowerment and Disillusionment in a Galaxy Far, Far Away', in Donald E. Palumbo and C. W. Sullivan III (eds), *Culture, Identities and Technology in the STAR WARS Films*, Jefferson: McFarland, 2007.

Eagleton, Terry, *Hope without Optimism*, New Haven/London: Yale University Press, 2015.

Ellis, Caron Schwartz, 'With Eyes Uplifted: Space Aliens as Sky Gods', in Joel W. Martin and Conrad E. Ostwalt Jr (eds), *Screening the Sacred: Religion, Myth and Ideology in Popular American Film*, Oxford/Boulder: Westview Press, 1995.

Farber, Stephen, 'George Lucas: The Stinky Kid Hits the Big Time', *Film Quarterly*, Vol. 27, No. 3 (Spring 1974): 2–9.

Gilbey, Ryan, *It don't Worry Me*, London: Faber & Faber, 2003.

Gordon, Andrew, 'Star Wars: A Myth for Our Time', in Joel W. Martin and Conrad E. Ostwalt Jr (eds), *Screening the Sacred: Religion, Myth and Ideology in Popular American Film*, Boulder: Westview Press, 1995.

Grimes, Caleb, *Star Wars Jesus: A Spiritual Commentary on the Reality of the Force*, Enumclaw: Winepress, 2007.

Hanson, Todd, 'A Big Dumb Movie about Space Wizards', in Glenn Kenny (ed), *A Galaxy Not So Far Away: Writers and Artists on 25 Years of Star Wars*, London: Allison & Busby, 2002.

Hearn, Marcus, *The Cinema of George Lucas*, New York: Abrams, 2005.

Henderson, Mary, *Star Wars: The Magic of Myth*, New York: Bantam Books, 1997.

Howe, Sean, *Marvel Comics: The Untold Story*, New York: Harper Perennial, 2012

Jarvis, Matthew, 'The Phantom Menace: Ballistic Missile Defence in Congress', Working paper 2001–4 of the Institute of Governmental Studies, UC Berkeley.

Jenkins, Garry, *Empire Building: The Remarkable Real Life Story of Star Wars*, London: Simon & Schuster, 1997.

Jenkins, Henry, *Textual Poachers: Television Fans & Participatory Culture*, London, New York: Routledge, 1992.

Jewett, Robert, *Saint Paul at the Movies: The Apostle's Dialogue with American Culture*, Louisville: Westminster/John Knox Press, 1993.

Johnson, Shane, *Star Wars Technical Journal*, London: Boxtree, 1995.

Johnston, Joe, *The Star Wars Sketchbook*, New York: Balantine Books, 1977.

Jones, Brian Jay, *George Lucas: A Life*, London: Headline, 2016.

Kapell, Matthew Wilhelm, 'Eugenics, Racism and the Jedi Gene Pool', in Matthew Wilhelm Kapell and Lawrence, John Shelton (eds), *Finding the Force of the Star Wars Franchise: Fans, Merchandise & Critics*, New York: Peter Lang, 2006.

Kapell, Matthew Wilhelm and Lawrence, John Shelton (eds), *Finding the Force of the Star Wars Franchise: Fans, Merchandise & Critics*, New York: Peter Lang, 2006.

Kaufman, Roger, 'How the *Star Wars* Saga Evokes the Creative Promise of Homosexual Love: A Gay-Centred Psychological Perspective', in Matthew Wilhelm Kapell and Lawrence, John Shelton (eds), *Finding the Force of the Star Wars Franchise: Fans, Merchandise & Critics*, New York: Peter Lang, 2006.

Kellner, Douglas, *Cinema Wars: Hollywood Film and Politics in the Bush-Cheney Era*, Malden/Oxford: Wiley-Blackwell, 2010.

Kenny, Glenn, *A Galaxy Not So Far Away: Writers and Artists on 25 Years of Star Wars*, London: Alison & Busby, 2003.

Kline, Sally (ed.), *George Lucas Interviews*, Jackson: University Press of Mississippi, 1999.

Koehn, Alexandre, 'DC Comics – TKO', *The Comics Journal*, No. 39 (April 1978): 47.

Kramer, Peter, 'It's Aimed at Kids – the Kid in Everybody: George Lucas, *Star Wars* and Children's Entertainment', in Yvonne Tasker (ed.), *Action and Adventure Cinema*, London: Routledge, 2004, pp. 358–70.

Kramer, Peter, 'The Best Disney Film Disney Never Made: Children's Films and the Family Audience in American Cinema since the 1960s', in Steve Neale (ed.), *Genre and Contemporary Hollywood*, London: British Film Institute, 2002.

Kramer, Peter, '*Star Wars*', in David W. Ellwood (ed.), *The Movies as History; Visions of the Twentieth Century*, Stroud: Sutton Mill, 2000.

Kramer, Peter, 'Would You Take Your Child to See This Film?', in Steve Neale (ed.), *Genre and Contemporary Hollywood*, London: British Film Institute, 2002.

Langley, Travis (ed.), *Dark Side of the Mind: Star Wars Psychology*, New York: Sterling, 2015.

Larsen, Stephen and Larsen, Robin, *A Fire in the Mind: The Life of Joseph Campbell*, New York: Doubleday, 1991.

Lawrence, John Shelton, 'Joseph Campbell, George Lucas and the Monomyth', in Matthew Wilhelm Kapell and John Shelton Lawrence (eds), *Finding the Force of the Star Wars Trilogy: Fans, Merchandise & Critics*, New York: Peter Lang, 2006.

Lee, Peter W. (ed), *A Galaxy Here and Now: Historical and Cultural Readings of Star Wars*, Jefferson: McFarland, 2016.

Lee, Robert E. A., 'The Lutheran', 13 July 1977, quoted in Robert Jewett, *Saint Paul at the Movies: The Apostle's Dialogue with American Culture*, Louisville: Westminster/John Knox Press, 1993.

Lucasfilm, *Star Wars: The Power of Myth*, London: Dorling Kindersley, 1999.

Lucasfilm, *Star Wars Year by Year: A Visual History*, London: Dorling Kindersley, 2016 (3rd edn).

Mangels, Andy, *Star Wars: The Essential Guide to Characters*, New York: Del Ray, 1995.

Mathews, Jack, 'Saber Rattler', *Los Angeles Times*, 17 January 1999, reprinted in Sally Kline (ed.), *George Lucas Interviews*, Jackson: University Press of Mississippi, 1999.

McDowell, John C., *The Gospel according to Star Wars: Faith, Hope and the Force*, Louisville: Westminster John Knox Press, 2007.

McNulty, Edward, *Praying the Movies: Daily Meditations from Classic Films*, Louisville: Geneva Press, 2001.

McVeigh, Stephen P., 'The Galactic Way of Warfare', in Matthew Wilhelm Kapell and John Shelton Lawrence (eds), *Finding the Force of the Star Wars Franchise: Fans, Merchandise & Critics*, New York: Peter Lang, 2006, p. 77.

Miller, Steven P., *The Age of Evangelicalism: America's Born-Again Years*, Oxford: Oxford University Press, 2014.

Mitchell, Elvis, 'Works Every Time', in Glenn Kenny, *A Galaxy Not So Far Away: Writers and Artists on 25 Years of Star Wars*, London: Alison & Busby, 2003.

Murdock, Maureen, *The Heroine's Journey: Women's Quest for Wholeness*, Boston: Shambhala, 1990.

Murphy, A. D., 'Star Wars', *Variety*, 25 May 1977, reprinted in Chris Salewicz, *George Lucas: The Making of His Movies*, London: Orion, 1998.

Phillips, Phil, *Turmoil in the Toybox*, Lancaster: Starburst, 1986.

Pollock, Dale, *Skywalking: The Life and Films of George Lucas*, London: Elm Tree Books/ Hamish Hamilton, 1983.

Pye, Michael and Myles, Linda, *The Movie Brats*, London: Faber and Faber, 1979.

Rinzler, W. J., *The Making of Star Wars*, New York, London: Ebury Press, 2007.

Rosenbaum, Jonathan, 'The Solitary Pleasures of Star Wars', originally published 1977, collected in Jonathan Rosenbaum (ed.), *Movies as Politics*, Berkeley: University of California Press, 1997.

Rubey, Dan, 'Not So Long Ago, Not So Far Away', *Jump Cut*, No. 41 (May 1997).

Ruppersberg, Hugh, 'The Alien Messiah', in Annette Kuhn (ed.), *Alien Zone: Cultural Theory and Contemporary Science Fiction Cinema*, London, New York: Verso, 1990.

Ryan, Michael and Kellner, Douglas, *Camera Politica: The Politics and Ideology of Contemporary Hollywood Cinema*, Bloomington: Indiana University Press, 1990.

Salewicz, Chris, *George Lucas: The Making of His Movies*, London: Orion Books, 1998.

Sammons, Todd H., 'Return of the Jedi: Epic Graffiti', Science Fiction Studies, Vol. 14, No. 3 (1987): 355–71.

Saunders, Ian, 'Richard Rorty and Star Wars: On the Nature of Pragmatism's Narrative', *Textual Practice*, Vol. 8, No. 3 (Winter 1994): 435–48.

Scanlon, Paul, 'George Lucas: The Wizard of "Star Wars"', Rolling Stone, 25 August 1977.

Schatz, Thomas, 'The New Hollywood', in Jim Collins, Hilary Radner and Ava Preacher Collins (eds), *Film Theory Goes to the Movies*, New York, London: Routledge, 1993.

Seabrook, John, 'Letter from Skywalker Ranch: Why Is the Force Still with Us?', originally printed in *The New Yorker*, 6 January 1997, reprinted in Sally Kline (ed.), *George Lucas Interviews*, Jackson: University Press of Mississippi, 1999.

SEFT Manchester Discussion Group, '*Star Wars*: Some Notes', *Framework*, No. 9 (Winter 1978/9).

Shone, Tom, *Blockbuster: How the Jaws and Jedi Generation Turned Hollywood into a Boom Town*, London: Simon and Schuster, 2004.

Silvio, Carl and Vinci, Tomny M., *Cultures, Identities and Technology in the Star Wars Films: Essays on the Two Trilogies*, Jefferson: McFarland, 2007.

Stuller, Jennifer K., *Ink-Stained Amazons and Cinematic Warriors: Superwomen in Modern Mythology*, London: I.B. Tauris, 2010.

Sunstein, Cass R., *The World according to Star Wars*, New York: HarperCollins, 2016.

Sweet, Derek R., *STAR WARS in the Public Square: The Clone Wars as Political Dialogue*, Jefferson: McFarland, 2016.

Taylor, Chris, *How Star Wars Conquered the Universe*, London: Head of Zeus, 2015.

Thomas, Roy, '*Star Wars*: The Comic Book That Saved Marvel!', *Alter Ego*, Vol. 3, No. 68 (May 2007).

Thomson, David, *The Whole Equation: A History of Hollywood*, London: Little, Brown, 2004, p. 371.

Time magazine, 30 May 1977, reprinted in *Star Wars: Forty Years of the Force* (*Time* Special Edition), New York: Time Books, 2017, p. 621.

Tulloch, John and Jenkins, Henry, *Science Fiction Audiences: Watching Doctor Who and Star Trek*, London, New York: Routledge, 1995.

Vella, Matt, 'Introduction', in *Star Wars: 40 Years of the Force*, New York: Time Books, 2017.

Windham, Ryder and Vilmur, Peter, *Star Wars: The Complete Vader*, London, New York: Lucas Books/Simon & Schuster, 2009.

Wood, Robin, *Hollywood from Vietnam to Reagan*, New York: Columbia University Press, 1986.

Star Wars fiction

Allen, Roger MacBride, *Star Wars: Ambush at Corellia*, London, New York: Bantam Books, 1994.

Allen, Roger MacBride, *Star Wars: Assault at Selonia*, London, New York: Bantam Books, 1995.

Allen, Roger MacBride, *Star Wars: Showdown at Centerpoint*, London, New York: Bantam Books, 1995.

Anderson, Kevin J. (ed.), *Tales from the Mos Eisley Cantina*, London: Bantam Books, 1995.

Bracken, Alexandra, *The Princess, the Scoundrel, and the Farm Boy*, Los Angeles: Disney Lucasfilm Press, 2015.

Daley, Brian, *Han Solo and the Lost Legacy*, New York: Ballantine Books, 1980.

Daley, Brian, *Han Solo's Revenge*, New York: Ballantine Books, 1979.

Daley, Brian, *Han Solo at Stars' End*, New York: Ballantine Books, 1979.

Foster, Alan Dean, *Splinter of the Mind's Eye*, London: Sphere, 1978.

Freed, Alexander, *Rogue One: A Star Wars Story*, London: Century, 2016.

Kahn, James, *Star Wars: Return of the Jedi*, London: Futura, 1983.

Karpyshyn, Drew, *Darth Bane: Rule of Two*, London: Century, 2008, p. 97/8.

Kogge, Michael, *Star Wars: The Force Awakens*, London: Egmont, 2017.

Lucas, George, *Star Wars*, London: Sphere, 1977.

Lucasfilm, *Star Wars from a Certain Point of View*, London: Century, 2017.

Revis, Beth, *Rebel Rising*, London: Egmont UK, 2017.

Rukha, Greg, *Star Wars: Guardians of the Whills*, London: Egmont, 2017.

Windham, Ryder, *Star Wars: A New Hope*, London: Egmont, 2017, p. 1.

Windham, Ryder, *Star Wars: Return of the Jedi*, London: Egmont, 2017.

Index

Adventures of Luke Skywalker, The
  66–7, 76, 78
agrarianism 72
American Graffiti 155
Alderaan 38, 74–5, 109, 113, 115, 119, 122
Amidala, Padme 105, 126
Antilles, Wedge 19
'anthology films' 125, 144–53
Arnold, Alan 25, 81–2, 85–6
Artoo-Detoo 19, 29, 46, 57, 61, 64, 72, 89,
  118, 129, 137, 138, 141
Attack of the Clones 18, 19, 32, 117, 125,
  126, 128, 129, 134, 173 n.24

Baxter, John 158–61, 163
Bell, Martin 123
Binks, Jar-Jar 40, 105, 117, 40, 105, 117
  Is he a Sith Lord? 132–4
biblical cinema 32, 148
Biskind, Peter 51–2, 59, 60
Blu-ray (release of *SW* films) 35, 128
Brooker, Will 33, 38, 102–4, 106, 107, 115,
  123, 131, 134, 160
Buddhism 26, 28, 33
  meditation 25–6

Calrissian, Lando 83–5, 140, 158,
  173 n.24
Campbell, Joseph 10, 32, 79, 87–91, 98, 99,
  104, 125, 131, 141, 159
  criticism of 96–9, 100
  see also myth
Carter, President James ('Jimmy') 6
  energy crisis 6, 43–4
Chewbacca 18, 27, 42, 60, 63, 68, 69, 72, 75,
  76, 78, 83, 106, 120, 123, 129, 137, 139
Chantrell, Tom 56–7
Chaykin, Howard 55, 58, 59, 62, 66, 70
Christianity/Jesus Christ 4, 6, 9, 20–4,
  26–9, 33, 37, 47, 56–7, 66, 69–71, 72,
  77, 79, 84, 94, 99, 101, 104, 107, 130,

146–7, 148–52, 156–8, 168 n.18, 168
  n.24, 174 n.7
Clarke, James 26, 105, 107, 161–2
Clerks (Kevin Smith) 95, 103, 126
Clone Wars, The (TV) 127, 140

Dagobah 70, 85–6, 91, 120, 124
Dameron, Poe 9–10, 140
Darklighter, Biggs 35–6, 60, 61, 97, 114
Death Star 14, 15–17, 19, 37–9, 42, 43, 47,
  55, 67, 75, 89, 90, 95, 105, 106, 115,
  117, 121, 122, 126, 132, 140, 144, 147,
  149, 150, 155, 157
Disney (corporate) 12, 13, 32, 118, 125,
  128, 136, 139, 142–4, 146, 147, 150,
  167 n.7, 176 n.4

Eagleton, Terry 9
ecology 44, 50, 74–5, 104, 106, 120–1
Empire Strikes Back, The 8, 10, 11, 14, 25–6,
  53, 67, 78, 81, 83, 85–6, 97, 106, 115,
  120, 128, 130, 140, 161
Ewoks 4, 45, 49–50, 52, 83, 93, 97, 105,
  120–1, 129
'Expanded Universe' 30–1, 108–14, 118,
  125, 131, 151–2

fans 2–3, 102, 128–9, 131–4, 162
  fan Studies 2–3, 102
Fanboys (film) 135–6
Flash Gordon 41, 58, 94
Force Awakens, The 5, 38, 137–9, 146, 148
Force of Star Wars, The (Frank Allnutt) 4,
  21–4, 27, 32, 33, 35, 39–40, 53, 61, 89,
  44, 157, 167 n.7, 167 n.8
Force, The 2, 4, 11, 14–18, 28–9, 32–3, 39,
  107, 128, 130–2, 137, 140–3, 145–9,
  151, 157, 173 n.16, 174 n.7
Ford, Harrison 67, 76, 139
Fisher, Carrie 117
Friends (TV) 116

gambling 72, 143, 173 n.24
genre 45–6, 57–8, 67–9, 81–2, 85, 159
    see also biblical cinema; Western
    (film genre)
Gordon, Andrew 89–90, 94
Grimes, Caleb 29, 33, 49, 120
Guinness, Alec 20

Han Solo at Stars' End (Brian Daley) 76–8
Herbert, Frank/Dune 72, 167
Heroine's Journey, The 96–7
Hero's Journey, The 87–91
Hildebrandt, Greg 24
homosexuality 22, 105, 109, 110, 107, 123
hope 5, 9, 10, 14, 44, 52, 103, 113, 125, 127,
    137–41, 164, 166 n.14
How Star Wars Conquered the Universe
    (Taylor, Chris) 33
Howard The Duck 158, 159

Industrial Light and Magic 118, 162
Islam 31–2

Jawas 23, 40, 41, 46, 63–5, 75, 97,
    110–14, 117
Jedi/Jedi Knights 2, 13, 17, 18, 29–32, 70,
    84, 105, 109, 110, 129–30, 132, 134,
    137, 141–2, 146
Jenkins, Henry 2–3, 102
Jewett, Robert 27
Jinn, Qui-Gon 106, 128, 168 n.24
Jones, Brian Jay 91, 163
Jung, Carl 87
Jung, Tommy 55–7

Kellner, Douglas 44, 107, 177 n.13
Kenobi, Obi-Wan/Ben 2, 4, 9, 14, 16–18,
    20–2, 29, 31, 38, 39, 42, 50, 60, 64, 66,
    67, 81, 84, 89, 90, 105, 110, 112, 115,
    117, 130, 131, 142, 151
Kershner, Irvin 25
Krämer, Peter 47, 126 n.4

Lars, Beru 23, 41, 90
Lars, Owen 23, 110
Last Jedi, The 10, 137, 140, 142–3, 148,
    173 n.24
Lawrence, John Shelton 97–8

Lewis, Clive Staples 32, 157
Lippincott, Charles 58, 59, 61
Lucas, George 1, 81–2, 91–3, 127, 132–5,
    141, 153, 166 n.12, 167 n.8
    biographies of 58, 91, 105, 155–64
    on myth 6–7
    on religion 25
Lucas Museum of Narrative Art 100
Lucasfilm 2–3, 10, 11, 24–7, 30, 33, 36, 53,
    55–60, 67–9, 73, 78, 81, 83, 91, 92,
    99–102, 105, 108, 110, 114, 118, 122,
    124, 125, 127–30, 132, 135, 146, 153,
    157–60, 162, 171 n.5, 176 n.4

McDowell, John 32, 33, 49
McNulty, Edward 27
'machete order' 128–9, 179 n.9
Making of Star Wars, The (television
    program) 57–8
Marvel Comics 57, 59–76, 101, 107, 142,
    146, 172 n.8, 173 n.16
Maul, Darth 98
Millennium Falcon 2, 4, 16, 21–2, 27, 39,
    59, 64, 66, 72, 84, 85, 89, 106, 137,
    138, 140, 167 n.8
myth 6, 37, 42, 45, 86–98, 100, 156, 159–60
    Lucas on 87
Mothma, Mon 20, 83, 109, 150

Nixon, President Richard 6, 15, 51
A New Hope see Star Wars (1977)

Obama, President Barack 52, 162
Organa, Princess Leia 4, 10, 11, 41–2, 46,
    50, 56–9, 63, 65, 68, 74–6, 84, 89, 109,
    115–17, 119–21, 137, 138, 140, 141,
    161, 163

Palpatine, Emperor 13–15, 22, 23, 28, 38,
    51, 61–2, 84, 85, 97, 105, 128–30,
    140, 160
post-modernism 101, 104
Phantom Menace, The 18, 32, 38, 46, 105,
    114, 117, 125–9, 132–3, 135, 136, 158,
    173 n.24
Phillips, Phil 27–8, 42
Pollock, Dale 82, 156–8, 160
post-modernism 101, 104

Power of Myth, The (television series) 91–2

racism 35, 40–6, 63–5, 108–10, 113, 117, 118, 147, 148

Raiders of the Lost Ark/Indiana Jones films 44, 51

Reagan, President Ronald 7, 43–9, 52, 103, 117

'evil Empire' 47–9

see also Strategic Defence Initiative (SDI/ Star Wars Project)

Rebel alliance 10, 13–19, 36–40, 42, 45, 51, 60–2, 67, 73–6, 83, 84, 97, 102, 103, 105, 106, 108, 110, 111, 113–15, 117–20, 123, 129, 136, 137, 139–40, 146, 150, 152

Return of the Jedi 14, 16, 19, 28, 30, 38, 47, 49, 67, 83, 92, 95, 103, 105, 113, 115, 123, 125, 127–30, 140, 150, 158, 174 n.7

novelisation 49–50, 60, 120–1

Revenge of the Sith 18, 38, 82, 99, 125, 128

Rey 137–42

parentage 142–3

Riefenstahl, Leni 40, 117

Rise of Skywalker, The 9, 38, 140, 142–4

Rogue One 12, 38, 49, 126, 144, 146–53, 181 n.28

Rosenbaum, Jonathan 41, 48

Rubey, Dan 4, 19, 37–43, 44, 45, 50, 51, 53, 92, 104, 163

Sandpeople/Tusken Raiders 18, 40, 89, 97, 110–14, 117

Scream 2 (Wes Craven) 82–3

See-Threepio 23, 29, 42, 57, 61, 64, 57, 61, 64, 94, 118, 129, 137

Sexism 35, 41–2, 96–7, 115–17

see also Organa, Princess Leia

Skywalker, Anakin 2, 31, 124, 127–30

Skywalker, Leia see Organa, Princess Leia

Skywalker, Luke 2, 4, 5, 10, 16–19, 21, 29–3, 35–6, 40–2, 46, 50, 56–9, 63, 65, 66, 68, 74–6, 81, 83, 86, 90, 92, 94, 96, 102, 105, 106, 108, 109, 112, 114, 116, 117, 120, 121, 124, 127–32, 137–43, 150, 157, 163

Solo (film) 144–6, 163, 173 n.24

Solo, Han 16–18, 21, 27, 29, 40–2, 56–8, 60, 63, 66–73, 75–8, 83, 85, 93, 94, 106, 107, 108–9, 116, 117, 120, 122, 129, 131, 137–40, 144–6, 151, 158, 161, 163, 173 n.24

Special Editions 83, 102, 114, 123, 155–6

Spielberg, Steven 44

Splinter of the Mind's Eye 66, 67–71, 76, 148

Soviet Union 36, 47–9, 52, 106, 169 n.2

Star Wars (1977) 1–4, 94, 126, 128, 137, 140, 143, 144, 155

Cantina sequence 4, 5, 11–12, 39, 41, 60, 63, 64, 68–70, 89, 110–11, 113, 114, 118, 124

promotion of 55–66

political readings of 35–53, 100–24

release 1, 163

religious readings of 13–33

retitling 1, 78, 81, 125

medal ceremony 40, 63, 117, 119, 123

novelisations of 57, 59–66, 118–22, 172 n.13

Star Wars Holiday Special, The 78

Star Wars: Identities 123–4

Star Wars: The Magic of Myth (exhibition/ book) 27, 92–3, 98, 123

Star Wars: The Power of Myth (exhibition/ book) 28, 92, 98

Strategic Defence Initiative (SDI/Star Wars Project) 10, 47–8, 160

Sunstein, Cass 1, 52, 116–17, 127, 130

Tarkin, Governor/Grand Moff 13–15, 19, 22, 55, 58, 119

Tatooine 5, 23, 35–7, 40, 43, 56, 57, 59, 60, 70, 75, 85, 105, 110–15, 126, 129, 144, 172, 155

Taylor, Chris 33, 82, 162

Thatcher, Margaret 7, 103

Thomas, Roy 58, 59, 69–71, 73, 75

Thomson, David 1

THX-1138 8, 61

Time Magazine 1, 7–8, 99

trilogy structure 81–3

Vader, Darth 14–19, 21, 22, 25, 28, 38, 39, 50, 55, 56, 62–3, 66–8, 72, 73, 81, 82,

84, 86, 90, 92, 99, 119, 122, 124, 127, 128, 130, 131, 136, 140, 141, 150
see also Skywalker, Anakin
Variety 8
Vietnam war 5, 38, 43, 49–51, 93, 127, 159, 170 n.17

'war on terror' 127, 133, 148
Watto 40
Western (film genre) 8, 68–70, 72, 75, 85, 145, 146

Whills
    book of 13, 61, 66, 148
    guardians of 148, 149, 152
Williams, John 94
Wood, Robin 1, 2, 16, 44–6, 51, 76, 91, 115, 120, 163, 176 n.4

Yoda 2, 28, 32, 42, 50, 86, 97, 105, 115, 120, 124, 130, 131, 140, 163